The Officer in The Tower

For Norman and Grainne

The Officer
in The Tower

Norman Baillie-Stewart

as told to John Murdoch

LESLIE FREWIN : LONDON

© NORMAN BAILLIE-STEWART AND JOHN MURDOCH, 1967

FIRST PUBLISHED IN GREAT BRITAIN, 1967

BY LESLIE FREWIN PUBLISHERS LIMITED,

15 HAY'S MEWS, BERKELEY SQUARE, LONDON W1

PRINTED BY ANCHOR PRESS

AND BOUND BY WILLIAM BRENDON,

BOTH OF TIPTREE, ESSEX

SET IN 12 ON 14 POINT MONOTYPE BEMBO

WORLD RIGHTS RESERVED

Contents

Destiny

FROM THE CRADLE my brother Eric and I were destined by long family tradition for service in Britain's armed forces.

Eric was three and a half years my senior and we were the only children in the family. I was born in London on 15th January 1909 and for many generations back there were distinguished Army and Navy officers among my father's and mother's ancestors.

Taking up a career in the uniform of the Army or Navy was, therefore, something that was regarded almost as a birthright for me. It was as natural as taking a breath of fresh air.

My father was Colonel Hope Baillie Wright of the Indian Army's 67th Punjab Regiment. He started with the Duke of Wellington's Regiment. My mother was born Miss Elsie Beatrice Stewart, daughter of General Hopton Stewart of the Hyderabad Cavalry. Her ancestors included Admiral Sir Edward Codrington, who from 1805 to 1808 commanded the *Orion* which played a conspicuous part in the Battle of Trafalgar. As Commander-in-Chief of Britain's Mediterranean fleet in 1827, he was in charge of a combined British-French-Russian force that destroyed a united Egyptian and Turkish fleet at the historic Battle of Navarino. Other maternal ancestors of mine were General Sir William Codrington, a Crimean War leader; Admiral Sir John Codrington, Lieutenant-General Sir Alfred Edward Codrington and

General Sir William J Codrington, a colonel of the Coldstream Guards.

So my brother and I were brought up to follow in the footsteps of a long line of illustrious ancestors and to be proud of their victories on land and sea.

But there is another equally important, perhaps more important, side to my ancestry – a paternal side that was not unconnected with my German sympathies before and during World War Two. On my father's side a forbear was a German, Baron von Krumme-Douglas, who was at one time ADC to the Kaiser. This Baron used to visit my grand-aunt in Bath. My great-grandmother was a German named von Krause – a name which I used when broadcasting from Berlin to Britain immediately after the war started in 1939.

The last of my mother's direct male line with the Stewart family was her only brother. He was Captain Christopher Codrington Stewart, who was killed at the Battle of Ctesiphon in Mesopotamia in 1915. Proud of my uncle's memory and in his honour, I changed my name on leaving Sandhurst in December 1928 from Norman Baillie Stewart Wright to its present form – Norman Baillie-Stewart. This was entirely my own decision.

Early in 1910, when fourteen months old, I sailed with my mother and brother to India, where my father was a captain in the Punjab Regiment. In India, as an infant, I travelled about the sub-continent for three years with my mother and brother, going everywhere with my father's regiment. Among my earliest memories in life were the native pipers in the Punjab Regiment ... a big march past which left the impression of a big drummer's leopard's skin ... the scorching heat ... the baked earth ... the smell of my father's cigar ... a native fakir crawling through my father's compound doing his penance. . . .

Another early memory around this period was the smell of the smoke from the funnel of the ship that took me back to England. On our return from India, my mother took Eric and I up to a country rectory at Laverton near Bath. There we were left in the care of a kindly, bearded old clergyman. That was the last we were destined to see of our mother for five years, because the 1914–18 war broke out and she was compelled to stay in India. We did not see our father for another nine years. This lack of a happy home life and motherly care at the most impressionable age may have left its mark on me in subsequent years. Life in the old rectory, although no substitute for a home life, had its attractions. There were other children of my own age there. And, of course, brother Eric, my constant companion, was there too. I looked to him for protection and guidance in almost everything in those years.

The outbreak of the 1914–18 war left an indelible impression on me, for I was then only about five and a half years old; I remember jumping out of bed with excitement when the news broke and dancing with delight. The boys in the rectory got a war map in which they stuck flags to mark the positions of the Allied armies in France and Belgium. Every day in the early stages of the war it was our painful duty to move these flags back as the gravity of the situation increased. The Allied armies continued to retreat before the German onslaught. Lorry loads of troops started to move in streams down the country roads near the vicarage.

The old parson had two daughters, Muriel and Phyllis, whom I considered very beautiful. They both used to encourage me to say which of them I liked better. To Muriel I would say, when asked the question: 'More than all the railway trains and cattle trucks in the world put together', and to Phyllis I would reply: 'More than all the houses and chimney-pots in the world put together.' I expressed my love for Phyllis by kissing what I called her 'duck pond' – the hollow at the base of her neck.

The halcyon days at the rectory came to an end when Eric was ready for a preparatory school at the age of eight and a half. As we brothers always moved together, I entered the same prep school at the tender age of five. I took a sorrowful last look at Laverton as I left in an open horse-drawn cab with balloons floating all around for my amusement. Our new school was at Clifton Downs, where we were cared for by the headmaster and his wife. Life at the Downs was happy but strict and I was always glad of the constant companionship of my brother to whom I went with all my most intimate troubles and complaints.

My closest friend at school was Pat, whose parents were also in India. The headmaster, his wife and boys whose parents were overseas always went on holidays together. Sally, the head-master's daughter, was a tomboy, joining in all our fights and games and working with us in the classrooms. The headmaster had a violent temper and many a storm raged over my head with the headmaster's wife acting as a buffer to stave off vicious physical assaults on my head. But the batterings I received from the headmaster came too often to encourage any mutual friend-ship between us.

For a considerable time the war did not affect the boys at Clifton Downs and it was sheer delight for us to see the airplanes flying out from a nearby aircraft factory. Exceptional excitement developed one day when an enormous semi-rigid dirigible flew very low over Downs and started the whole school running after it. Street lamps were blacked out and food became so scarce that for a long time we had not enough to eat. Bread was scarce and butter was almost unobtainable. There was a potato famine. Vegetables were scarce. Senior boys in the school were sent out to join food queues. On Wednesday and Saturday afternoons the school went out in a party to collect eatables from the country-side. In our forages for food we cut and collected young shoots of stinging nettles which, when cooked, tasted not unlike spinach. Elderberries were collected for jam-making. Dandelions were tried as a substitute for salad. They were never a success, being far too bitter for us. Sugar became gradually more scarce and finally disappeared from the tables at Clifton Downs. But the boys were never downhearted.

There were times when the war came particularly near to Clifton Downs in a personal way. News came through that fathers and close relations of boys had been killed in France. Snobbishness held sway in the school, especially among boys who could taunt others that their fathers held high rank on the battlefield or in the Navy. One unspeakably snobbish boy caused jealousy because his father was a colonel. And when the Colonel came home to die of wounds some of the younger boys were secretly glad because snobbery and boasting from one source had ended. Small boys are often notorious for their lack of sympathy or pity for each other.

Returning from holidays one summer, some of the boys waited at a London station to see a hospital train arrive from a south coast port. We watched with awe and great wonder as we saw men on crutches; others without arms; some were blind, others were so heavily swathed in bloodstained bandages that they were unrecognisable and there were hundreds of stretcher cases. Evidence of the human slaughter on the battlefields of France was before our childish eyes. At another platform we watched German prisoners arrive, miserable-looking, half-starved, unshaven men in dirty field-grey uniforms covered with caked clay. Was this war? Why? What was it all about? Silent, bewildered, we had no answer. We could not understand.

A few months after the end of the war my brother was ready to enter a public school and, of course, I had to move too. We went to Bedford, one of the oldest and best public schools in England. After only one term at the 'Incubator' or Junior School, I was accepted as a junior in the 'Big School' at the early age of ten.

At Bedford chastisements came hard and often, but I soon learned to stifle the cries that came to my young lips. It was not done to cry. My days at Bedford were unhappy. I felt alone in the world, with nobody to listen to my tales of childish fears and troubles. I was separated from big brother Eric, who was in the Senior School. I was always made to feel like an underdog, very much a junior to be beaten up and chastised by every bully who felt that way inclined. After two years I moved up to the Senior House. Here again my experiences were no better, although I was united with Eric. I soon learned that to hold my own I had to assert myself, be cynical and sarcastic.

Loathing school, I did not need to be asked a second time to accept a suggestion by Eric that I should enter the Royal Naval College at Dartmouth. Naturally the idea of a uniform at an early age appealed to me.

Hiring a private tutor out of school hours, I worked hard for my Dartmouth entrance examination and passed with high marks. At this time my parents had returned home from India and they both went up to London with me when I was going for the interview and medical examination. Even before I had been informed of my entrance examination successes I got orders to be fitted for my naval uniform. Leaving Bedford at the age of thirteen, I was thrilled at getting into a uniform before Eric. I relished the prospect of a glorious naval career. There could be yet another admiral in the family! My success in passing into Dartmouth pleased my parents and Eric. So one day in 1922 I left by train for Dartmouth, proud, happy and resplendent in my new uniform.

At Dartmouth all members of the most junior term report a day earlier than the other cadets and my train finally arrived at Kingswear Station full of excited new naval cadets. We all jumped out of the train with enthusiasm and were met by our term Lieutenant, term Captain and Junior Cadet Captain. At breakneck speed we were marched up the hundreds of steps leading from Sandquay to the RNC. As we were all small boys and carrying our regulation leather 'gladstones', we were in a state of almost complete physical exhaustion by the time we reached the top and found ourselves in the college building. Here we were handed over to a bearded chief petty officer who showed us our dormitories, sea chests and lockers.

Sitting on the floor of the 'quarter deck', we were addressed by our term Captain. He informed us that we were called the Grenville Term and we had inherited many fine silver trophies for sport from the departing senior term. We were under strict orders to retain those trophies.

From my narrow bed I felt proud to see the magic 'N B S Wright, RN' on my sea chest. But, bad as Bedford was, I was soon to discover that, for me, at any rate, the Dartmouth Naval College was much worse. Disillusionment came early. For a start, the senior term mates soon had us out individually in the Gun Room for an explanation of the 'guff' rules. A cadet earned six strokes on his behind from a chief cadet captain if he –

– Put his hands on his hips;
– Wore his lanyard too low;
– Spoke to a cadet senior to himself;
– Did not leap nimbly out of the way of a senior cadet even if he tried to walk through him and
– Did not pass a senior Gun Room at the double.

These were the main offences but as the guff rules were elastic we, the younger boys, were often engulfed in them and bewildered.

Great was the arbitrary power of the cadet captains and my experience was that they vied with each other as to the number of beatings they could give the young cadets.

At seven o'clock each morning the doors of the dormitory would be flung open and a bearded PO would shout such time-honoured phrases as 'Turn Out! Turn Out! Show a Leg! Lash Up and Stow!' Without a moment's hesitation we leaped out of our beds; divested ourselves of our pyjamas; seized a towel and rushed naked out of the dormitory. Dropping our towels anywhere, we plunged into icy-cold water, summer and winter; grabbed our towels; washed and cleaned our chattering teeth and rushed back to the dormitory. With hardly time to dry ourselves, we threw our clothes on our steaming bodies and rushed from the dormitory holding our boots, ties and other odd garments. Woe betide the straggler! He paid for it! If a cadet was early enough he could secure a cup of scalding-hot cocoa. Those who were not quick enough got nothing and had to go at the double with the others up to the roof of the building for physical training on an empty stomach. After the physical jerks we doubled back to get into line for breakfast. Everything was done at the double. Walking was almost unknown. As the term was graded in height from right to left the tall ones doubled into the Mess Room first, seizing all the food they could lay their hands on.

They held a monopoly of the food right through the term. Their smaller or less favoured brethren obtained their requirements by sheer personality or by the pernicious system of 'bags after you for the rest of the term'. Second helpings of anything were unusual and it was the survival of the fittest. The food itself was insufficient, badly served and of doubtful nutriment. I remember vividly the remark of my old CPO: 'I can't understand how you young gentlemen eat that food, why, they daren't give it to the lower deck.' At the RNC the physical training was hard and the brain work intensive. Games, sailing, running and hockey went on six days a week. And during one period I played rugby every day of the week except Sunday, with the result that I vowed that I would never play the game again!

The food and physical treatment at Dartmouth, as I found them, presented a bleak picture, but I also found that the College had much to recommend it in the way of education. My experience was that the educational system at the Naval College had much more to recommend it in a practical way than what is given at a public school. I learned a much wider variety of subjects of highly practical value from which I benefited for the rest of my life.

I registered a distaste for the Navy and longed for what I regarded as the free and more exciting life of the Royal Air Force. But the RAF was not for me. My parents objected on snobbish, social grounds, adding that they were afraid I would break my neck. At the age of sixteen I developed a severe attack of influenza which was followed by the discovery of a dark 'patch' on a lung.

That finished my naval career. Although the life at the Royal Naval College was unduly hard, I have always been grateful for my experiences there. I cherish them affectionately. I left one small colourful mark on the Royal Navy. I designed the Grenville tie, maroon with a sky-blue diagonal stripe split by a thin, dark-blue stripe. It has been adopted by all the members of the Grenville term, past, present and future. So, ironically, many a British naval officer is wearing, without knowing it, a tie designed by 'The Officer in The Tower'.

My report on leaving the RNC stated: 'As a student, this officer has passed his various examinations fairly well, and it would seem that he has brain power. His regimental work has been satisfactory. He has received a good report from OC Service Coys, for work done during Divisional Training.

'It is necessary that I refer to a casual manner which has been a cause of comment, and in his own interests this should be eradicated. He represents a general average of his rank.'

Spending a few months recovering my health, I had plenty of time to think about my future career. It had to be in a uniform, of course. I was still keen on the RAF but my father was adamant in his refusal. As a compromise I said that if I were to go into the Army nothing but a Highland regiment would suffice. Ancestors of mine had been in Highland regiments and I felt it was my duty to follow them. Highland regiments, I had discovered, had a superficial glamour which was quite unique and wholly acceptable to me.

It was with reluctance that my father agreed. I found that my father has a commonsense viewpoint. He had no use for the airs and fripperies that crack Highland regiments appeared to have and he favoured an ordinary line regiment in which soldiering was soldiering. I, however, clung to my Highland hallucinations and lived to regret bitterly the rejection of my father's advice.

I won a prize cadetship in my entry examination for Sandhurst which largely paid for my uniform and fees. This was a very good start for me. This success was followed up in my first term examination at Sandhurst with the winning of a cadet scholarship. I appeared to be on top of the world, with the promise of a successful military career.

Long before being allowed into Sandhurst I had to face an interview with the Board of Generals at the War Office. I was so successful that I received the same number of marks as the cadet who received the highest interview marks going into the Royal Military Academy at Woolwich. But I was surprised by what the Board already knew about me. They had my whole Dartmouth record before them. Unexpectedly one of them asked: 'Whilst at Dartmouth you invented a petrol engine, didn't you?' To this question, which came out of the blue, I replied, 'Yes' and was then asked to explain the engine's working principles. They were impressed and then suggested that I should join a technical corps and not waste my time in an infantry regiment. But I declined to accept this advice.

I was fifteen at the time I invented the engine and did the drawings. I showed them to one of the engineering lieutenants at Dartmouth, who said it was quite workable. The Lieutenant suggested sending the drawings to a motoring journal for their comment. Their opinion was that although the engine was complicated it could be commercialised if patent rights were obtained. Because of the expense, I dropped the idea. But I was not aware that an official record of this invention had been prepared at the Naval College.

At Sandhurst I was determined to let nothing stand in the way of making a success of my training and studies. During my first term, unlike all other gentlemen cadets, I refused to dine out or go on any leave. At weekends I stayed in uniform and worked in my room, much to the dislike of fellow gentlemen cadets. Drilling standards at Sandhurst were exceptionally high, as high, they said, as in the Brigade of Guards. I fixed a high target for myself: to excel in everything. At drill I made my feet ache with so much stamping and my shoulder sore with so many bangs from my rifle.

I was rewarded for this hard work and tenacity in my junior term by being one of five chosen to wear a lance corporal's stripe. At the end of the term I was promoted to the rank of corporal.

B

My appearance made a strong impression on staff officers at
Sandhurst. My progress was such that I came under the notice of
Brass Hats at the War Office and an application was made for
me to perform the duty of orderly to Prince Henry, now the
Duke of Gloucester, at a big London parade where the Prince
was presenting a shield. In London I was presented to the Prince
and we had a short conversation. Whilst standing behind the
Prince at the saluting base I heard a voice from the crowd of
spectators: 'My dear, so you have taken over my old job at
Sandhurst, have you?'

Turning round, I saw that the speaker was none other than
General Girdwood, who had only recently retired from the
position of Commandant at Sandhurst. He was having a little
joke.

An embarrassing moment during the parade was when
Prince Henry lost a copy of his speech and I eventually
found it after searching through his overcoat pockets. The
parade over, all the Top Brass retired to the RAC Club for
lunch and I felt on top of the world because I was invited to
join the party.

At this time I had a particularly fresh, healthy complexion,
and I was about six feet two inches tall, and looking back on
it now I must say I was as straight as a ramrod. The Club
appeared to be full of blue-blooded military aristocrats,
their wives and escorts. The eyes of the women in the Club
were on me as I moved around, and I appeared to be conspicuous because I wore corporal's stripes and bayonet, while all
the other officers wore ceremonial dress-swords. I must
confess that I was not without pride at my situation in the
Club, and to be truthful I felt slightly conceited. After several
helpings of champagne, two Guards officers asked me if I
were destined for the King's Company of the Grenadier

Guards. 'No,' I said as pleasantly as I could, 'my ambitions are more modest than that.'

In a rather exhilarated state I passed from the RAC Club to the Mansion House, where I met the Lord Mayor and Lady Mayoress of London. I was in attendance on the Mansion House balcony when the Lord Mayor took the salute at another big march past. After tea in the Mansion House, the officers' party left for the posh Naval and Military Club, where again I was hurled into an atmosphere of high society champagne and caviar.

At the end of a sumptuous dinner I was driven back to Sandhurst with the Commandant in a chauffeur-driven limousine. It was a day to remember, and certainly my happiest as a young gentleman cadet. I appeared to have a successful military career within my grasp, which was not an easy achievement in the years between the wars. Being suddenly thrust into London's top social whirl was not so easy in those days either.

During my gentleman cadetship at Sandhurst I had many honours showered on me. One that tickled my pride most was being on the demonstration and lecture platoon that visited the Public Schools' OTC camp at Tidworth. The young schoolboys appeared to be much overawed at the appearance of the Sandhurst cadets like myself.

As a gentleman cadet at Sandhurst I was especially keen on all kinds of athletics and physical-fitness tests. But my first love was boxing. One of my most vivid recollections of those days was the slogging matches I used to have in the ring with a tall, handsome and powerfully built Indian cadet. He was none other than Ayub Khan, now the President of Pakistan and one of the world's rulers. Little did I think in those days when we gave each other many a bloody nose that he would rise to such eminence in his country. He is actually a field marshal. In our Sandhurst days he was just slightly senior to me, being about nine months older. We both got our commissions in 1928. He was assigned to the élite Royal Fusiliers. Later when I met him he was being transferred to the 14th Punjab Regiment. I suppose the next time he heard of me I was 'The Officer in The Tower'.

The Seaforths

AS PASSING-OUT time was approaching at Sandhurst, I now had
to consider the matter of choosing a regiment. At this stage a small
incident played a part in my future career. My original choice
was the Argyll and Sutherland Highlanders, Princess Marie
Louise's Own. As was the practice at the time, I wrote a letter
to a representative of the Regiment, making my application. It
usually happened that the applicant was sent for to be interviewed
or invited to tea so that an appraisal could be made. After weeks
of waiting I had not even received a formal acknowledgement of
my application. Disgusted at what I regarded as rudeness, I changed
my mind. So, urged by my uncle, who had a considerable influence with the Lord Lieutenant of a certain Scottish county, I put
down my name for the Seaforth Highlanders, with the Black
Watch as my second choice and the Queen's Own Cameron
Highlanders as third. Having abandoned the idea of becoming an
officer in the Argyll and Sutherlanders, I was approached by a
major in that regiment, who said, 'I understand you want to enter
my regiment.' 'No, I do not,' I answered sharply because I was
annoyed. 'I would have nothing to do with your regiment after
being treated so rudely.' Apologising profusely, the Major said
he had mislaid the application. He invited me to reconsider my
decision. 'No, thanks,' I told him, 'it is too late now.'

To enter the Seaforth Highlanders my name had to be placed on the Colonel-in-Chief's list for approval. This happened to be the Prince of Wales, now the Duke of Windsor. An interview followed with the Colonel commanding the First Battalion, then at Aldershot, and later with the Honorary Colonel of the Regiment, Colonel MacKenzie. I had a strong recommendation from General Girdwood and from my Company Commander at Sandhurst. These were necessary in order to enter an élite regiment like the Seaforth Highlanders. Then I had to get through a social check-up. But this was not lacking. I was fortunate in having not only the necessary military qualifications and the social background, but influence too. Between the wars only about twenty per cent of the applicants succeeded in entering the leading British regiments. Regimental snobbery was one of the chief causes of many failures.

Leaving Sandhurst, I almost blushed because I was handed such flattering reports. They were the last I was to get in the Army. It was at this time, December 1928, that I changed my name by deed poll, dropping one name and hyphenating the other. This change of name became the subject of some sarcastic jokes in the Army, causing me intense annoyance. I considered the change a purely private matter, but fellow officers, young and old, took a different view.

Filling up an entry form for the Seaforths, I had to state whether I preferred a home or a foreign battalion. I remembered that when my brother was asked a similar question he put down 'foreign battalion'. So Eric was kept at home. Another cadet, entering with Eric, put down 'home battalion'. He went overseas. So I decided to stymie the bureaucrats by answering, 'No preference'. I was ordered to report to my regiment at Dover.

It was almost with boyish delight that I received my new Highland uniform after innumerable fittings from an excellent

Edinburgh tailor. It cost £240 without full dress. Arriving in Dover one winter's afternoon, I found that the Battalion headquarters were in an old Victorian fortress named the Citadel. Most of the Citadel was many feet below ground. In winter the rooms were extremely cold and wet. The Citadel was reached by a steep military road which, when covered with ice, was impassable for all transport. My taxi could not descend the road down to the Officers' Mess on my arrival and all my luggage had to be unloaded and carried down by hand. My first entry into the Officers' Mess did not augur well for my future happiness. I was greeted by what I considered an ungracious Captain, who said: 'You Baillie-Stewart? Didn't expect you until tomorrow. Changed your name to something funny, haven't you? Come along now and I will show you your room.'

I was nettled by the stinging remark about the change of name which the Captain regarded as a joke. Then I was left alone in an enormous, freezing room. The room was almost bare and there was no carpet. It was a strange, ludicrous reception after my wonderful pipe-dreams in Sandhurst about life in a crack Highland regiment. Stunned by the appearance of everything and hurt by the Captain's comment, I felt like a pricked balloon as I stood in silence and alone on the floor. It was supper that night in the Mess and attendance was not compulsory. A quarter of an hour of the unpleasant atmosphere was enough for me. I left my fellow officers to their supper and made my way down to a little Italian café in Dover. There I supped in miserable loneliness and only mellowed a bit after a bottle of wine.

A thick fog was hanging over the town, maroons boomed continually as I made my way back to the barracks. Losing the Citadel in the fog, I walked up one side of the hill and down the other. Then I seemed to stumble on the place. There I spent the first of many miserable nights. On the following day two other young officers arrived to join the Regiment for the first time. In neither of these did I find a companion. They paired off together. My experience was that all new officers in the Seaforths and other crack regiments were put into Coventry for about the first six months. I and the other two new arrivals were ignored. It seemed to me that it was preferred that we should go on parade and make fools of ourselves rather than any brother officers should assist by giving a little helpful advice. All three of us new officers were, for instance, put back on the barrack square to drill in the ranks with the newest and rawest recruits. This treatment was intended, in my opinion, to be humiliating. It was. At the military college we had attained the highest standard in drill of every kind. In the Citadel we had to suffer humiliation in a variety of other ways.

As far as I was concerned, these experiences and rude remarks happened too often. During a lull in a reel on a guest-night in the Mess, for instance, I was called over to speak to Colonel Mac-Kenzie. The Colonel's introductory remark stung me: 'Hello, Baillie-Stewart, changed your name to something funny, haven't you?' In the presence of other officers and ladies I burned with resentment by what I considered an offensive remark. Throwing the restraint of discipline to the winds, I quickly retorted: 'It is true, sir, that I have changed my name, but I am not aware that there is anything funny about it.'

The effect on the Colonel was almost electric. Blood rushed to his face, but he kept his thin lips tight and silent.

The blunt truth was that I could not restrain myself from answering back to anyone – not excluding my Colonel – if I considered he had been downright rude. I was certainly not going to allow myself to be the butt for a rude and regular regimental joke. I was determined, if possible, to nip the whole thing in the bud as soon as possible. I feared that this attitude towards me might grow and become a regimental habit. As a result of this incident two confidential reports were filed against me. They included the phrases 'lack of respect for his seniors' and 'having a casual manner with his seniors'.

Not long after this incident another one occurred in the Dover Mess. This time, a monocled, music-loving major was involved. This particular Major was, in my opinion, conceited. He took a delight in snubbing young officers. I used to flee from the Mess when the Major entered, preferring the emptiness of my lonely room to the Major's company. He was a jazz lover and a composer of popular jazz tunes. One night before dinner he brought his wireless set into the Mess and started it booming. In common with other officers, I continued to read my newspaper, indicating an apparent indifference to the music. Suddenly there was a loud click and the wireless was switched off. As he stumped out of the room, the Major shouted at me: 'You are the rudest person I have ever met. I had the decency to bring my wireless set into the Mess and you have not the ordinary politeness to listen to it.' Downing their newspapers, all the officers with one accord stared in astonishment as the door banged behind the Major.

One unpleasant incident followed another and the more I became acquainted with my fellow officers, the more I developed a strong anti-snobbery outlook. I could not tolerate the 'county' talk about horses, point-to-points and hunting.

It did not take me long to discover that to talk and act 'horsey' was regarded as a sign of caste and the amount of Army time wasted on horses and talking about them was astronomical during my subaltern days. I was a particularly good horseman myself, but I had not enough money or the time to be bothered about them to the exclusion of my Army duties and ambitions. So in horsey matters I was clearly regarded by my fellow officers as a philistine. Probably that was why I was described in my confidential regimental report as 'an indifferent horseman'. I certainly agreed with Oscar Wilde's definition of hunting – 'The pursuit of the uneatable by the unspeakable'. I regarded talk on horses and hunting as snobbery. And it seemed to go on in the Seaforth Highlanders everlastingly.

As Colonel-in-Chief, the Prince of Wales visited his Regiment for Trooping the Colour, and the Seaforth officers noticed that the Prince had a perpetually bored expression on his face. Shaking hands with me, in the Dover barracks, the Prince asked: 'How long have you been in the Regiment? Do you like it?' I confided to a brother officer just afterwards that I would have liked to have expanded my answer to the second question by the Prince.

During firing practice we had to be out on the range at 6.30 am ready for the shooting to start at daybreak. After four days of continuous practice with the recruits and early rising I saw on the Orders Notice that I was not to attend the range until 9 am, as recruits would be firing. So I looked forward to an extra rest in bed. But at 7 am I was roused by a runner from the Company Captain.

'With the Captain's compliments, sir,' said the runner saluting, 'he would like to see you at the firing point immediately.'

But I decided to have breakfast first, otherwise I would get none. 'Go back to the Captain,' I said to the runner, 'and ask him would he mind if I had breakfast first.'

Saluting, the servant dashed off at speed, but returned later, panting.

'The Captain's compliments, sir,' the runner began, 'you may not have breakfast but must report immediately.'

The situation looked ominous, but I decided, come what may, that I must eat immediately. I would face whatever might come with a full stomach. Slipping over to the Mess, I had a quick meal of scrambled egg and marmalade. I then strolled over to the range and saluted the Captain smartly. The Captain fumed, but fortunately did not know that I had had breakfast.

'What the hell have you been doing?' thundered the Captain. 'Why weren't you here at six o'clock?'

'I am sorry, sir, I had no idea I was expected at six o'clock.'

'Haven't you read Orders?'

'Yes, sir, but my name appeared as being for duty at 9 am.'

'Didn't you know that the recruits were classifying?'

'Yes,' I said, getting annoyed, 'I noticed that.'

'Well, why the devil weren't you here with them?'

'I am not a recruit.'

'No, you bloody fool, but you have got to shoot with them.'

'Well, I couldn't very well guess that, could I?'

It was typical military dialogue in my time. As a result of my last remark I was ordered before Colonel Fortune for insolence. The interview was what diplomats would call 'Unilateral'. I was told off like a common pickpocket. . . .

This was a particularly humiliating experience for me because only a few months earlier I had been a Sandhurst marksman, which is quite a creditable achievement even at Sandhurst. Yet I had to fire all the recruits' course over again.

Other unpleasant and humiliating experiences followed until I finally applied to be posted to the Seaforth's foreign battalion in India. It may have been due to an unduly sensitive nature, but I felt that I could no longer tolerate the pin-pricking clashes with senior officers. Being a mere inexperienced second lieutenant, I usually got the worst in these encounters. They left me bitter, disillusioned and frustrated.

In due course the application for a transfer was granted. I was, however, really only taking a step from the frying pan into the fire – intensified by Indian heat.

After six weeks' embarkation leave I returned to Dover complete with tropical kit. The night before sailing was the last I spent with the Home Battalion of the Seaforths. Throughout the night the noise of carousing troops was heard as they enjoyed the last binge with old comrades before they disappeared to an uncertain future. At 2 am I was roused to have breakfast with all the other officers who would see the troops off. There was only one other officer in the contingent for India. The other was a captain who was in command.

A full brass-reed band turned out at 3 am to march the troops down the hill to the railway station where they entrained for Southampton. It was a crazy, hysterical last march. The troops got a little out of hand either from drink or excitement or both. They just sauntered behind the band like a disorderly rabble. The lights of their cigarettes presented a queer picture in the darkness as they moved down the steep hill.

As a junior officer, I had to march in the rear. Here another side of the picture showed itself. The last section of fours just in front of me consisted of men linked together with heavy chains. They were under punishment and it was assumed that they would have bolted if they could. It was not a pleasant sight. No wonder an early start had been made for the station, because the wives and sweethearts of the entire draft were waiting there to see them off. The draft just disappeared into the arms of their women. Nothing could stop them. They were allowed some considerable time together before being separated.

As the couples courted, the band with its bright drums and glittering accoutrements played appropriate airs. Despite my own unhappy feelings towards several of the officers, they all surprisingly trooped into the carriage and said goodbye to me. I was naturally pleased at the parting honour.

Right in the centre of India, in the United Provinces at Jhansi,

I joined the Second Battalion. I felt the impression that there was greater ease in the Indian Battalion. A big improvement in conditions compared with procedure in the Home Battalion was evident. Above all, there was a better atmosphere in the Mess. No longer was a junior officer treated as a dog's body, jumping up out of a chair when a captain entered the room, and offering his senior whatever journal or newspaper he might be reading. But snobbishness was there too, although it was kept under more control by Colonel Cope, a likeable pure-bred Englishman and proud of it, who had a puckish and acid wit. Colonel Cope was a real character who took a delight in debunking and deliberately flouting all the Seaforth's hocus pocus. He never wore six bow tassels (the regulation number) to his sporran in the Mess. He may have had six at one time. If so, he probably lost one and never bothered to replace it. He had five and stopped at five. To see him riding up to the Mess on his bicycle was a sight that everybody turned out to see.

He struggled along on a bicycle that was much too small for him, with his kilt around his naked thighs, his sporran twisted round and hanging over the back of the saddle. He might have been taken for a fool. He was far from it.

He was a shrewd old man with a super-abundance of tact in the handling of men. Ironically, he held the same name as a certain English gentleman who, when beaten by the Scots, was forced to bring the news of his own defeat to the enemy. Oddly enough, the tune that the Seaforth pipers played so often was *Hey, Johnny Cope, are you walking yet?*

At home hunting was the thing for officers to do in the élite regiments like the Seaforth Highlanders, but in India it was polo, definitely polo. Personally, I considered polo the finest game in the world but it was fiendishly expensive. I was naturally anxious to join the polo-playing set in my regiment but I had no intention of running myself into debt immediately on arrival in India. As a matter of financial prudence, therefore, I decided to take such things slowly for a start. But for a small private income from my parents, being a second lieutenant of the Seaforths in India would have been impossible financially. But polo-playing was a regimental tradition in India. It appeared to me that this tradition in the halcyon days between the World Wars was more important than the Army. To ignore polo or sport generally was regarded as reprehensible. In 1930 in Jhansi only a few officers did not indulge in the polo passion either for reasons of impecunity or because they were not horsemen. The price of polo ponies in India was exorbitant at this time, although they could have been bought through the Regimental Polo Fund on hire-purchase terms. But I preferred to keep my head above financial water for a while.

Eventually I was precipitated on to the polo ground in a way that was to put another nail into the coffin of my Army career. This resulted from a complaint by a senior officer to the Company Commander that I did not appear to be much use to the Regiment. The Commander took up the cudgels on my behalf and remarked that I was very useful to him.

'Well,' said the top brass, 'he doesn't take any interest in sport.'

'On the contrary,' said the Commander, 'he plays hockey every afternoon with his men and they have won quite a lot of trophies.'

'I dare say,' commented the top brass, 'but he doesn't throw his leg over a horse.'

Later the Commander told me that he had left the senior officer with annoyance when the complaint had been made. He added, 'You can see the position for yourself. You have two courses open to you: you either play polo, which would seem the easier, or make yourself so indispensable that nothing matters. I

am no good on a horse myself so I don't play polo, but then I
am sufficiently senior not to fear the consequences. My advice
to you is to play polo.'

And polo it had to be. My financial predicament was to some
extent eased when I was presented with Judy, an Irish grey mare,
by Colonel Cope, who was, unfortunately, leaving the Regiment
to go home and manage his estate. Colonel Cope made the gift
on condition that Judy was looked after well and never sold to a
native. With one pony I was able to play in two or three chukkas
in an afternoon.

Gradually I accumulated a small string of ponies by borrowing
until I was able to have three or four ponies on the field. And the
more I played polo, the more I liked it – in fact I became infatuated with the game.

Unfortunately Judy often went lame after one or two fast
chukkas because of her shaky legs. The vet was never able to
discover the reason. It was during one of these frequent periods of
lameness that I was asked by a senior officer in the Mess for the
loan of Judy to play in the infantry polo tournament. I refused,
saying that Judy would be completely crippled as a result.

'So you refuse to lend a gift horse to your regiment?' demanded
the officer.

'I certainly do,' I told him emphatically. 'She is a gift horse, as
you say, but she was given to me personally and I have some say
in her disposal. Please don't imagine that I am unwilling to help
the Regiment in the tournament, but I know Judy would become
increasingly lame and I would have to shoot her as the result.'

After weeks of treatment, poor Judy remained lame. So in
desperation I told my Indian servant to take the mare away and
have her destroyed. Some weeks later a senior officer approached
me at a dance in the Officers' Club and remarked: 'By the way,
they all say you sold Judy to a native.'

So disgusted was I with this despicable accusation that I didn't even reply. But by now I was sickened with the atmosphere in the Regiment. I tried to get seconded to my old love, the Royal Air Force, but the War Office regulations at that time did not permit such a move. I was determined, somehow, to get out of the Seaforths.

During my first year in India I took no leave. I stayed down in the plains doing the work of about eight officers whilst they were on leave. I found that the work was too much for me. Daily I had to cycle around in broiling heat of 118 degrees in the shade. No wonder, then, that I suffered agonising prickly heat and at night the effects of the heat were mental and physical torture. Living on stale water and lacking vegetables, I soon became run-down and boils developed all over my body. Unable to stand the mental and physical strain any longer, I cycled up to the hospital. There the RMC doctor pulled my eyelid down and commented, 'You haven't got a drop of blood left in you. You will have to go to the hills straight away.' The hills are the Himalayas. I told the doctor that this was impossible. Giving a list of the duties I had to perform, I said that there was no officer available to take my place.

'All right,' said the doctor, 'I will give you another four days. Knock off all polo and take as little exercise as possible. I will not be responsible for you if you remain down here.' After four days I was weaker than ever. So I was ordered to the hills immediately to escape the savage heat and to restore my broken health.

To a friend in England I wrote at the time:

Much has been spoken of the hills in India and the life which is led up there. I indeed found not one word of exaggeration in what I had heard and read. Love is free and plentiful and life gay and charming. Great dances and then drink

Norman Baillie-Stewart, aged about nineteen, resplendent in his Sandhurst cadet uniform

(*Above*) India 1911: Baillie-Stewart, aged two, is the toddler in the middle. His brother, Eric, is on his left. Baillie-Stewart was fourteen months old when the family arrived in India to join his father, a captain in the 67th Punjab Regiment. (*Right*) Aged thirteen, in his Dartmouth Naval Cadet uniform: 'I relished the prospect of a glorious Naval career.'

and dances again. To a young officer who has been compelled to lead a life of celibacy under trying conditions, the hills are a veritable haven. It is not the unmarried girls or the 'fishing fleet' who provide the pleasure. It is the married women.

The exotic nature of their surroundings, the adulation of handsome and virile young officers, the brilliant uniforms, the drink and the music under a clear and starlit sky with a view of the moonlight gleaming on the sugared slopes of the Himalayas, are too much for them. Strangely, the overtures very often come from the women and many a young man of twenty has been led up the flower-strewn path and had his outlook widened. Women of all ages, married to men who hold high positions with sometimes great seniority, gather in their multitudes, intent, seemingly, on one thing – love. They just cannot stand the heat of the Indian summer and so in a body they take to the hills, returning to the plains when the cold weather sets in. The husbands, in the meantime, are confined to the plains. And when they get to the hills themselves they often go off the rails too. Many of them forget about their own wives and I have seen them freely taking someone else's. There have even been open exchanges.

I have witnessed many astonishing scenes. Indeed, these scenes have been so common that they did not even arouse gossip. In this place amused tolerance takes the place of gossip. To tell the truth, few people here are in a position to throw stones, except, as usual, the unattractive, the stupid or spiteful.

If I may be forgiven mentioning it, one of my own experiences was amusing and difficult. I had just arrived up at this delectable station and was sitting with a group of people one night when I noticed an extremely attractive middle-

c

aged lady with whom I had a most amusing and witty conversation. I was impressed by her intelligence and wit and, as she was the wife of a senior civilian official, a judge, when making a round of calls on the next day I dropped my card in her box.

'Cards', incidentally, means in high falutin' Anglo-Indian society the simple act of going around on a horse with a jacket full of cards and dropping them in the little black boxes at front gates which usually had painted on them, 'Mrs So-and-So, Not at Home'. At the same time Mrs So-and-So may be watching the caller surreptitiously from her home.

The first fruits of my card-dropping on Mrs X was a perfectly formally worded invitation to dinner, to which I replied with equal formality, accepting. In due course I arrived suitably attired, just a little late of the specified time. I was the first to arrive which seemed odd to me having been late. I chatted to Mrs X, enjoying her cocktails. Time went and nobody arrived. As I was wondering if I had not been mistaken in the time, the butler arrived to announce that dinner was ready. With a charming smile, Mrs X said, 'Shall we go?' and there for me was a *dîner à deux*.

I maintained a friendship with Mrs X. It was most pleasant because she was extremely clever and beautiful, until I was suddenly recalled from my verdant pastures by a mobilisation order from the blue.

This mobilisation order was unfortunate for me because it prevented me from taking over the Hill Depot Adjutancy, a very responsible job for which I had been selected.

More unpleasant incidents followed between me and my superiors. They continued during the mountain warfare exercises at Rawalpindi in the North-West Frontier. One of the final incidents that climaxed my association with the Seaforths took place during the campaign against the Afridis, the powerful war-like tribe in the North-West Frontier's Khyber Pass.

It happened after a surprise rifle and machine-gun attack on the Seaforths, during which encounter one officer was killed and several officers and men were wounded. I was marching up a narrow, rocky pass with my men when I saw a colourful native banner flapping from the end of a stick. 'Ah!' I thought, 'a souvenir for my platoon!' I ordered my runner to jump up and fetch it. From my position I could not see to what the flag was attached. Soon the runner was back, smiling, with the flag in his hand. At our next halt in the Pass, I proudly displayed this flag to another officer. 'Where did you get that?' he snapped, eyeing the flag, and then pointed. 'Was it from that graveyard back there?' Sure enough, it had been taken from a native graveyard. 'Well, it can't be helped now,' I told him; 'in any case, no harm has been done and native graveyards are not so sacred.'

My comment was prompted by the fact that my father, a colonel in the Punjabs, had told me that his battalion had on one occasion camped in a large Indian graveyard. Without further discussion, my officer friend went to our Company Commander and reported me for committing sacrilege on a native graveyard. Nothing was heard of the incident until the platoon had completed its withdrawal. My men had been lying along the crest of a ridge covering the last troops of the native rearguard when I was called by the Company Commander.

'I hear you have taken a flag from a native graveyard,' said the Commander with a furious look.

'Yes, I am afraid so, but I thought it was an ordinary banner, I could not see the graveyard from where I was.'

If anyone could have said 'liar' with a facial expression it was the Commander.

'You bloody fool,' was his retort, 'take your runner with you and go and put it back!'

What made me furious was that the ticking-off had been given to me in the presence of my own men, including native troops. I had been made to feel like a worm. If ever I felt like striking an officer with my fist it was on this occasion. To make matters worse, my Commander had not merely humiliated me but he had ordered me to carry out a very dangerous operation, which I considered very unnecessary. It was almost like sending me out to be executed. The last covering troops had come through and I had been asked to place back the flag on a spot that was then out of sight of my own troops and within easy range of the Afridi sharp-shooters. As I started out, flag in hand, with my servant to run to the graveyard, the Commander rubbed salt into the wound by shouting after us, 'At the double!' I executed the order without incident but for me that was the last straw with the Seaforth Highlanders. Without waiting to regain my wind after the race down the rocky Pass to the graveyard and back, I sat down and wrote out my resignation. I asked for leave pending its finality. My next move was to send a cable to my father in England: LAST STRAW APPLIED FOR LEAVE PENDING RESIGNATION.

It may be mentioned, incidentally, that Mr Ramsay Mac-Donald's 1929–31 Labour Government was in office at the time and orders had been given by the War Office to the effect that kid-glove methods were to be used against the native fighters in the Khyber Pass. Trouble-making incidents were to be avoided because important talks were pending in London with Mahatma Gandhi over India's future. A most serious view had been taken of the flag incident.

Having sent in my resignation and the telegram to my father, I waited for the next move. I had not long to wait, for I was sent for by the Colonel. In a subsequent interview I wisely decided to avoid any kind of a scene. Being a very junior officer, I was certain to come off second best, so I avoided answering my Colonel's questions. Returning to my tent I heard another senior officer remark, 'The bloody swine kept masterly silence.'

I was then sent for by the Staff Captain, who suggested that I should withdraw my resignation until I had thought things over more quietly. Meanwhile it was reported around the camp that because of the flag incident the Afridi warriors had thrown a mass of fresh troops into battle against the British.

Pending a decision on my future, the Colonel put me on his own personal staff for a month's trial. Having reported to Brigadier Robertson, I took up the duty in the Brigade Headquarters as liaison officer in a large tent. There I met a friendly and sympathetic Irish officer to whom I confided my troubles and that I was disgusted with the Seaforths in India. The Irishman suggested that I should apply for service in the Irish Free State Army. I did so, but was informed that the Irish only accepted men from their own Staff College. (This application was used against me during the 1933 court martial, following my imprison ment in the Tower of London.) After working at the Brigade Headquarters the friendly Irish officer confided in me, 'The Brigadier has been talking to me about you. He said he could find nothing wrong with you.'

I felt deeply gratified and more so when Brigadier Robertson sent for me privately. He said: 'I understand you want to leave the Regiment. In the circumstances I think this is the best thing you can do. How would you like to be transferred to the Indian Army? I am prepared to give you my personal recommendation into any regiment you like.'

I deeply appreciated the Brigadier's proposal and told him so.

But I turned down his suggestion, saying that I didn't like living in India and did not like the Indian people.

As I liked Brigadier Robertson personally and especially the work he had been doing of interviewing Afridi spies, I withdrew my resignation. I had, however, been under a test and as I had proved satisfactory and efficient I had to return to my battalion. Here I found things much more smooth and friendly. At the end of the operation I was delighted with my official report. I was described as having 'led my platoon well whilst on active service'. A medal was struck for the Afridi campaign.

After our part in the North-West Frontier skirmishes the Regiment returned to our headquarters at Jhansi. This proved to be an unhappy return for me, for I clashed with the new Company Commander who would not allow subalterns to enter the Company office except during orders. Naturally I felt humiliated. All we young officers were forced to wander about in the open under a roasting sun or hide in the Company store where we could sit around chatting on sandbags. The Colour Sergeant's office was also barred to us. Life for us became unbearable. At this time the Divisional Commander sent for me for a private talk. He urged me to stay in the Army and settle down.

'You are doing well now,' said the Commander, 'your reports are good. You come from a distinguished military family and you appear to have a very good future in the Seaforths.'

The final episode came at a dinner in the Officers' Mess in the presence of all the officers in the Regiment. Presiding at the dinner was the Company Commander. At the other end of the table was a second lieutenant who happened to be the Orderly Officer. Cabbage was brought in and the Commander considered this a plebeian vegetable.

'Are you responsible for this?' shouted the Commander to the

Orderly Officer at the other end of the table. Surprised and embarrassed, the young subaltern replied, 'Yes, sir.'

'Well,' retorted the Commander, 'as soon as you learn to eat like a gentleman the better.'

It was like a bombshell and all the dumbfounded officers stopped eating with their mouths open in astonishment. I smiled.

'What the hell are you laughing at, Baillie-Stewart?' thundered the Commander in the otherwise silent room.

With considerable hesitation, I gave the schoolboy reply, 'Nothing, sir.'

'Very well, come and see me in my office in the morning at 8.30.'

'Ah, Baillie-Stewart!' said the Commander from his office chair next morning. 'About last night. I am a sick man and I am not responsible for what I say.'

I accepted what was intended as an apology but knew what was really wrong with the Commander – his liver.

I had been receiving good reports recently and felt that now would be an opportune time to get out – with a clean sheet. I would go while the going was good. So I wrote out an application for a transfer to the Royal Army Service Corps and left it on the Adjutant's office tray. Promptly I was sent for by the Colonel. Entering the Colonel's office I was faced with the Adjutant too.

'Why are you doing this? I can't accept it,' said the Colonel.

'I merely wish to leave the Regiment, sir.'

'But why? Why? I suppose you know that this will make you out to be a failure? I hope this has nothing to do with an incident in the Mess the other night.'

I was surprised that the Colonel knew. I felt compelled to say, 'No,' because the Commander had offered an apology, shabby though it was.

The Colonel said he would not accept the application at that stage. He suggested that I should go away for a couple of weeks and consider it further. A fortnight later I came back with the written application in my hand. It was accepted, recommended and forwarded.

Irma Steidelmann

AS THE APPLICATION for a transfer to the RASC would take a considerable time, I secured three months' leave and wired to a relation in South Africa saying that I was coming out for a holiday. I was tired of the *pukka sahib* and horsey gentlemen in India. At Bombay I boarded a new ship, the *SS Hypatia*, and sailed across the Indian Ocean to Mombasa in Kenya. Among the visitors boarding the ship at Mombasa was an amazingly beautiful blonde girl. Her beauty, graceful movements and perfectly proportioned figure captured my attention immediately. She was destined to have a far-reaching effect on my life, including my imprisonment in the Tower of London.

I was in the bar of the ship with three other young men when I saw what to me was like a feminine vision passing the open port. We were all equally struck by her extraordinary attractiveness. After a discussion my friends challenged me to make her acquaintance but I had no opportunity of doing so until the ship sailed. Then I persuaded a Dutchman to secure an introduction by arranging a game of deck tennis with the beauty.

She was Irma Steidelmann, a German, aged about twenty, who was on her way down to Dar-es-Salaam on a visit, after which she was returning to her coffee plantation in Kenya.

In the three days that it took the ship to sail from Mombasa to

Dar-es-Salaam via Zanzibar, my friendship with Irma ripened with extraordinary rapidity. Aboard the ship we were inseparable. We sat together in the dining saloon, played deck tennis, chatted and laughed together. At Dar-es-Salaam we went ashore together and bathed in the soft warm waters of the beautiful bay. Irma returned with me to the ship and we sat together until the warning notes of the ship's siren cleared the deck of visitors. We were mutually infatuated. Before she left the ship Irma implored me to cut short my stay in South Africa and come and stay with her in Kenya. But I told her this would be impossible because of my limited leave. It was sad saying goodbye to Irma, a girl with soft blue, dreamy eyes and an attractive German way of speaking English.

The last siren had sounded and the *Hypatia* slowly got under way and proceeded up the channel to the open sea. Leaning disconsolately over the rail I was fascinated to see a fast motor boat shoot out from the shore and head for the ship. Closer it came as it rapidly overhauled the ship. And then in the stern of the boat I could distinguish the slight figure of a girl. Could it be Irma, leaning forward and shading her eyes with her hands as she gazed at the ship's rail? It was! At once I raced for the stern rail and nearly fell overboard in my efforts to draw Irma's attention to where I was. Then she saw me and waved. In this way we proceeded to the open sea. I was hanging over the stern and Irma was in the motor boat racing along immediately below me and all the time looking up, her lovely pearl-like teeth gleaming in the sunshine as she smiled. The white foam of the wake of the ship raced and parted in flashing streaks on either side of the small boat, as it bounced, scudded and danced over the foam.

This romantic scene of the parting lovers attracted the attention of the passengers who were ambling around with nothing to do. They crowded around the rails to see the unusual spectacle which caused some amusement. Somebody laughed and called out 'Play soft music,' but I was oblivious of everything except Irma. When the ship reached the open sea, the motor boat was forced to turn back. Slowly the waving figure of Irma receded and finally disappeared from view. Thoughts of Irma were on my mind for the rest of the journey to South Africa.

It was like a lovely dream and I despaired of ever seeing her again. In Kimberley I was entertained lavishly by my uncle, Thomas Pickering, who was then managing director of the De Beers diamond mines. In South Africa I observed all the rules of an officer of the Seaforth Highlanders abroad – I shot Springbok, rode horses, played tennis and golf and generally lived like a *pukka sahib* and a sportsman. A colonel of a local volunteer force in Kimberley asked me to go and see his troops. As a regular officer of the Imperial forces, although only a second lieutenant, I was regarded as a man of some standing.

It was the custom in the British Army on such an occasion for a visiting officer to 'Leave his cards' with the colonel and officers of a local regiment when calling to see them for the first time. This is exactly what I intended to do a couple of years later during a most unfortunate visit for me to the German Army in Berlin. On the Kimberley occasion I asked the adjutant where I could leave my cards, and the officer, unaware of the military social custom, brought me down a corridor and pointed out the lavatory to me!

During my stay in South Africa my thoughts were haunted day and night about my dream girl Irma in Kenya. I then discovered that if I cut my South African visit short I could get a boat to Mombasa on my way back to India. That would mean two weeks with Irma. Promptly I sent her a cable and got a warm invitation to be her guest. Irma was in Nairobi to greet me on the platform. Laughing together we went off in her car for coffee and that night we danced in the famous Torrs Hotel. Here the band played the most popular foxtrot of the evening, *If You Were the Only Girl in the World*. The romantic strains of this delightful melody put life on wings of song for me in Irma's company. The more I saw of her the more I became infatuated. She was tall and she possessed a character and personality that completely captivated me.

At this time I wrote to a friend: 'Irma is an entrancing, lovely girl and I am now her slave. From her I learned my love and sympathy for the German race. My exchange of ideas with her and her many compatriots made me long to be one of that race and share its sufferings. To marry Irma and to embrace German nationality is my dearest wish. Our love for each other grew from the very moment our eyes first met. Our eyes seemed to talk to each other long before our lips moved. I spent six delightful days on safari with Irma, shooting game all the time, absorbing some part of her personality until I was quite under her domination. I lived each day for her alone.'

Probably one of the reasons for my infatuation for the lovely German girl was the fact that on my father's side I was a German myself. This also no doubt counted for my German sympathies. Irma and most of her German compatriots talked about what they considered to be the injustices of the Treaty of Versailles and of the East African colonies that had been taken from Germany under the 1914–18 war settlement.

I was in entire agreement with Irma and her friends. From the time I visited East Africa the Versailles Treaty became a burning question with me. In a subsequent discussion with a brother officer in the RASC about the Treaty of Versailles I was, of course, reminded of the other side of the picture. I was told that the Germans and their sympathisers conveniently forgot the crushing peace-treaty terms that the victorious German Army imposed on the Russians at Brest Litovsk in March 1918 when they thought the war was over.

I must say now at this stage that I became a German sympathiser at the time of the Weimar Republic and, unlike people such as William Joyce, I was not climbing on Hitler's bandwagon. was never a Nazi.

My parting with Irma was miserable and we both spent a lot of money on ship's cables exchanging terms of endearment. Up to the time of my arrest and imprisonment in the Tower of London I corresponded regularly with Irma. I had planned to stay with her on a holiday in Bavaria, to which she had returned, but my imprisonment in the Tower prevented our meeting. From the time I met Irma I felt that Germany was my spiritual home. I was drawn to it by some irresistible force.

Some weeks after I had returned to India and in the middle of mixing drinks for friends I was notified that I would be sailing for England from Bombay on the liner *Rajputana*.

So I left my regiment, unwept, unhonoured and unsung, but considerably happier. I was to do a probationary course at Aldershot with the Royal Army Service Corps.

Just before sailing from Bombay in the *Rajputana* I learned, to my disgust, that Mahatma Gandhi would be sailing in the same boat as the head of a big Indian delegation to a round-table conference in London. Gandhi's entourage included HH the Rajah of Malaviya, Mrs Sarojini Naidu, the famous Indian poetess, and Miss Slade, the daughter of Admiral Slade and Gandhi's ardent English disciple. She had gone 'completely native', dressing in Hindu clothes and ministering to the Mahatma's most intimate needs, including bathing his feet. The spectacle of Miss Slade, a lovely European girl, scurrying up and down the deck with goats' milk and dates for Gandhi, angered me.

There were five young Army officers aboard the *Rajputana*, all from famous British regiments. The fun soon began. Two of them grabbed Gandhi's *charpoys* (native beds) which were propped up outside the Purser's Office and unwound all the linen tape which constituted the springing. They then proceeded to walk the whole length of both gangways between the cabins tying the tape in intricate knots to the door handle of each cabin. They had just completed their handiwork when the Purser arrived to catch them red-handed. He sternly ordered them to undo the tape and remake the beds.

On another occasion a dance was taking place after dinner on the first- and second-class decks when someone ran up from the lower quarters shouting: 'There's a fire in the second class.' One of the two jokers again distinguished himself by grabbing a chemical fire extinguisher, bumping it on the ground and rushing forward with it. A thick jet of chemical foam spurted from the machine as he ran. The jet caught the dancers in the second class nicely in the middle of their pirouetting. Black dinner jackets became white, white jackets became cream, and ladies frocks just adhered clingingly to their shapely limbs. To bring an end to the chaos one of the second-class males, too wet to care further, dashed forward and started to grapple with the young officer. Instead of directing the stream over the side the jet played first on the heads of the dancers, then on their feet, and finally swept in circles as the struggle for supremacy went on. From behind a friendly bulwark of a pillar, I cautiously watched the scene and felt a real disappointment when the extinguisher finally ran out. Had the joker not taken to his heels he would certainly have been lynched. Only an abject and humiliating apology to the captain of the ship on the following day saved him from being placed in the ship's cells more for protection than punishment.

Gandhi travelled second class, but to the annoyance of me and my friends the Mahatma made free use of the first-class deck and had his favourite hymns sung there at Divine Service on Sundays.

I was sitting up late one night with the five officers drinking when one of them suggested that it would be a good idea, and they would be doing the world a good turn, if we seized Gandhi and threw him overboard. In our foggy and inebriated condition we were unanimous in the view that the idea was eminently sound and could solve India's troubles. Getting ourselves together in a bunch, we proceeded with our drunken determination to the place on the second-class deck where the Mahatma slept. To our chagrin nothing but Gandhi's blankets could be seen. Owlishly we considered venting our rage and disappointment on the bedclothing, but decided, on second thoughts, to return for more drink. On reflection, I felt quite certain that but for the call of nature that took Gandhi away from his couch he would have slept that night the deepest sleep of all on the bed of the Indian Ocean.

We did not, of course, realise that our drunken escapade could have had terrible consequences both for ourselves and the peace of the world. I was later able to appreciate the value of Gandhi as a patriot, social reformer and the moralist leader of world renown.

A stout Hindu lady was the particular object of cold stares from me and my brother officers. We did not learn until later that she was no other person than the distinguished Indian poetess, Mrs Naidu. Great, therefore, was my surprise and change of feeling when a friend of mine, an ex-Governor of an Indian province, called me aside and said, 'By the way, Baillie-Stewart, you know Mrs Naidu. Have you ever spoken to her?'

'No,' I replied.

'Well,' said the ex-Governor, 'that's funny because she thinks the world of you and says what a fine type of Englishman you are. She says she loved to see you walking along the deck so proud and handsome like a thoroughbred race-horse.'

She subsequently said to the ex-Governor when she saw me on board the Orient Express at Marseilles: 'I am so glad he is travelling on the same train.'

(*Above*) A line of Seaforth Highlanders – Baillie-Stewart second from right – inspected at Dover by the regiment's Colonel-in-Chief, the Prince of Wales, now the Duke of Windsor. With him (*centre*) is the Honorary Colonel of the Regiment, Colonel MacKenzie, with whom Baillie-Stewart clashed more than once. (*Below left*) In Kenya with Irma Steidelmann: 'An entrancing, lovely girl and I am now her slave,' Baillie-Stewart wrote to a friend. 'From her I learned my love and sympathy for the German race.' (*Below right*) Baillie-Stewart pictured in Alt Aussee in the last weeks of the war. He was still wearing the *lederhosen* when brought to trial at the Old Bailey in 1946

(*Above*) Baillie-Stewart, shielding his face from the photographer, arrives for his court martial on 20th March 1933 from the Tower of London (*courtesy: Radio Times Hulton Picture Library*) (*Below*) During an adjournment of the court martial, Baillie-Stewart talks with his counsel, Mr Norman Parkes (*extreme left*) in the grounds of Chelsea Barracks (*courtesy: Associated Newspapers*)

Major Müller

BACK IN ENGLAND I went straight to my parents' home and wrote to the Adjutant of the RASC at Aldershot. I was told that I need not report for duty for another month. So I had managed to get five months' leave in the year. My thoughts were that this was pretty hard on the British taxpayer.

With plenty of time for contemplation my main thought was the futility of everything. I felt that I had got a raw deal in the Army. Germany had been played foul. Irma was suffering and the German people were suffering. At this particular time I felt Germany was more than ever my spiritual home. Thoughts of Irma naturally coloured my views of Germany. My prevailing thought at this time was one of self-pity and despair. I would like to become a German, but how could I fit in with the Germans? What use could I be to them?

With the RASC at Aldershot I had to learn an amazing variety of subjects: equitation, baking bread, engineering, mechanised transport, accountancy, driving tactics, administration and other subjects. I was doing well and getting good reports. A riding accident, however, interrupted my training for six months. I was in hospital with a serious leg injury and then had to start my studies all over again.

As the summer came and Ascot week arrived I arranged with

D

some friends to see the Ascot Gold Cup Race in the RASC's four-in-hand coach. Such an arrangement was all part of the regimental procedure in those days. I was asked to join the party with senior officers and strange ladies. It was a glorious episode on a brilliantly warm sunny day. We went in a major's car to the Household Cavalry Barracks at Windsor where the coach and horses were stabled. Immaculately attired, I waited for the coach. Several coaches were in the yard and, pointing vaguely in the direction of a red coach which was just going off, a very horsey-looking captain said to me 'There you are. Get on board.' Being used to obeying orders of any kind without question, I called to the driver to halt. I climbed aboard from a ladder which was lowered to me.

The driver of the coach, an artillery man, turned to me and said politely, 'You don't belong to this coach, do you?' With an air of certainty I said 'Yes' and settled down. But only the frantic shout and waves of the haughty-looking Captain again halted the coach as the horses were trotting off. I was able to join the correct coach which was being pointed out to me with much gesticulation.

The day had started well. I was allotted a seat opposite the Captain with my back to the horses. Off we started for our drive through Windsor Great Park to the racecourse. After a while, being in the need of a cigarette, I took out my case, and offered it to my companions. All refused, but I lit one and started to smoke unconcernedly. Then the Captain drawled at me: 'Baillie-Stewart, it is not done to smoke cigarettes when on a coach. If you wish to smoke, you should smoke a cigar.'

I was secretly delighted at this exhibition of snobbery. Apologising I said: 'I hope to learn in time', and threw my cigarette overboard.

The driver of the coach, a titled civilian, was a member of the exclusive Coaching Club. He must have heard the comedy being enacted because he promptly took out his own case and offered it all round. Very soon everyone except the discomfited Captain was smoking cigarettes. I enjoyed my cigarette with unusual relish.

Passing through Windsor Great Park with courtly, old-world gestures to the occupants of the other coaches as we met, we came upon a colourful flowering shrubbery. As conversation was flagging, I asked someone, quite innocently, the name of the plants. The Captain replied from his regal and horsey height. 'Do you really mean to say you do not know what that is called, Baillie-Stewart?'

Not having the vaguest idea and not being interested I admitted ignorance, to which the Captain replied, 'Good Lord, have you lived all your life in towns?' This time I was incensed by the 'country gentleman' attitude of the snobbish Captain who hunted five days a week and did no work. From that moment I set myself out to annoy the Captain. I ran down the country and horses in particular for the benefit of the Captain. The fun was good but not calculated to improve a subsequent confidential report on my behaviour.

To announce our progress a footman blew fanfares from a yard of highly polished brass. The crowd, less well bred, answered with rude noises made between their forefinger and thumb. Our ostentatious progress ended at the special coaching enclosure where our horses were unhitched and the ladder lowered for us to descend. There to greet us was old Prince Monolulu, who shouted with a wave of the hand, 'Ah! This is not the working class.'

I, descending first, proceeded with polished courtesy to assist the ladies down. Unfortunately, as the first lady started to come down, the ladder slipped away and I received some eleven stone of femininity in a billowing Ascot frock on top of me. A mixed gathering of racing folk out for a day's fun laughed and cheered. It took me some time to disentangle myself and straighten out my disarranged appearance. My hat required more than a little attention.

It was a hot, cloudless June day. At lunch in our special tent everyone was so genteel that the champagne was almost untasted and the food was just nibbled. I was interested to see, from the top of the coach after lunch, the footmen and grooms polishing off whole chickens in their hands and swigging quantities of good drink. My heart bled and my stomach groaned. My feelings were outraged as I longed to join them. Unhappily, I was playing a part and the rules did not permit me to leave at this stage. For me the whole day was a riotous farce.

As the summer of 1932 approached I had talks with a few other young officers in the RASC about holidays. There was no definite plan, but there was a suggestion with which I agreed – that we should make up a party and spend our holidays in Germany. For a variety of reasons the others dropped out and I decided to go to Germany alone. I was deeply disappointed that Lieutenant Cromwell, my best friend since Sandhurst days, was unable to accompany me. I relished the idea of a will-o'-the wisp trip to the capital of my spiritual home, where I felt sure I would make friends.

In August I accordingly proceeded to London's Liverpool Street Station where I left for Harwich, the Hook of Holland and Berlin. It was an uneventful journey. Arriving in Berlin, I proceeded to a small hotel in Mittelstrasse, called Hotel Stadtkiel. I signed the hotel register giving my own name and British Army designation. Without knowing it I had stumbled upon a hotel where, it was proved afterwards, there was a German hotel porter in the pay of Britain's MI 5. I later blamed what I said were the lies and false reports of this hotel porter for my downfall.

In Berlin I knew nobody, but I was given the address of a young German Jewess, Olga Israel, by an English girl acquaintance. She was, naturally, a German speaker and as I knew no German I spent a considerable amount of the early part of my time in Olga's company. Olga Israel introduced me to a son of Walther Rathenau, the cultured German Foreign Minister, who had been shot dead in the street by extremists in 1921 because he was a Jew and because he tried to implement some of the provisions of the Versailles Treaty.

Being on holiday in a foreign country I intended to get the maximum amount of experience and enjoyment, so all three of us went to an exotic nudist colony at Halensee.

It did not seem to me at all strange to be formally introduced to girls in their birthday costumes in the baths of the colony. The piquancy of the situation did, however, make me laugh. I found that the morning bath itself was a magnificent affair, with bathing going on to music accompaniment from loudspeakers. There was an immense gallery fitted for table tennis and a wide, sloping shore on which artificial waves thundered. For half an hour the water would be calm and then, for the next half-hour, rough weather and turbulent water would be turned on. On the roof were rows and rows of small metal and canvas beds upon which the nudists reclined and sunbathed after having covered their bodies with sweet-scented oils. The whole atmosphere was exotic.

In the afternoon we saw a physical-training class. A magnificently proportioned instructor stood at a small table with a drum in his hand. With his knuckles he kept time with a big group of men and women of all ages doing exercises. The participants appeared to be taking their exercises most seriously. At the final drum-beat they all clapped – why, I do not know. I left the colony with a bundle of liberally-illustrated nudist literature which was later produced at my London court martial. I was amused to see that when the nudist literature was passed round to members of the court for their scrutiny one officer's monocle fell off.

I was only a short time in Berlin when I was introduced to a German film star who was also a beauty queen. In her company I set out to enjoy myself to the full at many places of amusement in the city. The lovely blonde actress had only to walk down any Berlin street to attract public attention for her photograph was displayed all over the place. People stopped and stared at us in the street. I was also an impressive-looking figure. I was more than six feet tall, erect, young and handsome. In Berlin people had told me that I had a striking sartorial bearing, for my well-cut Savile Row suit was in strong contrast to the comparatively dowdy dress of most Berliners in those days. So we both made an impression everywhere we went, and I say that in all modesty. I found the Berlin people mostly poor and shabby; shops were badly stocked; few motor cars were in the street and signs of general decadence and decay were everywhere. Germany had not recovered from the 1914–18 war. I, of course, blamed this all on the Treaty of Versailles. So I became more sympathetic towards the German people.

With the actress in a fashionable Hungarian restaurant one night I was in a cheerful mood after some Hungarian wine, so I thought I would like to hear the Second Hungarian Rhapsody played by the restaurant's real Tzigane band. Following the English custom, I called a waiter and sent a message requesting my selection to be played. A gracious bow was the immediate response from the bandleader, indicating that the guest's wish would be met with pleasure. Throughout the rendering of the piece the fat, cheerful celloist kept the actress and me in a constant state of hilarity with his antics, adding enjoyment to the pleasant evening.

He would suddenly lean forward and prod the nearest violinist in the stomach with his bow and then shake all over with laughter, waving over to us as he did so for our mutual enjoyment. The music over, I called the waiter again and sent over an invitation to the band to have a drink. To my surprise, the request was for a modest 'coffee'. Having paid my bill I got up from the table with the actress to move out. Immediately the band stopped playing, all the musicians downed their instruments and rushed over to the door. They made sure to reach the exit before me and my actress friend. They promptly formed a gangway. As each stood with his hand out, I nonchalantly shook hands with them and my actress friend bowed smilingly as she passed. I discovered later that the musicians expected a hundred-mark tip! It was a lucky escape.

Having become more familiar with Berlin, I decided to contact Germans with whom I was likely to have more in common and, being a military officer, I immediately thought of soldiers and military subjects. I had to rely almost completely on guidance from the English-speaking porter at the Stadtkiel who also happened to be an ex-soldier. I had had many friendly conversations with the porter since I arrived at the hotel. The porter alone amongst the hotel staff spoke excellent English. When I enquired about the German War Office for the purpose of seeing the military ceremony of guard mounting and to present my card as I had done in South Africa, the porter was most helpful. That was the only actual substance of this enquiry, but the point was stressed with emphasis at my court martial.

On the strength of this enquiry, the hall porter contacted a Russian, who in turn informed the British Air Attaché in Berlin that a man claiming to be an officer in the Seaforth Highlanders had been enquiring about how to contact the German Secret Service. This was the real start of all my troubles. But I was most insistent and emphatic on this point that the German hall porter told a lie to the Russian. At any rate, from that time it appears that my movements in Berlin were watched by British agents. The most casual remark I made to the hall porter was noted and passed on. But my claims were that the porter let his imagination run riot, telling of alleged events that never could have happened. It was my inference that the more tales that were told by the porter the more he qualified for financial reward. It was a big temptation for the porter, for he was playing the role of being a useful MI 5 agent. He knew, of course, that I would not be in a position to deny anything he had said, because at that stage I did not know that I was being spied upon.

My approach to the German military authorities was simple and direct. I telephoned the German War Office from a public call box in the Unter Den Linden and asked for somebody who could speak English. Eventually a man came to the phone. This man tried to cross-examine me, but I insisted on meeting the man personally outside for a talk. Having told the War Office man where I was speaking from we arranged to meet.

The War Office man, tall, dark and wearing horn-rimmed glasses, would be carrying a newspaper in his left hand. I walked a short distance to the rendezvous and within about ten minutes a taxi drew up and a man with a paper in his left hand stepped out. Without hesitation I went forward to greet him as if I had met an old acquaintance. In greeting we took off our hats, as is the German custom, and shook hands. The stranger looked so astonished that I almost laughed. We turned quickly together, as if we had been performing the same routine act for years and walked off. When I told the German that I was a British officer the German appeared to be impressed and remarked: 'We won't talk any more in the street. Let's go somewhere for lunch and have a chat.'

Walking down the Unter Den Linden, I had a good look at my German companion. He was about forty, nearly six feet tall, with square shoulders and a military bearing. He had a deep scar, like a duelling wound, down the left side of his cheek. He was a serving major in uniform and I could tell from the crimson stripe down his trousers that he was on the German General Staff. He appeared to be a pleasant, jovial type and this had the effect of putting me at ease. As we walked in smart military fashion down the Linden, we chatted freely, as if we had known each other for years. Then suddenly we swung left into a restaurant where there were a large number of officers in uniform and only a few civilians, sitting round the tables. At the coffee stage of the pleasant lunch my friend and I started to talk. The German said his name was Müller and in return I gave my name, rank and regiment. As proof of my identity and in good faith, I pulled out my passport to let Major Müller have a look.

For some reason that I cannot explain, Major Müller immediately assumed that I wanted to sell British military secrets, for he made the remark that I was probably in debt.

'If that is so,' he said in good English, 'I will soon put that right.'

Unfortunately for me, at that early stage I did not attempt to put the German Major right. Frankly, I did not take him seriously. Instead, I repeated that I wanted to contact the German Army to leave my card and to see the guard-mounting ceremony. Leaving a card was the British military custom on such courtesy calls and I had observed it in South Africa. It was looked upon as an almost duty-bound action by officers of the élite British regiments in those days.

My subsequent troubles would not have arisen if I had made

myself clear to the German officer, but subconsciously in my mind there were reasons for this. I was glad to have made this military contact in Berlin, because being alone in the city I wanted to make a friendship and particularly with the Major who was able to speak such excellent English and who appeared to be friendly. I did not want to do anything that might upset that friendship.

After the lunch Major Müller and I arranged another meeting for the following evening. Before adjourning the German decided, however, to put me through a knowledge test, apparently to prove that I was, in fact, a genuine British military officer. This test comprised a series of written questions on tanks, armoured cars, automatic rifles, organisation and army instruction. The questions were scribbled on a scrap of paper and the Major suggested that I should furnish the answers on the following day. As it happened, this scrap of paper was found months later in my Aldershot headquarters in the search after my arrest. It became a highly important document – Exhibit Number 9 – at the court martial. I saw no reason for destroying it. To me it had no significance, but for the prosecution it was a vital document. The answers to the questions were freely available from military publications.

Relations between Major Müller and myself continued to be friendly. After our first meeting we met almost every day and went to a variety of places of amusement.

The Major asked me if I needed money and I replied that if any money was given or lent it would be entirely at the discretion of the Major. Cash was, however, necessary for me to help cover the cost of my holiday and to replace the second-hand car that I had sold in England before going on holiday.

Small payments were made to me, but they had no relation to anything. I never gave this German officer any information of a military nature that he could not have obtained himself from

British military publications. It is conceivable that Major Müller gave me money as an inducement for possible future services to him. Altogether, including sums sent to me through the post from Berlin to Aldershot, I received just over £100. Before leaving Germany for Aldershot, I arranged with the Major that we would write to each other.

I arrived back in Aldershot a few days before the expiration of my leave. Before returning to my RASC duties I bought an old second-hand Morris coupé car with £30 that Major Müller had given me. My intention was to use the car for further trips to the Continent to meet the Major. I had the old jalopy re-painted, re-upholstered and another engine was put in by the RASC.

Soon after arriving back at Aldershot I was attached to an RASC company for practical work and divisional manœuvres. I enjoyed the work immensely and, for the first time, I really liked being in the Army. It was a pleasure for me to work with my Company Commander, who interviewed several senior officers in an effort to get me permanently posted to his company. This was not possible because I had not yet been established as an RASC officer. I was still on probation. I did, however, receive excellent reports for my work.

Having natural liking for all things mechanical and being an inventor of gadgets myself, I visited the Mechanical Warfare Experimental Establishment at Farnborough in company with another officer. It is part of the RASC officer's duty to study such mechanics as I saw at the Establishment. I inspected the latest type of lorry and the most secret tanks.

Strange things started to happen to me even before I left Berlin to return to Aldershot. It was evident that the British Secret Service felt that they were on the scent of something. And I must, at the same time, have come under the scrutiny of the German Secret Service agents, too.

On my way out of Germany on the train I had been shadowed by a Cockney who, it seemed clear from subsequent events, was either a German or British secret agent – such is the strange world of espionage and counter-espionage. This Cockney got into my compartment when the train was leaving Berlin. We were the only passengers in the compartment and he appeared to be unusually keen on starting a conversation. I was not. But I remember inviting him into the dining car for something to drink. He declined politely. It was not until I returned to the compartment that I realised I had left my valise carelessly on the seat. It was unlocked and I discovered that my papers had been handled, for they were not in the position I had left them. I thought little of this at the time. But it all came back to me most vividly when the Cockney made a dramatic and mysterious reappearance at my court martial. I still do not know whether he was working for the British or German Secret Service. But, despite his accent, I suspect that he was German.

I should have seen the red light from the condition of my letters from Müller in Berlin. They were all opened and closed in such a crude way that the tampering could not have deceived an infant. A thin line of shining glue was all around the flap of the envelope. I sent one of these envelopes back to Müller, with the warning that the letters were being opened. Both Müller and I used pseudonyms and their use became a feature of my court martial. It was obvious that my letters to Müller were also being opened by MI 5. The use of the pseudonyms must have startled the British spy-catchers. Major Müller asked me to write to him at an accommodation Berlin address and to address the letters to 'Herr Otto Waldeman Obst'. He would sign any name that came into his head – and it happened to be 'Marie Louise'. I thought of the name 'Alphonse Poiret', which I signed.

Another disturbing piece of information reached me. It came

from my batman. It was that during my absence in Berlin my room had been broken into and articles examined. But nothing was missing. MI 5 had been at work. Yet another pointer came from a brother officer. It was that enquiries had been made at the RASC library to find out what books I had borrowed. I had, in fact, borrowed military manuals in an ordinary straight-forward way to further my studies. It was assumed, wrongly, that because I had one manual on loan for ten days that it had left my possession.

Then there was a further most disturbing incident which added up to a chain of evidence all pointing in one direction. It should have become as clear as a pikestaff that there was going to be a bombshell when I heard that an inebriated senior officer made an unambiguous remark to a subaltern about myself. This senior officer said: 'Let me give you a word of advice. Don't go about with Baillie-Stewart. It is not good for you. I'll say no more.' The junior officer later repeated the remark to me as a tip-off. Tackled a couple of nights later by me about the remark, the senior officer made the excuse that he had taken a lot of drink at the time. He offered a humble apology. He said he meant to say that the subaltern was spending too much time enjoying himself; his position was most insecure and he was in danger of not passing his examinations.

In an atmosphere that was becoming increasingly charged, I carried out my duties as usual at Aldershot. I was innocent and I had nothing to fear.

Socially and as an RASC probation officer I was enjoying myself with hosts of friends. A contribution to my gaiety at Aldershot was that I played the drums in the RASC officers' band and dances reg-ularly at the Officers' Club. From women who frequented the Offi-cers' Club I had the reputation of being a 'divine dancer'. How this came about I don't know, but I had overheard the remark a few times.

During the late summer and autumn of 1932, despite the grave incidents and whisperings, I went to Holland three or four times to see Major Müller. I signed the leave book as going to 'London' because nobody ever took the leave book seriously. It was, however, an offence to go abroad without permission.

Before leaving by the 8.30 pm train from Liverpool Street Station I had dinner with a French lady, Madame de Sales, whom I had known in India. She saw me off on the train and I made no secret of the fact that I was going to Holland. Unfortunately for me, Madame de Sales sent me a Christmas card, on which she scribbled: 'I thought Holland had swallowed you up.' This Christmas card was discovered by security officers when they searched my quarters at the time of my arrest in Aldershot.

Further proof of my visit to Holland came as a result of my amorous overtures to a girl in the train and on the boat. Having said goodbye to my French friend, I looked along the corridor of the train and saw a quite handsome dark-haired girl. Without wasting time, I went to the girl and engaged her in conversation.

She was Lotte Geiller, a German girl, whose father was a Professor at Heidelberg University. She had been visiting her fiancé in Glasgow. She spoke excellent English and she was of a romantic turn of mind – what they called in those days 'cinema-minded'.

We struck up an immediate friendship on the train, so Lotte asked me to escort her on to the boat and to look after her. Being young and catholic in my tastes, I accepted the invitation, hoping that it was in the nature of an invitation. It was a glorious night crossing the Channel with the moonlight shining brightly on a glassy sea, but Lotte's resistance remained unbroken. She said she would be my soul mate but not my physical mate. Before we parted she begged me for my address. Unwisely, I gave her my card.

In Rotterdam I met Major Müller and we had a very pleasant time for several hours. I then returned to Aldershot by boat and train.

Arrest

FROM THE TIME I started my course with the Royal Army Service Corps on returning from India, until the third week in January 1933, I had been doing reasonably well in the Army. I had passed all my examinations with distinction, obtaining top place in most of them. Brother officers were predicting that I would eventually be a high-ranking 'Brass Hat'. Frankly, and without boasting, I had most of the attributes that send a young officer rapidly to the top – a great Army and Naval tradition in my family; a good military bearing and physique; a public school education, and the standard of my work, shown by the results of the examinations, was above the ordinary. Added to a record in Sandhurst of which any officer could be proud, I had some very valuable training in the Royal Navy. I also had social standing, and a certain amount of influence.

Undoubtedly my prospects appeared to be rosy when the bombshell burst. It happened on an icy-cold day on 20th January 1933, when I was keeping warm for a few moments before a big blazing fire in the Orderly Room at Aldershot. Unexpectedly I was called to the Adjutant's Office. A document was suddenly thrust into my hand immediately I entered the room. Would I sign it? That was the Adjutant's startling request as he offered me a pen.

The document stated simply and bluntly in a few words that Second Lieutenant Baillie-Stewart was unlikely to become an efficient RASC officer. I was being asked to resign. This was a tremendous shock and it came without any hint or warning of any kind. Apart from the surprising nature of the order it would mean my return to my regiment, the Seaforth Highlanders, as a reject from the RASC. Because it was a military order I was compelled to sign, but I could find no explanation for my extra-ordinary and unexpected dismissal. My Company Commander and brother officers were equally astounded. Gathering around me, they expressed their sympathy, but nobody could throw any light on this sensational turn of events in my military career.

Another shock was soon to follow. Determined to fight my case, I immediately wrote a letter asking for an interview with the Brigadier. I had not long to wait for a reply. The Brigadier would see me at Command Headquarters, attired in kilt and claymore. This order struck me as being odd. I was further surprised when the Colonel suggested I should go down to the Headquarters with him in his car immediately. Things were moving fast. I was bewildered. Soon I was ushered into a room where the Brigadier stood waiting. With the greatest politeness and cordiality the Brigadier greeted me and said immediately: 'Oh, Baillie-Stewart, before we go into our business, there is someone else who wants to see you. I am sure you will be able to offer a satisfactory explanation.' With those cryptic words, the Brigadier left me alone. Just as the Brigadier left the room two men in civilian clothes entered. They seemed pleased to see me and came forward to shake hands. The elder was the first to speak.

'I expect you remember me, don't you?' he said.

'No,' I told him promptly.

'What, you don't know me? Surely you have been to my lectures.'

I then recognised him as Colonel F N Syms of the Judge Advocate's Department, who used to lecture to the officers of the Command.

'This,' he said turning to his companion, 'is Captain "B".'

'How do you do,' I said politely, and waited for the next move. A strange coolness came over me. I was offered a cigarette. The Colonel dropped his frigid attitude and became affable. He asked me to sit down and then said: 'We have come to see you over a rather unpleasant matter; perhaps you will read this and then offer some form of explanation.' With these words he handed me two typewritten sheets of paper. One described how a mysterious Russian had laid information against me in Berlin and the other was a charge which read:

–That when you stayed in a hotel in Berlin in August 1932 you made enquiries for the address of and the means whereby you could get into touch with the German Intelligence Service.

– That later in that hotel you were visited by a German Officer and that an interview took place in your room in the same hotel.

– That on or about 12th November 1932, after your return to England, bank notes for £50 were obtained in Berlin and remitted to you from there by a person using a foreign name which appeared to be one of a code.

– That on or about 26th November 1932 you acknowledged receipt of the money so remitted to you by a letter in your own handwriting addressed to another person in Germany, also apparently using a code name.

– That you signed this letter in a fictitious and foreign name chosen from the same code.

– That on or about 5th December 1932, English bank notes

E

for the sum of £40 were obtained in Berlin and remitted to you from there by a person using a foreign and apparently an assumed code name.

– That you intimated to the person above referred to your intention to re-visit him during your next expected leave.

– That you did withdraw from the RASC Training Corps library and retain in your own possession for a month a book relating to modern formation which was issued for official information only.

I took time to read the documents because I required time to think. Handing them back to Colonel Syms, I remarked: 'It is all too absurd.'

'If it is absurd,' said the Colonel, 'you can doubtless easily provide a satisfactory explanation. Here is a pen and paper, write down your explanation, and I will submit it to the Commander-in-Chief who has asked me to obtain it.'

I was determined neither to be rushed into giving an explanation nor into committing myself in writing. I needed time to think. So I replied to the Colonel: 'The implications of this questionnaire are so serious and I must have time to think after which I will provide you with a satisfactory explanation.'

'The truth comes out easily enough,' said Colonel Syms, 'and you should require no time to think about it. Come on, here is the pen and paper, write it down.'

As the Colonel was speaking I was wondering how this had all come about. I felt incensed about the hotel hall porter and the Russian in Berlin.

'May I please read that first paper you gave me again?' I asked.

But the Colonel read it through himself and then snapped, 'No, you may not.'

Colonel Syms continued to coax me for an explanation as

Captain 'B', a Secret Service agent, sat silently beside us.

Colonel Syms then dropped his voice confidentially. 'Now look here, young man,' he said, 'it is our opinion that you know something about the German Secret Service and you have had dealings with them. You probably know their codes and we want you to tell us what you know. It is quite natural to be interested in Secret Service work and you are not the first one to have become interested. Make a clean breast of it,' he coaxed. 'I can promise you nothing, but I rather think that the Army Council will probably consider you're just resigning your commission if you tell us everything. Whatever happens they want no publicity, now tell us all you know.'

By this time I could not suppress my feelings of amusement at the Colonel's coaxings and pleadings.

'All this is just too ridiculous,' I said. 'What on earth have I got to do with the German Secret Service or their codes? I can assure you I know nothing about them whatsoever. I deny all these accusations.'

But as the Colonel persisted in coaxing and questioning me about things which I denied, I replied finally, 'If you don't believe me, put me under arrest and do what you like.'

I protested to the Colonel that I had been subjected to a form of third degree and was being badgered. But the Colonel denied this and was supported dutifully by Captain 'B'.

After a long silence Colonel Syms suddenly asked, 'May we search your quarters?'

'Certainly,' I replied, and signed a paper to that effect, as requested.

The questioning lasted for exactly four hours. Then the Colonel and the Captain left the room. Within seconds of their departure, the Major-General in charge of Administration entered the room accompanied by the Provost Marshal – the head of the Military Police.

'I place you under arrest, charged under the Official Secrets Act,' said the General, glaring at me.

I was now a prisoner in military custody.

'Take off your sword and belt,' snapped the General, and when I complied he handed them over to the Provost Marshal. The General then seized hold of my sporran.

'What have you got in here?' he demanded.

'Nothing,' I said firmly. The General then dropped the sporran back into place after sticking his fingers into the pocket in the back. Though I had been deprived of my principal weapon I was not unarmed because the searchers had overlooked my skenedhu, which projected from my hose top. I was not deprived of this for another two days when it was taken out of a drawer in my room by the Adjutant.

'Take him away,' ordered the General, 'see that he does not go near his own quarters.'

Having given these orders, he left.

From Command Headquarters, where I had been interrogated, I was taken by car back to the RASC Mess. I was kept in an office, unable to return to my room. Whilst waiting I got permission to telephone a firm of solicitors in Aldershot.

When the solicitor arrived I gave him a brief outline of the situation. The solicitor then left, saying his partner would call and see me in due course.

The room where I had been placed was immediately below my own quarters. The thud of heavy footsteps, mingled with the crash of furniture by the searchers, shook the ceiling. My old batman came down pale-faced and almost trembling.

'There's an earthquake going on in your room, sir,' said the batman sadly. 'And all your clothes are in a terrible state being thrown about everywhere.'

In their search for German codes the officers stripped the wall-paper from the room and even the linings of my coats were ripped open. There was nothing they could find, I knew, except jottings which would show the times of the boats and trains on my trip to Holland. Everything was available for inspection, nothing being hidden or locked up.

The officer in charge of me was sympathetic, for he knew that I had been to Germany.

'Look here, Baillie, old boy,' he said, 'you still have the key of your garage and your car is there. If you think it will help you at all, give me a knock on the jaw and good luck to you. I won't come around for some time.'

I declined the offer, which I deeply appreciated. I was not going to run away. I had nothing to hide.

My next move was to telephone my parents, but the Adjutant insisted on standing in the telephone box with me. My parents were shocked and horrified. I assured them that everything would come all right. They were not to worry.

Then I wrote to 'Otto Obst'. I handed the letter openly to the Adjutant for posting and, of course, the Adjutant passed it on to the Military Intelligence. It was never sent. This letter stated:

Dear friend,

I am afraid through making your acquaintance and that of Marie Louise that I am now involved in trouble with the Military Authorities here, who give me to believe that you are connected with the Intelligence activities in your country.

As you know, nothing connected with such matter has passed between us.

My affection for Marie Louise, which prompted her to finance me in the manner she did, has taken a direction which I never dreamt of and has placed me in the terrible position which I am now in. In the face of things and in the circumstances I must sever all connection with you and Marie Louise, to whom I send my love and ask her and you to forget me entirely.

As I used to sign myself 'Alphonse Poiret' I now sign myself by my proper name and regret very much that this is goodbye to both of you.

Yours very sincerely,
Norman Baillie-Stewart

Bewildered by all that was going on, brother officers at Aldershot accorded me the most kindly treatment while I was under arrest. I was lent a wireless set and a gramophone and received gifts of bottles of whisky. On one occasion an officer rushed along the corridor to his room.

'They are searching Baillie's quarters,' he shouted, 'and I am going to set fire to mine before they get there.'

The Tower

ON 26th JANUARY, six days after my arrest, the Colonel of the RASC training battalion came to me at 11 am and told me to prepare to leave.

'When am I to leave, sir? Where am I to go? How long am I going for?' I asked.

'Be ready to leave at 2 pm. I cannot answer your other questions,' said the Colonel curtly as he left. I turned in bewilderment to the Australian officer who was guarding me.

'Don't worry, Baillie, old boy,' said the Australian. 'As long as one gets three good meals a day and a bed I always say what does anything matter.'

It was a good philosophy, but not very comforting. Before leaving I asked permission to telephone my legal advisers at Aldershot. The Adjutant refused. I then asked the Adjutant my destination.

'I am afraid I cannot tell you,' said the Adjutant. 'But take no mufti.'

I then called for my batman and had my valise fetched. I packed my bedding, spare clean sheets and pillow-cases. My largest suitcase was filled to bursting with changes of clothes, washing and shaving tackle. At the bottom of my suitcase was a bottle of whisky, a parting gift from a brother officer. My close

friend, Lieutenant Cromwell, came in to say goodbye, remarking:
'Mark my words, you will be back with us on Wednesday.'
Unfortunately this prophecy was not to be fulfilled.

As 2 pm approached I looked out of the window and saw many
staff cars outside. They were flying their distinguished flags.
Through the window I could see generals fussing around. It was
all like a horrible nightmare and so hard to believe. Military
luminaries and 'Brass Hats' were agog with excitement. What
could it all mean, these hurried, serious conversations in small
groups all over a young subaltern like myself?

Punctually at 2 pm with military precision I was off. I shook
hands with the Australian and walked down the corridor with
the Adjutant. At a side door a private saloon car was waiting
with all my luggage stacked on board. My old batman stood by,
speechless and with tears in his eyes. He saluted, bareheaded as
he was. I climbed into the back of the car. When we started off I
noticed that there were four of us altogether. A captain of the
RASC was driving, the Adjutant beside him and in the back the
Assistant Adjutant and myself. In the car I was a bit dazed about
it all and I did not respond to efforts to start friendly conversation.
We travelled fast.

Leaving Aldershot I soon realised we were on the London
road. I still wondered and worried where I was going. 'Where
the devil are they taking me? Is it to the War Office for further
examination?' I thought, but had to give it up. I sat back and
tried to enjoy the drive.

In what seemed a short time we were driving through the
thick of London's traffic in parts that I had known only vaguely
as a boy.

Suddenly a notice flashed by: TO THE TOWER OF LONDON.

'Good Lord!' I thought. 'Is it possible that they are taking me
to the Tower of all places? Surely this couldn't happen to me!'

I had a feeling of shock. Suddenly there was a weakness in the pit of my stomach. I felt faint as the terrible realisation grew. It was like falling, falling down a deep dark abyss. Staring out of the car and wondering what the next turn might reveal, perspiration broke on my brow. My hands gripping my knees felt clammy. I gulped.

As the car swung swiftly into the entrance to the Tower, my thought was, 'Good God, has it come to this!'

Not until then did I know in my own mind what terror and panic really were, and these were, no doubt, largely prompted by my personal knowledge of the dreaded Tower of London.

In the confused state of my mind, being arrested and in military custody faded into insignificance compared with the ghastly prospects of imprisonment in the Tower of London.

Once as a schoolboy from Bedford, and again as a Dartmouth Naval cadet, I had been on conducted educational tours of the Tower and the succession of nightmares I had as a result of the gruesome atmosphere are still vivid in my memory. It was all probably due to an oversensitive nature and maybe an over-developed schoolboy imagination.

All that I had seen and much of what I had read about the Tower crowded around my mind during the fleeting minutes that elapsed after we had reached the Tower gates. Flashing through my mind were the thoughts of the royal heads that had rolled repeatedly from the Tower's execution chambers . . . the imprisonment there of the great Queen Elizabeth I by her sister Mary . . . the number of fallen favourites Elizabeth herself had later ordered to the block . . . the incarceration of King Henry VI . . . the executions of Queen Anne Boleyn: Robert Devereux, Earl of Essex; King James I of Scotland; Sir Walter Raleigh . . . the Bloody Tower where King Edward V and his brother, the Duke of York, were murdered . . . Sir Roger Casement . . . Traitors'

Gate . . . the execution block alongside the massive, razor-edged axe . . . the ghosts . . .

I was abruptly jerked out of my horrible reverie when the car suddenly braked at the Officers' Mess. We all got out. We were greeted by a magnificently attired Coldstream Guards officer whose regiment was on duty at the Tower at the time. He had been expecting us. He knew my name.

Taking me into custody, he half-whispered to me in a voice that appeared to be sincere, 'This is rather bad luck on you.' I was grateful for his sympathy. Physically, I tried to maintain a military bearing. Mentally, I was plumbing the depths of despair and degradation.

Seeing a sentry with rifle and bayonet approach to guard me, my adjutant turned to the Coldstream Guards officer and said: 'This is hardly in accordance with Army regulations. In Aldershot he always had an officer guard over him.'

My officer escort who had driven me from Aldershot went into the Mess for a drink while I was shown to my room. Before leaving the Tower for Aldershot they came to shake hands with me and wish me good luck. Left to myself I began to take stock of the situation. My room was cheerless and perishingly cold, for it was now about the third week in January. I examined the bed that had been prepared for me with a thick, discoloured sheet and two thin Army blankets. I thanked my foresight for having prepared for such an emergency with my own bedclothes and other needs to make myself 'at home'.

The Coldstream Guards officer returned to tell me that his servant would see to my wants and if I required him personally I was to inform the sentry outside my room. I then had a good look at the sentry. If not the tallest he was certainly the biggest soldier in the Battalion. In his towering shaggy bearskin, heavy long grey overcoat and rifle topped by a length of glittering steel, he looked really gargantuan. I was most impressed and his presence outside my door made me immediately conscious of the fact that I was a special State prisoner – one of the few for many generations back – in the Tower of London.

The officer who was temporarily commanding the Battalion, a major, then came in and said sympathetically: 'I know what it is like to be a prisoner of war myself. Is there anything I can do for you?' I thanked him and told him there was nothing I required. He then left.

My room was not a dungeon, as was popularly supposed. It was not an officer's quarters either, but a picket officer's room. It was described as such on the door. It had never been occupied for more than one night at a time. As far as I was aware, there never had been a prisoner of my category in the Tower of London before, certainly not in peacetime. My room had a medieval appearance, as was to be expected in a fortress built way back in the Middle Ages. There were three slits for windows and the semi-darkness necessitated electric light night and day.

Quite rapidly, I settled into my quarters, strange as they were. They reminded me grimly of my desperate situation. At first the constant tramping of the sentry, with his big, heavy hobnailed boots, on the stone flags of the passage immediately outside my door was merely disturbing. But later the continual clatter got on my nerves completely. In the silence of the night, added to my shocked mental condition, the sentry's steel-shodded boots seemed to clang like a blacksmith's hammer on an anvil. Non-stop for twenty-four hours a day, it was most wearisome and monotonous. And every two hours, day and night, came a thundering rat-tat-tat on my door that used to make my heart miss several beats. In marched a corporal with a relieving sentry. This military procedure was adopted because one sentry had to hand over his charge, my august body, to the next relief. He had to view the body in my presence to make sure it was there. It was a physical discomfort but my sense of humour helped to retain my sanity.

In the morning this odd military procedure excelled itself. On arrival I had been deprived of my safety razor and nail scissors. So each morning these 'dangerous implements' were produced for my use with dignified pomp and ceremony. A servant brought them in with an air of solemnity and produced them before me as if he were presenting a sovereign with a bejewelled crown. He was accompanied by a sentry with rifle and fixed bayonet who stood over me in military posture as I shaved and cut my nails. The ceremony over, the servant picked up the razor and scissors and left with military precision with his sentry escort.

This was the daily procedure and it appeared all the more fantastic by the fact that I had the use of three sharp steel knives at my meals without anyone being present in my room.

There was an amusing incident involving the ceremony of the safety razor and scissors. The Guards officer came in one afternoon and was horrified to see that the scissors were reposing on the dressing table, for the servant had forgotten to take them away that morning. The officer was so horrified that he picked up the scissors immediately and dashed out of the room to institute an enquiry – leaving his sword and belt on my bed! A few moments later I discovered the sword and belt. Calling for the sentry, I had the equipment restored to their embarrassed owner.

During my imprisonment in the Tower the weather was so bitterly cold and the draught so great in my room that when I sat down by the fire I had to lift my feet off the floor and place them on a chair. On the floor they would have been chilled with an icy, piercing draught. In this room I lived day and night except for my short period of daily exercise in full view of the public.

The commanding officer of the Coldstream Guards in the Tower showed me great kindness and consideration while I was in his custody. He chatted with me nearly every day and supplied me with two packs of cards to play patience. With my knowledge of the Army, I knew that he might well have been differently disposed.

For some weeks the monotony of my solitary confinement was broken only by the half-hour exercises in the morning and afternoon. Times for exercise were never fixed. They depended entirely on when the guard officer could find time, for he had to be my constant guard during these outings. They would take place any time between 10 am and 3.30 pm. Because of statements that had been made in the House of Commons and in the Press, I would like to make it clear that never at any time had I a choice as to time or place.

Soon after my arrival in the Tower I was awakened one morning by the crashing strains of a familiar marching tune from immediately below my window. Leaping out of bed in the cold, I peered at the black bearskins and the steel-tipped rifles of the guardsmen swinging past my narrow slit windows. It was the changing of the guard. The last time I had heard this rousing marching tune was when a detachment of German troops followed their band down Berlin's Unter Den Linden. But how different were the occasions and the circumstances!

For the first couple of weeks when I was awaiting court martial the general public, and, in particular, the thousands of sightseers who paid their money to look around the Tower, did not know of my existence. During this time I roamed the Tower freely as I was being exercised, always under the gaze of an escorting Guards officer. And all the time, in addition to the Army officer, at my heels was a regimental police sergeant, constantly on the watch in case I should make a dash for freedom.

During those outings I admired the Crown Jewels and watched the ancient Ceremony of the Keys at night. Then the publicity bomb burst and the world at large got to know that a mysterious and unidentified officer was imprisoned in The Tower of London.

When I was being questioned by Colonel Syms at Aldershot he informed me that at all costs the Army Council wanted to avoid publicity. But if they had deliberately organised a show to attract the maximum amount of publicity not only in Britain but in every country in the world they could not have succeeded better. It was like a master stroke by a public relations officer or an advertising agency. It is a fact that the presence of 'The Officer in The Tower' captured the imagination of the Press and public from China to Peru. While the British Press were naturally restricted in their reporting before my court martial, due, I suppose, to the dangers of contempt of court or libel, the American and Continental Press, being outside the jurisdiction of Britain, gave my incarceration in the Tower unrestricted coverage.

My identity was known in Fleet Street a long time before the War Office made the official disclosure. But the British Press was naturally cautious at that early stage. They were unwilling to make my identity known to the public without official confirmation. But this did not stop the representatives in London of the American, German, French and Italian Press from publishing details that were unknown to the public in Britain. Representatives of the foreign newspapers and magazines called on my parents, seeking information about my career and looking for photographs. Whole pages were devoted to me and to members of my family and the Tower of London long before I faced my court-martial. In fairness, I must say that the foreign Press said nothing against my character.

The War Office was bombarded so much by Fleet Street for

information about 'The Officer in The Tower' that officialdom decided to lift the veil of secrecy. But this was done in such a way as to make matters worse. It was on 8th February 1933, exactly two weeks after I started my imprisonment and nearly three weeks since my arrest at Aldershot, that the War Office disclosed the identity of my regiment. That had the effect of merely whetting the public and Press appetite. Who was this 'tall, handsome young officer who is being paraded in the Tower in mysterious circumstances?' was the gist of the public and Press demand. Public attention had been aroused in a way that was probably unprecedented in British history. Naturally the public were curious, for the unknown officer was regarded as an exceptional State prisoner. 'Who is the mysterious Seaforth Highlander? What has he done? Why is he imprisoned in the Tower?' The Press in Britain could publish only what they legally dared without official backing. But I know that my brother officers and my parents were bombarded with these questions. So was the War Office.

It was on 19th February, eleven days later, that the War Office named me. At the same time they said that my court martial would be held 'early in March'.

There was considerable public concern about the way I had been treated in the Tower since my arrival. There were complaints that I was being exposed unfairly to the public and Press, especially photographers, when being exercised in the Tower; that a soldier was standing over me with a rifle and fixed bayonet while I shaved and that my removal from Aldershot and away from my legal adviser was making the defence difficult.

But as far as I was concerned the Tower of London show went on, so much so that I have been known ever since as 'The Officer in The Tower' – a name that I will carry with me to the grave.

I could never understand why I was singled out for such

exceptionally unfair treatment when awaiting trial in the Tower. It was all so blatantly contrary to the principles of natural British justice, for even the lowest petty thief is given protection from the public and publicity until he has been found guilty. For some curious reason, I, a commissioned officer in His Majesty's forces, was placed in a different category from other people awaiting trial.

A few days before my identity was disclosed by the War Office an effort was made dramatically in the House of Commons to put an end to the Tower of London exhibition and to give me fair treatment. According to the parliamentary record, Mr Valentine McEntee, the Labour MP for West Walthamstow, asked Mr Duff Cooper, the Financial Secretary to the War Office, what were the alleged offences for which 'a gentleman holding His Majesty's Commission is under close arrest in the Tower of London and when it is proposed to hold his trial?'

Another Member, Mr T Levy, asked why the officer was compelled to exercise 'exposed to the gaze of the general public?' They were joined in their questioning by Mr James Maxton, the Glasgow Communist. He wanted to know the reason for maintaining the anonymity of the Seaforth Highlander and why the Tower of London had been chosen for my imprisonment.

Mr Duff Cooper replied that I was in the Tower because it was the most convenient military establishment for the purpose.

'This officer,' he said, 'is under no compulsion to take his exercise at a time when he can be seen by the general public.'

He added that the officer's name would be announced 'as soon as public interest permits'.

Mr McEntee then asked: 'Will you take steps to prevent photographs being taken when the officer is at exercise.'

Mr Duff Cooper replied: 'I have no power and the authorities in the Tower have no power to prevent the general public taking photographs in parts of the Tower to which they are admitted and permitted to be there.'

Mr Winston Churchill: 'Will my Honourable Friend, in reply, say why it is not possible to detain this officer under arrest in the Aldershot Command in the usual way?'

Mr Duff Cooper said there were many reasons why I should be detained in London. One was to help me to prepare my defence. Wellington Barracks, he said, was more exposed to the public eye than the Tower, and Chelsea Barracks was not convenient. I could not be allowed bail.

That was on 21st February, but, dissatisfied with events, Members raised the issue again on 1st March. Mr Duff Cooper, replying to questions, insisted that my removal from Aldershot to London was to help my defence.

Mr Maxton: 'What is the idea of the fixed-bayonets business?'

Mr McEntee asked when the charges would be made known to me; why was I guarded by soldiers with fixed bayonets when shaving and why I had been refused a request to consult my solicitor before leaving Aldershot.

Mr Duff Cooper said that in the 'early days' of my arrival at the Tower a private soldier 'carrying the ordinary weapons' watched over me when I was shaving. Later the commanding officer had replaced the private with an officer when I was performing my toilet.

But Mr Duff Cooper did not tell the House that 'ordinary weapons' were, in fact, the rifle and fixed bayonet.

Further questions, I see, were tabled but before they were answered I was at last furnished with the charges. That was on 13th February, three weeks after my arrest.

But the Tower of London show went on and I was regarded as the star turn on the stage. I was afforded no protection from the sightseers wanting a curious peep at the now celebrated 'Officer

F

in The Tower'. Hundreds of curious people swarmed into the Tower daily to have a look at me. They crushed and scrambled for the best vantage points for a maximum view. Many of them were armed with cameras. They took pictures of me at exercise with the Coldstream Guards officer escort and the regimental military policeman following close behind us. I was powerless. Of course, Mr Duff Cooper must have known he was misrepresenting the situation when he told the House that I was 'under no compulsion to take exercise at a time when he could be seen by the general public'. It is only common sense to say that I had to await my officer escort. It was the officer's convenience, not mine. And the only way I might have been able to avoid the public gaze would have been to exercise in the dark.

I was horrified by the publicity and by the way the sightseers crowded around me in the Tower. At times the crush was so great that my escorts had to push their way through the crowd. On these excursions I wore my Glengarry, a khaki greatcoat and tartan trews. The sightseers got some historic pictures for their souvenir albums!

On one occasion two Press photographers were waiting for us at the steps leading up to the Officers' Mess, a place where they had no right to be. On another occasion a national Sunday newspaper published a half-page picture of me at exercise. The picture was taken with a telephoto lens from a distance.

We normally walked briskly from the Officers' Mess, down the front steps past the White Tower, through the Byward Tower and into the Moat. Usually the sightseers stood aside, forming a gangway to let us pass. But when the weather was fine and unusually big crowds gathered we had to push unceremoniously through the mob. As we walked into the Moat hundreds of people who had been waiting on Tower Hill flocked to the railings to get a closer view. I was in a speechless rage and felt deeply humiliated. If I had been an exhibit in the zoo I could not have been more closely scrutinised.

Oscar Wilde, the irrepressible Irish wit, was not lost for an answer as I was, when he was in similar humiliating circumstances. He was being transferred from Reading Jail to London for bankruptcy proceedings and had been kept standing at Clapham Junction Station handcuffed and in his convict clothes. A crowd gathered to laugh and jeer at him. 'If this is the way Her Majesty treats her convicts,' said Wilde, 'she does not deserve any convicts!'

On another day I was forced by a mob of sightseers to run from exercising on the Wharf, alongside the Thames, to exercise on the Moat. And from the Moat I was forced to run again, this time to a very confined space on Raleigh's Walk, where Raleigh exercised during his twelve years imprisonment in the Tower. I remarked to my officer escort that I was surprised that Raleigh was able to obtain exercise in such a small space. The young officer, who stuttered badly, replied, 'I expect he–e–e did p–p–p–p–p– . . . press-ups!' So we moved on again, this time time to an uninteresting cobble stretch between the walls in front of the Yeoman Warder's quarters where I was free from public gaze.

Press and Parliamentary criticism of my treatment in the Tower eventually brought about improvements in my situation, but they came long after the damage had been done. Efforts were made to stop the sightseers and to prevent the photography. But by that time many hundreds of photographs of me had been taken. A carpet was laid down for the sentry to march on outside my room to deaden the sound. An officer replaced a corporal guarding over me when I shaved. The sentry had his rifle and bayonet replaced by a swagger cane. And my room was no longer entered at night. My period for exercise was extended.

I summed it up in a letter to my parents, written on official notepaper:

Coldstream Guards,
HM Tower of London,
1/3/33.

Dear Mummy and Daddy,

The authorities are now most terribly and painstakingly careful to avoid my photograph being taken these days. I had arranged to go to Church in the Tower to-day and special instructions were issued as to how I was to be conducted to the Church. I was finally led down by all the cookhouses, at the back of the men's barrack room, and smuggled in that way. I could see no photographers before I started either. The change was perfectly astounding. But the gate has now been closed when the horse has walked out! I was, of course, curious as to why I was led round by the cookhouse and was told it was on account of the photographers. The devout worshippers in the Tower Chapel of course *may* have abandoned their Prayer Books for cameras! One never knows!

With much love to you both.
From Norman

In a leading article the London *Weekend Review* stated, three weeks before my trial, what many people had been thinking at the time.

The War Office have provided the public with a first-class sensation, flavoured with medievalism. It should have been apparent to the military authorities from the outset that if an officer, serving away from his own unit, is placed under close arrest for an offence under the Official Secrets Act, it can only be a question of time until someone in the know, either civilian or soldier, will find it impossible to keep the secret to himself. The competition for journalistic scoops turns the likelihood of such news becoming public property into a practical certainty, for the temptation of gain is added to the satisfaction derived from the possession of exclusive information. It is hard to believe that of all their advisors none suggested to the Army Council the advisability of taking the Press into their confidence and asking them to forego a possible increase in circulation in the interests of fairness to the accused. As far as records go back, there is no instance of a British Army commissioned officer being convicted to traitorous conduct. If this is the charge, it is a pity that lack of imagination should have given the case such unnecessary publicity.

All the letters written by me to my parents when I was a prisoner in the Tower awaiting court-martial are in my possession. Here is one which reflects my situation and mental outlook at the time.

> Coldstream Guards,
> HM Tower of London,
> 5/1/33.

Dear Mummy and Daddy,

I am getting a little fed up with this place and its associations, even with the kind C.O. who lent me the patience cards. The unfairness of keeping me in close arrest for all these weeks before trial under these conditions is beginning to tell on me. Nothing to do, too little exercise and the permanent necessity for electric light in this gloomy room.

No privacy and sentries popping in and out throughout the day.

Your efforts have certainly eased things off a bit and must have tickled the War Office's conscience, if it has one!

One paper has referred to me as the modern 'man in the iron mask' and has severely criticised the War Office's medievalism. The handle of my door is not even rattled at night now, but the sentry still marches up and down immediately outside and follows me to the bath and to the lavatory.

John Bull, on the other hand, ingeniously states in this week's issue that the sentry is stationed a long way off and says they are nowhere near my room but only glance in the direction of my room occasionally!

I can hear the damn noise the sentry is making while I write. You know how the ticking of an extra loud clock can irritate one? Well, I listen to the thud of a sentry's military boots day and night, week in and week out!

With much love to you both.

From Norman

It was ironic for me to read the newspaper reports of some British engineers who had been arrested in Russia and were awaiting trial in Moscow on charges of spying. There were protests that the engineers had been in custody for nearly a month without being charged. The point was also emphasised that armed Russian guards were standing over them pending their trial. No charges were submitted to me until three weeks after my arrest.

Public and Press curiosity was aroused over my case for a variety of reasons. And, of course, I cannot blame the Press and public for their attitude. Not the least reason was the way my arrest and incarceration in the Tower was handled by the War

Office, which, I had been informed, wanted absolutely no publicity. Another reason was that my case was the first in which a court-martial was being permitted to try an individual under the Official Secrets Act in England in peacetime. An added titbit for the public was that I was an officer in a famous British regiment. The Tower was reserved for exceptional State prisoners. So, it was reasoned, my case must be sensational.

There were brighter sides to my imprisonment in the Tower and some incidents that helped to relieve the boredom that nearly drove me to insanity. Being greatly in need of exercise, especially because of my physical training in the Army, I sometimes used the small gymnasium in the White Tower. I was not allowed mufti but I was able to borrow gym shoes. So in tartan trews and khaki shirt I exercised on the parallel bars and on 'the horse'. I also used to take the physical-training sergeant on at bayonet fencing and I was not a little proud of the fact that I beat him every time.

One afternoon the sleet was falling so heavily that my Coldstream Guards officer escort and I decided to go to the gym instead of exercising in the open. It was here that an accident happened to my escort that could have been fatal. The result could have been that I would have found myself in an alarming situation for a sinister accusation could have been made.

There was a rope passing over a pulley in the ceiling. At one end of the rope was a loop for the feet. By pulling on the other half of the rope with the hands the gymnast could raise himself to the ceiling. There was an art in this, because unless balance was retained the feet could shoot away and the danger was of falling to the floor fifteen feet below. I had pulled myself up to the top when my escort said he would like to try. But he made the mistake of trying to perform the exercise in full-dress uniform – bearskin, grey overcoat and sword. He was almost at the ceiling when his feet shot away from him. For a few seconds he remained suspended in the air. Off fell his bearskin. Then his sword slid out of the scabbard and crashed to the ground. Finally, the officer came hurtling down and with a heavy, dull thud fell on top of his sword. He was knocked senseless, but I revived him by slapping his face several times with the palm of my hand. He reported the accident to the Colonel and praised me for my help. He said that I could have escaped.

It is strange that at the time there was so much talk in the House of Commons and the excuse given by the War Office for putting me into the Tower – to help my defence and make it easy for me to be near my counsel – I had not even decided to employ one. It was only on the advice and kind offices of a Coldstream Guards officer that I was able to employ a civilian counsel at all. I could have employed a legally qualified officer, but was advised by the Coldstream Guards officer to employ a civilian. I told him that I could not afford one.

So he drafted a typewritten application for financial aid from the War Office, which I signed. A most inadequate grant of £100 was given, but I had to be thankful for small mercies. It was due to this major alone that I was able to employ counsel. In the Tower when I wished to telephone my solicitor in Aldershot, which was often, I had to give the required number to the Guards officer who got me through. I was not allowed to make a call myself. It was an expensive procedure, for almost as soon as I got the call my three minutes were up and I had to get more money for an extended period. It was evident that my line was tapped by MI 5 – the prosecution – who were also censoring my letters. Living in the Tower alone cost me £20 a month, a substantial sum in those days and more than my pay. I had to pay for the privilege of being incarcerated in HM's Tower of London. I was compelled to mess at the same expense as Coldstream Guards officers, who were mostly wealthy men.

On one occasion, in emulation of Lady Jane Grey and others, I was persuaded by my fellow officers visiting me from Aldershot to leave my mark for posterity on the door as was the time-honoured custom of all London Tower prisoners. Taking a poker I made it red-hot in the fire and had succeeded in burning one initial on the panel of the door as my friends watched in amusement. The smoke of the burning wood and paint made them cough and then the Coldstream Guards officer who was with us in the room lost his nerve. He said he wasn't looking. But when the commanding officer came into the room the following day my artistic efforts were not appreciated. He said I would have to pay for a new panel, which I did.

I had one strange visitor. Her name was Ann. What a surprise she was! One morning the Adjutant came to see me.

'I wonder,' said the Adjutant, 'do you know anyone named Ann Pilchard? She sounded to me like an American. She was on the phone and wants to come and see you.'

Sensing something interesting, I replied that the lady's name was familiar. I thought I must know her. Could I have her to tea? My request was granted. Cakes were brought in and I sat with the Guards officer waiting for Ann to arrive at 4 pm. I felt some keen anticipation, since I had not enjoyed the company of the other sex for several weeks. Being confined as I was, I needed some distraction. I thought, however, that this girl Ann must have considerable nerve to push past all the War Office regulations and the sentries in order to reach me in the London fortress. I waited almost with excitement.

Punctually at 4 pm there was a knock at the door and a young girl was ushered in by a sentry. She was pretty but poorly dressed and seemed nervous. I had never set eyes on her before. But, rising to the occasion, I hurried forward to meet the girl, shook her hand and said, 'How do you do, Miss Pilchard, I am so glad you have come.'

'Call me Ann, call me Ann,' were the hotly whispered words I received in return.

'Well, Ann, do come and sit down, will you? It was very nice indeed of you to come and see me.'

I now covertly glanced at the Guards officer, who was gazing in amazement at Ann with wide eyes.

'Please excuse me,' he said tactfully, 'while I go out for a moment to tell my servant to bring my overcoat and sword down as I have to go out after tea.'

The Guards officer should not really have left the room, but this gave Ann her chance to come close to me. She hurriedly introduced herself as a sergeant-major's daughter in the 'Dumberland Fusiliers'. There was no such regiment, of course.

'I had to come and see you,' said Ann. 'I read such a lot about you. How are they treating you? May I write to you? Will you write to me?'

'Certainly,' said I, touched by her interest.

'Where shall I address my letters?'

'Tower of London.'

'Just Tower of London?'

'Yes, just Tower of London. That will always get me.'

At that moment the Guards officer returned and we all settled down to tea. But Ann refused to talk. We could not get a word out of her. The Guards officer played up to the situation manfully, despite the fact that he cast puzzled and doubtful glances occasionally at me. Feeling that something ought to be done to entertain her, we offered to show her around the Tower, as it was closed to the public, being Sunday.

'Would you care to see round the Tower?'

'I don't mind.'

'Lots of nice things in it, you know, Bloody Towers and all that.'

'I don't mind.'

'Well, would you like to?'

'I don't mind.'

This defeated us. Taking it that she would really like to see the sights of the Tower, we started off in a shower of icy sleet. The tour over, we returned to the dungeon and Ann again sat down and relapsed into silence that was only broken by monosyllables. It became late and she showed no sign of moving. Something had to be done. It was nice of her to have come, but she could not sleep here. Then I reminded the Guards officer that I had quite an imaginary picket to mount and this finally moved Ann.

As she moved out, she whispered, 'I'll write, I'll write.'

That was the last I ever heard of her. She vanished as suddenly as she came. As the door closed behind her the Guards officer turned suddenly and looked quizzically at me. Feeling that some explanation was needed, I told him frankly that I had never seen her before in my life.

'Well, as a matter of fact,' said the officer, 'I could think of no other explanation for her except that she was perhaps the product of some low evening you had spent in your murky past!'

It was a strange and memorable tea party on that winter's evening in the Tower of London.

During my incarceration in the Tower there were some amusing incidents over the password for admission. One involved the Colonel of the Guards. Returning from a jovial dinner one night, he was challenged by the sentry, who demanded the password. It was 'rifle', but the Colonel said 'rissoles', according to the sentry, who refused to let him pass. Only after a considerable cajoling from the Colonel could the sentry be persuaded to let the Colonel know the password which he had forgotten. This accomplished, all was plain sailing, and the curtain dropped on a military pantomime.

I never spared my escorts when out exercising. My intention was to get exercise, and exercise I got. The discomfort for my attendants was considerable, particularly for the officer, who, garbed in full-dress uniform and bearskin, sweated profusely. Since they wore Wellington boots, there were very few of the officer escorts who did not develop blistered feet. So many, in fact, developed sore feet that the medical officer complained to me that I was crippling all the officers in the Tower! As I was, of course, walking continuously my feet had become hardened and I was taking on the Guards officers in relays.

One evening I was permitted to ring the old sunset bell by the Yeoman warder whose duty it was to ring it. The bell has been rung at the same time throughout the centuries and I considered it an honour to be allowed to perform this historical function.

I was friendly with the officers in the Tower and particularly with the Drum Major of the Coldstream Guards band. For that reason the military band at the changing of the guard always counter-marched under my window. The ceremony enlivened my spirits and helped to relieve my boredom each time the Drum Major marched his men up to my window before turning. When the drum-and-pipe band beat retreat the Drum Major always played Scottish tunes for my entertainment.

Whilst I was in custody in the Tower, one of the sentries posted near the Crown Jewel House 'saw a ghost', left his post and refused to return. The punishment for such a dereliction of duty in these circumstances in the Tower is not severe. A certain amount of credence is lent to the stories of scared sentries because, within the Tower, so many people have been executed or murdered.

During this period of nine weeks' imprisonment I amused myself, in a fight against reaching the depths of despair, by carrying out a variety of practical jokes. One was at the expense of an old Yeoman warder and his family. On the part of the wall where I used to stand watching the traffic going up and down the Thames the chimneys of the Yeoman warders reached up to knee level. One of them was belching smoke so much that it interfered with my enjoyment of the morning air, so I thought of a plan to give the warder and his family the benefit of their own smoke.

Taking off my overcoat, I laid it over the top of the chimney. Very soon the warder and his family hurriedly evacuated their dwelling, coughing and gasping as they ran. As soon as I saw the effect, I removed my coat and innocently resumed my sight-seeing. When the smoke gradually cleared from his home the warder and his family returned, and my escort and I had a good laugh.

In the Tower I was able to read a great variety of newspapers and magazines. I was astonished and bewildered at the space I was getting. I was tickled by the harmless imaginative writings by many of the journalists. One referred to me as 'The Man in the Iron Mask' and another said: 'The Highlander in the Tower is a greater draw than the Crown Jewels'. Most of them conjectured about the dungeon I was in and whether it had been occupied by any famous characters in history. A French magazine suggested that I had been engaged in the export of arms to Japan, which country, at that time, was in the process of liquidating Manchuria. A Hollywood writer said that because I had been imprisoned in the Tower, Anny Ahlers, the celebrated German actress, had committed suicide!

The First Trial

AFTER WEEKS OF waiting I was at last informed of the date or my court-martial. The receipt of this information coincided with a startling incident. My solicitor in Aldershot, having prepared all the documents for the defence, sent his brief by post to his counsel in London. When the packet reached the London lawyer it had been broken open. An attached Post Office note stated that the packet had been found open and re-sealed. My counsel, furious and perturbed, started investigations but never obtained any satisfaction.

As was expected, my trial received world-wide Press coverage. It started in the Duke of York's headquarters at Chelsea on 20th March 1933 – fifty-nine days after my arrest. Presiding over the General Court Martial was Major-General W J Dugan, Commander 56th (First London) Division, Territorial Army. The Judge Advocate was Mr P N Sutherland Graeme and Major H Shapcott prosecuted. Defending were Mr Norman Parkes and Mr Connolly Gage.

Accommodation was provided in the court room for the Chief of the Imperial General Staff and his representatives; the Adjutant-General; the Judge Advocate-General and Military Intelligence officers. It was an all-ticket affair. There was seating for seventy-five reporters representing the Press and agencies in every country.

There were ten charges under the Official Secrets Act. I was accused of having, in Berlin between 1st August and 20th August 1932, made a note concerning tanks, armoured cars, automatic rifles and organisation of brigade tanks in association with Otto Waldemar Obst, for a purpose prejudicial to the interests of the State – information which might be useful to an enemy. There was an accusation of obtaining information which might be useful to an enemy at or near Aldershot between 1st July and 30th November 1932, for a purpose prejudicial to the State. Another charge was that for the commission of the alleged offence I made an arrangement with Obst to meet him in Holland on 28th August 1932, to give him information. Another was that I made notes for a journey to Holland and that I had visited Holland twice for purposes contrary to the Acts.

To each of the charges I pleaded 'Not guilty'.

Immediately the officers of the court had taken the oath, there was a disturbance at the back of the courtroom. A tall, middle-aged clergyman was on his feet with a bible in his hand. Everybody turned to look at him.

'I protest in the name of Jehovah against this young man being committed to the Tower,' he said in a loud, clear but quivering Scottish accent. There was a stunned silence in the courtroom.

He stood as if surprised that he had not been pounced upon immediately by the Red Caps and flung out. Encouraged by this, he shouted again, 'I protest, I protest'. The President ordered his removal and he was grabbed by two hefty military policemen. Gripped by the Red Caps, he left shouting.

When silence had been restored, Major Shapcott told the court that part of the proceedings would be *in camera*, during which the evidence of certain foreign nationals would be laid before them.

I write the following account of the proceedings from *The Times* report:

Major Shapcott said that a watch had been kept on me and about 14th November a letter addressed from Berlin to me at my private address at Southsea had come into the possession of the authorities. It was dated 12th November 1932. He read it aloud:

My dear Boy, I often think of the nice days we spent together in Berlin last summer. I hope you are very well and you have not forgotten me. You were so kind in lending me some money. You remember my father stopped giving money to me because he did not wish that I should continue studying. Meanwhile, he has altered his opinion and it is all right. Unfortunately, I cannot pay you back the whole sum at once, but I hope I may be able to send you the rest before Christmas. I look forward to seeing you again next year. Please write to me again if you can come.

> With very kind regards,
> yours,
> Marie Louise

In the letter were ten £5 Bank of England notes.

Major Shapcott told the court that the prosecution had in their possession my banking account and knew from this that I did not have, at this material time, £50 to lend anyone. I went on record as saying that there was no lending of money and that this letter was not true in that particular. The case for the prosecution was that the money was for information which I had collected and communicated to a person to the prejudice of the State. In other words, they alleged that I had sold my country for the sake of £50 and any more which might be forthcoming.

Major Shapcott outlined my movements: On or about 16th July I applied for leave to go to Germany from 1st August to

31st August. Leave was granted and I went to Berlin, he continued, but on 20th August I came back.

Then the prosecution read out another letter, addressed to Herr Obst: It was dated 26th November, from Aldershot, and read:

Dear Friend, Thank you very much for your letter and the prompt way in which you settled our small debt. It is very good of you to ask me to stay with you and I shall do my utmost to take a holiday. At the moment I think I shall be able to manage at the beginning of March.

When you write to me in future, may I make a suggestion that you use much smaller seals, as such large ones are apt to arouse the curiosity of unscrupulous people. I say this because, from the appearance of your last letter, I should imagine someone had opened it to have a look inside before it reached my home address.

The weather here is not too good at the moment and nearly everyone seems to have colds. I hope you are fairing better in Berlin.

I shall look forward to hearing from you soon and seeing you in the Spring.

Again many thanks.

Yours ever,
Alphonse Poiret

Major Shapcott said the letter was in my handwriting and that I was 'Alphonse Poiret'. The man 'Obst', he said, was a foreign agent.

He went on to say that on 7th December another letter came into the hands of the authorities. It was sent from Berlin to me

G

at my Southsea home. It was in similiar terms and was from 'Marie Louise'. The letter contained four £10 Bank of England notes.

Major Shapcott then described the questions of Colonel Syms and Captain 'B' put to me at Aldershot on 20th January, and of the eight questions that were submitted to me.

The Major said that I had insisted that an entirely wrong construction had been placed on the whole matter; that I had said that the money had been sent by the woman in consequence of a love affair; that it was in fact money sent to me 'for services rendered'; that she had sent me the money to help me because I was not well off.

He also alleged that I had handed to an officer a letter addressed to 'Otto Waldemar Obst' explaining to 'Obst' that I now wanted to have nothing more to do with him or 'Marie Louise' because I had been informed that they were connected with the Intelligence of Germany. The Major emphasised that I signed the letter Norman Baillie-Stewart.

In the Tower of London, the Major continued, I had told my escort, Lieutenant Preston, that while in Berlin I had enquired about seeing the ceremony of Mounting of the Guard and about the location of the German War Office. He said that I had met a military officer, presumably 'Obst', and that I had picked up a girl named 'Marie Louise'. I had told Lieutenant Preston that 'Marie Louise' and I had become great friends and that she had sent me £90 so that I could return to see her.

The £90, he pointed out, was partly for the journey and partly for services rendered. When my rooms were searched they found a document containing the address of the German Military Defence headquarters and its telephone number. On another piece of paper there were details of time-tables of trains and boats to Holland. On the back of that piece of paper was the address of a film star whose name, the Major added, he did not propose to mention.

He went on, in the words of *The Times* report: 'Another document in his possession is one of the most remarkable documents in this case.

'It is written on a piece of paper which must have come from Berlin. It is an invitation to some stores in Berlin in which an exhibition of sports trophies was being held. The document contained the words "organisations, tanks, AC's" – which we say means armoured cars – "equipment, arming and structure".

'The submission of the prosecution is this, that someone wanted to get information concerning those things. The documents also contained the words "automatic rifles, pattern extent". It may be that "extent" means extent of distribution or range. That we do not know. The document also contained the words, "organisation of brigade" and underneath was the word "tanks".

'We say that this document was eminently one which had been dictated and the submission of the prosecution is that it was dictated to the accused at some time by some person who was a foreign agent and sought the information required.'

This was Exhibit No 9, the prosecutor's trump card.

'On 27th August', said the Major, 'Baillie-Stewart breakfasted at the Mess at Aldershot and left Liverpool Street Station on the boat train for Harwich.'

On the train I had met a lady who would say she saw me disembark in Holland. I was supposed to have told her I had 'something difficult to do' in Holland and she was not to ask what it was. The submission of the prosecution was, said Major Shapcott, that I went to Aldershot to get information and take it to Holland. The Major produced a photograph of a tank which he said had been found in my possession. I had borrowed from another officer a book called *The Textbook of Small Arms*, *1929*, and that officer would say that I had returned the book saying that it was too technical.

Major Shapcott went on to say that I had borrowed from the Aldershot library a book on modern formations. It was for official use only. I obtained it on the very day when, according to the prosecution, I should have received what Major Shapcott termed the first reward.

Colonel Syms, in evidence, told the court about the interview he had with me at Aldershot on 20th January. He said that I had explained that I had not lent any money to the German girl, but that she had given it to me for services rendered.

'I asked him,' said the Colonel in the Press report, 'what sort of services? He said that he had had a liaison, a love affair with her. I asked him to give me the name of the hotel where he registered. He said that the relationship with the girl could take place otherwise than in a house. I told him that I had heard of a motor car for such a purpose, and asked for the address of a garage where he had hired a motor car. Baillie-Stewart said it did not take place in a motor car but in an open place.'

Colonel Syms said that I could not give him the address of the girl or her relatives but that I had told him she was about twenty-two and was fair. Colonel Syms said he had asked me why I acknowledged the receipt of money from a girl by writing to a man named 'Obst'. According to the Colonel, I replied that that was the arrangement between us; that I did not know 'Obst's' profession and could not give any particulars about him except that he was about thirty-six years old.

'In fairness to him,' added the Colonel, 'I must say he showed considerable surprise when I told him that "Obst" was German for "fruit"; "poiret", French for "little pear" and that "Marie Louise" was the name of a pear. He said that that was pure coincidence. He denied from the beginning that he had attempted to get into touch with the German War Office or the German Intelligence Service. He denied that he had any German officer or any other man in his room in his hotel.'

When he was cross-examined by Mr Parkes for the defence, Colonel Syms said: 'When he told me the remarkable story of getting £90 for one act of intimacy in a public park I was so astonished I asked for an explanation.'

Mr Parkes: 'You regarded it as remarkable? I think that it is astonishing.'

'He did tell you he used the name "Poiret" to keep the military name out of it?' – 'Yes. Something of that sort. He said he wanted to keep his military status out of the letters.'

'As I understand it, he explained to you he had written to her under an assumed name to avoid placing on paper any record of his military identity in this transaction?' – 'I don't consider that an explanation. He had only to call himself "Norman". That would have kept his military status out of it.'

'I dare say you have come into contact with cases of blackmail?' – 'Yes.'

'You know when persons are engaged upon matters which are rather discreditable they place themselves in great jeopardy if they place upon paper their names?' – 'Yes.'

'I am suggesting that it was the desire of the military authorities at this time to keep the matter secret?' – 'Certainly.'

'And that you indicated to this officer that if he had admitted this matter he would get out by being allowed to resign his commission, and he rejected that suggestion?' – 'Nothing of the sort.'

'Did he say to you, "If you say these are Secret Service agents I will help you when I go over there in the spring"? ' – 'When I was asking him whether he could give me any details concerning

"Obst", he said: "If you will let me go over in March I will find out for the Army Council".'

Colonel Syms said he had been instructed to invite me to give an explanation by way of the eight questions that had been submitted to me. He said he thought that I could give a short explanation which was an innocent one and give some particulars that could be checked. He said that I had told him I had received money payments from a woman following a love affair I had had with her in Germany, but not by way of explanation.

Mr Parkes: 'And he told you the reason he wrote to her through "Obst" was to avoid the possibility of other people knowing of the association, as they might object?'

'He did not say a word of that sort.'

'Did he give you no explanation as to why he wrote to "Obst"?' – 'No. All he said was that that was the arrangement made between them.'

'If Captain "B", who was present at the interview, were to say that the accused said he wrote to "Obst" because the girl's parents might object, that would be quite untrue?' – 'I have no recollection of it.'

'Do you deny it specifically?' – 'I say he did not say it.'

'He told you he wrote to this young woman under an assumed name because he did not want to put his military identity on paper?' – 'Yes.'

'He denied that the names constituted a code?' – 'No, he did not deny it, but he showed surprise when I read out the word "code". He seemed genuinely surprised.'

Colonel Syms said that I had told him the girl was fair and aged about twenty-two. He said that I had confided that I had been intimate with the girl in the open beside a lake. He added that I did not realise the importance of the interview at Aldershot in so far as a court-martial was concerned.

Mr Parkes: 'You appreciate that his explanation was discreditable to him?' – 'It was not an explanation at all, it was a statement and I didn't believe it.'

Mr Parkes: 'I am not asking you whether you believe it or not. Did you understand he was admitting to you discreditable behaviour? I mean it is not creditable behaviour to receive sums of money from women?' – 'I quite agree with you.'

Colonel Syms said that he had not requested me to write down there and then for the information of the Commander-in-Chief an account of what he called my discreditable behaviour.

Mr Parkes: 'Had he committed in detail that statement to writing, it would not have made attractive reading as regards the character of an officer in the Seaforth Highlanders?' – 'It certainly would not.'

The Judge Advocate asked Colonel Syms: 'Lieutenant Baillie-Stewart told you that he received the money for services rendered?' – 'Yes.'

'Are you positive that he said that intimacy only took place once?' – 'Quite positively.'

'Then it would be possible that he might have meant that the money was received not merely for one act of intimacy but for general association with the woman?' – 'I do not know.'

'Did you gain the impression that the money he had admitted he had received from the girl was for one single act of intimacy?' – 'I did not gain anything because I thought he was putting me off with a story simply to gain time. I did not believe a word of it.'

'Did you in your report to the Commander-in-Chief say that the accused had told you he received the money for one act of intimacy?' – 'No, I wrote that he had had a liaison with a German girl and that she had paid him money in respect of that liaison.'

'If you had put in your report that the liaison consisted solely of one act of intimacy that would have been more prejudicial to the accused than the report as it appeared?' – 'I think it would.'

Captain L P Causton, MC, Assistant Provost Marshal at Aldershot, then gave evidence of searching my quarters with the help of two other officers. He found a tweed suit and some bank notes, he said. The *Tactical Handling of Tank Battalions* was found in a drawer beside my bed. He mentioned that nothing was under lock and key.

Another witness called by the prosecution was my fellow officer, Lieutenant Cromwell, RASC. He said he had been friendly with me since we passed-out together from Sandhurst in December 1928. In the summer of 1932, he recalled we had discussed going to Germany together on holiday but he could not go for financial reasons. He said that I went alone in August. On my return from Berlin, I had mentioned to him the great time I had in Berlin in night clubs and things like that. He pointed out that I did not mention having a liaison with a German girl or receiving sums of money. Major Shapcott handed Cromwell a book called *Textbook on Small Arms*. The Lieutenant explained that I had borrowed it from him for two or three days and that I had returned it, saying it was too technical for me. This book, Cromwell said, could be bought at the Stationery Office.

Mr Parkes asked Cromwell: 'Was there anything secret about the accused's visit to Germany?' – 'Nothing whatever. He was quite open to me about it and to the other officers. I had hoped and intended to go with him. He asked two or three other officers to join the party.'

Cromwell said he was in and out of my room when we were doing the same military course and that I kept all my books and papers quite openly. He described me as a keen soldier, interested in all branches of the profession. Cromwell pointed out that I had volunteered to give up my holiday in Germany in August in order to attend a small-arms and light-guns course at Hythe.

Lieutenant D W S Miller, formerly of the Royal Tank Corps, was summoned to give evidence on the point that I had borrowed a photograph of a light tank from him. The tank was out and about in the open in Salisbury Plain, Miller explained, and he believed that similar photographs of it had appeared in the public Press.

Before calling me to the stand, my counsel, Mr Parkes, said that the story the prosecution asked the court to believe was one which not merely involved the unbelievable conclusion that an officer had acted in this way, but was a story that was full of all sorts of improbabilities. The books and journals that had been mentioned were not brought by me to Germany. A photograph, in a newspaper cutting, of a Vickers gun and of a tank had already appeared in the public Press. Was that the sort of thing the German Secret Service were paying £90 for?

While in Berlin, Mr Parkes went on, I was introduced to this woman whom I knew only as 'Marie Louise'.

'He was alone in Berlin and not unnaturally became on more and more intimate terms with her,' said Mr Parkes. 'I ask you to draw the inference that she became infatuated with him. The accused has always been a man having peculiar attraction for women, and himself having a peculiar attitude towards them which, perhaps, I might describe as rather a lack of chivalry. This young woman apparently had plenty of money. The accused, while not in financial difficulties, was not well off, and they soon drifted into the habit of this young woman paying for their joint entertainment.'

He said that towards 20th August I decided to return home, knowing that my brother, Lieutenant Eric Wright, would be on leave at our parents' home at Southsea. He said that when I left

'Marie Louise' I said we might meet again. She replied that she would be in Holland on 27th–28th August, and we agreed to meet there.

Mr Parkes said that during the progress of the trial some corroboration had been forthcoming, for the defence. A man of eminent respectability would tell the court that during the same month he was introduced to a young lady who gave the name of 'Marie Louise'. He had seen the reports of the proceedings in the newspaper and had decided to volunteer the information.

I was then called to give evidence. I said I met 'Marie Louise' on holiday in Berlin in August 1932. I explained that I got into conversation with a man in a café in the city who introduced me to Fräulein 'Marie Louise' on the following day. Before I left Berlin we discussed the idea of meeting in Holland and went so far as sending a waiter for time-tables. That, I explained, was the origin of the notes about Holland that were found in my room. Subsequently I received a total of about £90 sent in letters from Berlin. It was partly for services rendered and partly to pay my fare.

When Colonel Syms questioned me about allegedly giving information that might be of use to an enemy, I told him it was rubbish. I explained that it did not dawn on me for a very long time that the accusations were most serious. I said I wanted time to think and to give an explanation but the Colonel could not agree. I said I would offer to help in the enquiries if Colonel Syms believed my friends in Berlin were intelligence agents. Colonel Syms said that was impossible.

I said in reply to Mr Parkes that the visit of the two officers to my Aldershot quarters was a great shock to me because I knew they were from the War Office.

Mr Parkes: 'Did Colonel Syms say anything about publicity?' – 'Yes, he said that the Army Council were absolutely frightened and that they did not want any publicity in the matter. They wished to keep it out of the civil courts. I complained to him about all the questioning which lasted nearly four hours. I complained that I was being badgered and subjected to third degree.'

I went on to describe how the Major-General came in and I was arrested. Almost immediately I wrote the letter to 'Obst' stating that I was severing all connection with him and 'Marie Louise' because I had been informed they were secret service agents. I said I never obtained or attempted to obtain any information for a purpose prejudicial to the interest of the State at any time. There was no possible reason why I should commit such offences. I had never been in debt in my life.

When I was cross-examined by Major Shapcott, I said I met 'Marie Louise' nearly every day in Berlin. The Major suggested that she looked like a shop girl. I said she was definitely above that.

The President asked me: 'Did she strike you as a mystery woman?' According to *The Times* report, I replied: 'All foreigners are mysterious in a way.' I went on to say that I felt she had become increasingly infatuated with me. I denied, in response to a prosecution suggestion, that I left her in Berlin to go back to Aldershot for information and then return to Holland.

The Judge Advocate then asked me about the sum of £50 I mentioned in one letter. 'Is it your view that this £50 was sent to you for immoral services rendered. You know what I mean?' – 'I do know what you mean. I think it was given for the whole of our friendship. It was more as a gift.'

'You know what the expression "keeping a woman" means?' – 'Yes.'

'Have you heard the contrary of a woman keeping a man?' – 'Yes, I have heard.'

'Do you think that comes within the latter category?' – 'Yes, it does, sir.'

The President: 'It also includes payment for entertainment, going to cinemas and other shows, does it not?' – 'Yes.'

Asked about 'Marie Louise', I explained that I wrote to her through 'Obst' because I did not know her address. That was the arrangement. They asked me why I used the signature 'Alphonse Poiret'. I said it was never agreed that I should use any particular name.

My counsel, Mr Parkes, then asked me about a document which bore a number of train times on one side and the name of a German film actress on the other. I explained that I had corresponded with this actress for some years previously.

Mr Parkes: 'The suggestion was that you did not know her until you got to Germany?' – 'That is quite wrong.'

I then identified a letter which I had received from the film actress. This document was in my quarters when I was arrested.

One of the witnesses called at my trial was the well-known dance band leader, Mr Victor Sylvester, who was then principal of a dancing school in London's West End. He said that until he had read about the case he had never heard of me. In August 1932, he said he was in Berlin with his wife. They were giving an exhibition of dancing on the roof garden of the Eden Hotel. On Friday 19th, after their demonstration, a gentleman came over to him and said there was a lady who would like to dance with him. A girl was then introduced to him as Fräulein Marie Louise. She was pretty, young and had fair hair. She was 'very, very German', said Mr Sylvester. He thought it was funny that she was German and asked her, because of her name, if she was French. She said she was very fond of 'ze Englishmen'.

Mr Sylvester was then shown a photograph by Major Shapcott. Mr Sylvester said that that was not the woman he had met in Berlin.

The trial was now drawing to a close. My counsel stood up to make his closing speech. He told the court: 'This is no ordinary court-martial held in the quiet of a barrack room at Aldershot. In this case this officer's life is ruined, whatever the result of it may be, and he knows it. His career in the Army is ended.

'Any possible life he may continue outside the Army will be a life which is wholly worthless, whatever the result of this case may be. He knew that when he went into the witness box and during the months he has spent awaiting trial. He knew when he went into the witness box that he would have to confess shameful matters of his association with this woman, and for weeks he has been awaiting to undergo that ordeal.'

My trial lasted seven days. I had been sixty-six days in custody. I was found guilty on seven of ten charges and I was sentenced to be cashiered and to five years' imprisonment.

Now I must say that my court-martial was held in an international atmosphere of growing world tension that was not calculated to help my case. There was increasing nervousness in Britain at the rise of Hitler and the Nazis in Germany. Step by step, Hitler had been gaining supreme control in Germany and only ten days after my arrest in Aldershot, on 20th January, he was appointed German Chancellor. The Fuehrer was then poised for his first move into what the democracies regarded as a dangerous military dictatorship.

At that time Germany was still obliged under the Treaty of Versailles to keep her armed forces reduced to 100,000 men. She was forbidden to have such weapons as military aircraft and tanks. Her Navy was also vastly reduced as a striking force. But secretly Germany was rearming and, naturally, everything that Germany's Secret Service could find out about such matters as tanks and military equipment was acceptable from any source.

The *Glasgow Bulletin* on 14th April 1933 had this to say in a leading article about my trial in relation to the world situation:

THE FIRST FRUITS OF RE-ARMAMENT?

In some ways the most serious side of the Baillie-Stewart court martial is just that it seems like the ground-swell of a new tide of armaments in Europe. Military spying has not been much heard of in recent years – though no doubt there have been attempts at it in many countries. But if the movement for rearmament in Germany begins a new arms race on the lines known before the war, we may expect trouble of this sort everywhere.

Unless Europe can contrive to keep its armaments under control we shall have a growth of treachery and suspicion that will push the nations straight into the state of mind which leads to war. We are getting a pretty complete exhibition of that state of mind in Russia now, but there are other countries in which its appearance would be far more dangerous to peace. This case ought, in fact, to be a warning to British people to do their utmost to make that sort of development impossible.

There was world-wide unrest. World disarmament conferences were flopping. Spies and spy-catchers were active in many countries. Russia had seized some British engineers in Moscow just about the time I was thrown into the Tower. They were accused of spying for Britain. War clouds were gathering in the Far East. Japan had seized Manchuria and had set up a puppet government there. She was digging herself in during the London and Moscow spy trials.

With the limitless publicity that my trial provided, Britain had an opportunity of telling the world that her counter-espionage agents were not asleep. Any foreign agents contemplating obtaining secret information about Britain's Army and secret equipment were warned publicly to abandon any such attempts or take the consequences.

Immediately the gates of prison clanged behind me there was a flood of speculation in the Press everywhere about my trial. Any kind of theory that seemed to have even the ghost of credibility was published to satisfy the insatiable appetite of the public for this *cause célèbre*. A controversy raged and some of the leading newspapers in Britain published highly critical articles on the way the case was handled. They referred in particular to the drama in the medieval atmosphere of the Tower of London. The issue of whether or not I got a fair trial was raised but official-dom remained discreetly silent on the way I was treated before the trial. In the public free-for-all that followed the conviction and sentence, suggestions were made that I was Britain's Dreyfus.

Writing in the *Sunday Dispatch* on 30th April 1933, Lieutenant-Colonel Balfour Macnaughton, DSO, asserted that 'The Officer in The Tower' was innocent.

He stated: 'The most terrible disgrace which can overtake a soldier has blasted his life, broken his mother's heart, brought his father near to death, and jeopardised his brother's Army career.'

Colonel Macnaughton said that 'Obst' and 'Marie Louise' had laid a trap for me and that I was being blackmailed. He added: 'Let us look to it that a lasting injustice is not done in this case, lest we, like France, should have an indelible blot on our memory. I refer, of course, to the famous 'Dreyfus Case' when an entirely innocent man was wrongly condemned and doomed to spend the greater part of his ruined life in exile on Devil's Island, his entire innocence only to be proved after years and years of untold suffering.'

Brigadier-General W H H Waters, CMG, CVO, in the same newspaper on 21st May said: 'The evidence against Baillie-Stewart was purely circumstantial. I think a terrible miscarriage of justice has been done in this case.'

Mr William Bronson, an ex-investigation officer with the British Army of the Rhine, in a circular on my case, said he flew to Germany to make his own investigations. He wrote: 'The feeling there was generally in his favour and the name "Dreyfus" was frequently recalled . . . I am definitely convinced that he is definitely innocent of the charges. I am also definitely convinced that he has been disgracefully outraged, cashiered and cast into prison unjustly, for a crime he did not commit and was incapable of committing.'

Mr Bronson said that all the references to 'The Officer in The Tower' in the newspapers before the trial must have influenced the War Office. When the court-martial was convened it was noticed, said Mr Bronson, that four officers came out of the offices of the Judge Advocate-General; the principal witness for the prosecution, Colonel Syms; the prosecutor, his assistant and the deputy Judge Advocate-General. Beside these, two officers came from the Intelligence Department of the War Office. He said it was a great mistake to have the case tried by a military court. The proper court would have been a civil one.

Much speculation after the trial was concentrated on the mystery of 'Fräulein Marie Louise' and the equally mysterious 'Otto Waldemar Obst'. Now what are the facts? Everything that was said about 'Marie Louise' by me during my examination at Aldershot by Colonel Syms, and later at my trial, was, in fact, a figment of my own imagination. I assert that 'Obst', as such, never existed. 'Obst' was the alias used by Major Müller and the address given for 'Obst' was an accommodation address for the Major.

When Colonel Syms gave me the eight-point document at Aldershot before my arrest I fully realised the seriousness of the situation, especially after my sensational, unexplained dismissal from the RASC a short time earlier. Colonel Syms confronted me with a demand about the identity of 'Obst', suggesting that he was a German secret agent. At once I realised that a battle of wits was being started between me and MI 5. Without much consideration I countered with the not very convincing story of the love affair with 'Marie Louise'. There was a ready-made opportunity for me to use this story because the name was already known to the Colonel through the censored letters. It was, of course, Major Müller who had signed himself 'Marie Louise'. During the trial the prosecution tried to prove the existence of 'Obst', the secret German agent, and I tried to prove the existence of 'Marie Louise'. I can state with certainty that neither of them existed.

Exhibit No 9 is said to have damned me at the court-martial. But it had been lying in my room among other papers for several months. It is, however, such things, rightly or wrongly, on which convictions are often obtained and on which assumptions can be drawn.

I realised, too late, that if I had told the entire truth about Major Müller and the reason for the scrap of paper I would probably never have been convicted; nor would it have been necessary to invent 'Marie Louise'. I would, of course, have been dismissed from the Army.

Why did Major Müller want the written answers? Why did he not ask me for oral answers on the spot? I could certainly have given them there and then.

H

I cannot understand why he asked me to write them down. It was his way of doing it. Not mine. Of course, as a junior officer I was always accustomed to doing what I was told by superior officers. This was probably in my mind subconsciously when confronted across the table by the German Major in the Berlin restaurant. The whole thing seemed so unimportant to me at the time. I remember the Major appeared to be in a hurry to keep an appointment that evening and, as I had arranged to meet him the following morning in any case, I decided that I could give him the answers when we met again. Major Müller was so unaffectedly pleasant and companionable that it irked me to think he might regard me as a collaborator.

After much mature consideration it seems highly probable that Major Müller sent the money in order to maintain me as a contact for future use. I admit freely and frankly that I was responsible for getting myself into this highly dangerous position with a major in the German War Office for I accepted the money. But I never had any intention of giving the German any military information of a nature that could be used against Britain. I had none to give.

There was never any proof, direct or indirect, that I ever did so. Any military matters I discussed with the German were freely available in widely circulated official books. I was found guilty on suspicion and assumption. In any court of law I would have been entitled to the benefit of any doubt that there might have been in the minds of the court.

In the flood of speculation that followed my conviction, many things happened to the mythical 'Marie Louise'. She was 'shot', 'buried' and 'imprisoned' in several countries.

One of the many strange characters who turned up every day at the court martial was Captain Franz von Rintelen, a self-confessed German master spy. He was in court to defend the honour of his lovely daughter, also named Marie Louise. Von Rintelen, then an anglicised German, had a highly developed dramatic sense, and made himself conspicuous at the trial. With a flourish and considerable amount of affectation he produced an enlarged photograph of his daughter and presented it to Victor Sylvester. Mr Sylvester had said that he danced in Berlin with a fräulein named Marie Louise. But the photograph that Von Rintelen produced of his daughter was not, said Mr Sylvester, the Marie Louise he had danced with in the fashionable Eden Hotel. Determined that his daughter would not become involved in my spy trial, Von Rintelen wrote to all the newspapers threatening to destroy 'the whole German Secret Service', if necessary, in order to protect his daughter. His daughter's photograph appeared in the popular Press at the time.

In order to ensure that no injustice was done to the German Captain's daughter and to exonerate her, I wrote a letter on official Tower of London notepaper to the Press, while I was awaiting the verdict of the court-martial. This was duly published. I apologised to Von Rintelen for the misunderstanding which had associated his daughter with the case. I disclaimed all knowledge of the girl.

Another surprising appearance at the court martial was that of the Cockney from Berlin who was a German Intelligence officer. He turned up in mysterious circumstances. I was having a walk with my escort during a short interval in the grounds of Chelsea Barracks when I saw something that startled me. As I passed the main entrance of the building I happened to notice a man standing under the portico holding a newspaper up to his face and visibly shaking in every limb. He looked so suspicious to me that I presumed he was another of the numerous MI 5 men scouting around. I was determined to let the suspicious stranger know that I had noticed him lurking there. So, walking up the steps past him, I deliberately peered round the newspaper and into the man's face until our noses almost touched. To my astonishment, the stranger said in a low voice with an unmistakable Cockney accent, 'Good morning, sir.' But I naturally could not stop and passed on having noted his greeting. I had seen that face before. Where on earth could it have been? I paced up and down racking my brain. At last I had it; it was the Cockney in the Berlin train! I turned back trying to find the man, but without success. It seemed to me very likely that the Cockney had been sent from Berlin by Major Müller to contact me during my trial and to give me some message. It was strange how this mysterious Cockney agent turned up to give a celebrated spy trial a real cloak-and-dagger atmosphere. I have no doubt he was German, not Cockney. He had slipped through the surveillance of military and civil police in order to communicate with me. But the opportunity had been missed and all we had been able to do was to exchange greetings.

Naturally I felt very bitter over the careless way that Müller had sent me unsolicited money through the post. Admittedly, it was most damning, on its superficial value. It was Major Müller's false assumption that had landed me in all my difficulties and not the least was the sending of the £90. But in fairness to the Major it must be said that he did his best to help me when I was arrested. He had despatched the Cockney and he had also written letters to me. The Major tried to come to my aid by writing silly letters signed 'Marie Louise', knowing that they would be intercepted. One of them was to the effect that she was so sorry that this situation had been brought about but, 'unfortunately "she" could not come forward to give evidence for family reasons'. At that time such letters seemed so futile.

Miss 'D', the foreign witness who gave evidence against me, was none other than Miss Lotte Geiller, the German girl whom I had escorted from London to Holland. When she returned to Germany she wrote me many flattering and sentimental letters. I was, therefore, astonished when I learned that she had come specially from Germany to give evidence for the prosecution. Impressively Major Shapcott announced 'the evidence of certain foreign nationals will be laid before you. I am instructed that if their names are given in public it would be exceedingly detrimental to them on their return to their country of origin. Their future life might be jeopardised.'

Miss Geiller's evidence consisted of telling how I had accompanied her from London to Holland, a fact that was admitted. After the court had been cleared of the public and Press, she entered leaning heavily on an officer's arm and weeping. In the witness chair she languished and sobbed, but she was soon brought sharply to her senses by Mr Parkes. She was asked had she ever heard of an old English adage, 'there's no fury like a woman scorned'. Her love letters to me were read out in court and the reading of them was the cause of many uncomfortable moments for me. Miss Geiller had said in evidence that when she met me on my way to Holland I had told her I was going there 'to do the most difficult thing I had ever done in my life'.

Now can anyone imagine a spy making such a ridiculous confession? I deny having made it, but, assuming I did would not such a remark be consistent with innocence?

The only other witnesses who gave evidence *in camera* were military officers who told of the contents of certain Army manuals, most of which were on sale at the Stationery Office.

Now the 'fruit code'. The choice of the names used in the correspondence was sheer coincidence. Even Colonel Syms admitted in evidence that when I mentioned the code at Aldershot, I appeared 'genuinely surprised'. It was pointed out that 'Marie Louise' was the name of a particular pear; 'Poiret' was a small pear in French, and that 'Obst' was the German word for 'fruit'. Major Müller had told me in Berlin that when he wrote to me he would address me as 'dear friend' and he would sign it under any name. 'Marie Louise' was his inspired choice. I followed his difficult lead with another bogus name which I invented. It was 'Alphonse Poiret', the surname of a leading Paris dress designer with whose daughter I was on friendly terms. 'Obst' was the name Müller had chosen for himself.

The uncovering of the alleged fruit code was accomplished by the late Major Hinchley Cooke of MI 5, then known as Major 'A'. He won a reputation in Britain for spy catching.

It was emphasised by counsel for the defence during the trial that the use of code names for a surreptitious correspondence was not the exclusive right of spies. It could be for business reasons or during a lovers' illicit liaison.

No proof of the physical existence of 'Obst' was ever put forward at the court-martial. Yet the name of this mythical person 'Obst' was included in charges against me. At the same time Major Hinchley Cooke stressed that 'Obst' was a well-known ex-military intelligence officer on the Western Front in the 1914–18 war! The fact remains that I was convicted and sentenced for allegedly giving information to a character whose physical existence nobody ever attempted to prove.

I admitted quite openly that I had been to Holland twice. I had gone there each time to see Major Müller, but I could not abandon my initial mistake of saying I had gone to see 'Marie Louise'. Having invented 'Marie Louise' on the spur of the moment I had to stick to that story. I thought little of making such trips and pointed out that frequently I had travelled from Portsmouth to the Isle of Wight in the boat solely for the purpose of getting drink when the pubs had closed on shore, and to enjoy myself. This, I maintain, was a common practice.

I went to Holland to see Major Müller to have talks but not to give him military information. It was all highly suspicious, I admit, but people do strange, innocent things. In Holland Major Müller was in his civilian clothes, but he always wore his uniform in Berlin.

Other points arise from my trial. How could any young second lieutenant, for instance, be in possession of highly secret information that would be of use to the enemy? I was never in any position of responsibility to possess such secrets. My knowledge was limited to information that might be of use to me to pass examinations and to further my own Army career. After returning from India I spent about seven months off duty. I was in hospital recovering from a riding accident. Then I was convalescing and afterwards on holiday. The time I spent at Aldershot was thus very limited. Why should the German War Office pay in such paltry instalments for information? Is it not clear that they would have sent all the money, a mere trifle for a War Office, in one lot? Is it not evident also that if Major Müller had been paying me for military information he would have safely handed over the money when we were in Holland? Yet the money was sent through the post without even being registered when both of us knew the letters were being opened.

Another feature of the case is that if I had been given secret information about the new British light tank I would have required a blueprint of the internal mechanism or a photograph of the inside of the tank. There was never any evidence or suggestion that I had either. A picture of the outside of the tank had appeared in the public Press.

A fair and reasonable inference is that Major Müller regarded me as having treasonable intentions, but it would be wrong to jump to the conclusion that I had intended to oblige him with co-operation. There was no evidence that I would, although, admittedly, the circumstances were suspicious. In law, however, suspicion is not good enough to secure a conviction. Being partly German myself, I liked the Germans and I liked Major Müller. I wanted to maintain that friendship.

Within a few days of my being lodged in Wormwood Scrubs Prison, I was visited by a high ranking MI 5 officer who held out an inducement to me that if I made a detailed disclosure of all I knew about the German Secret Service and their codes I would be released forthwith. With this object in mind, I signed a type-written confession that was handed to me. But when my release was not forthcoming I promptly repudiated it.

Mr Duff Cooper was asked about this 'confession' in the House of Commons on 23rd November 1933 and replied: 'If Baillie-Stewart made a statement that he was induced to make a confession by a promise that he would be released, there is no truth whatever in that statement.'

What, then, could my object have been in making the 'confession'? Surely what I wanted most in life was my freedom and, in the circumstances, I was only being human in signing the statement. There could have been no motive other than freedom.

Recriminations

I KNEW THAT all my letters from the Tower were being read by War Office officials and, of course, Military Intelligence officers.

So, on 29th March 1933, whilst awaiting the promulgation of the court-martial's findings, I sent a letter to my parents, but my message was, in fact, to the War Office. I knew my parents were convinced of my innocence. This was it:

> Coldstream Guards,
> HM Tower of London,
> 29/3/33.

Dear Mummy and Daddy, After months of protracted strain I have at last been found 'guilty' of the dreadful things I have been accused of. This verdict is the greatest shock I have received since the day when I was first arrested and when I underwent that four-hour interview, the details of which have never been made public, as those concerned in it have thought it best in their own interests to keep quiet.

In that interview the offer of resigning my commission was held out to me but it was only if I gave them codes or information relating to the German Secret Service. Being unable to do this, I naturally did not accept it and told them that I knew no codes or information, nor had I anything to do with the German Secret Service. I, however, offered to find out all I could for them when I returned to Germany in the Spring. This last fact, in the accounts of that interview by the two officers concerned, was denied by one and admitted by the other! Does not this point to the nature of the rest of their evidence?

I chose the path of a court-martial, when I knew the consequences should I fail, with the faith that I should completely clear myself.

That my true story is highly discreditable I frankly admit and make no attempt to excuse myself, but that the other story profferred by the prosecution should have been accepted, when there *was not one shred of direct evidence* is almost unbelievable. Did not the Judge Advocate himself warn the court against acting on surmise and suspicion? The case for the prosecution was based on these two things alone!

Surely I have suffered enough and have expiated my moral crime after all this time?

It has been said to me that I bore myself well at my trial but I do not take credit for that. I was conscious throughout of my absolute innocence of those ten formidable charges and I was confident that the issue would be in my favour. This, and this alone, enabled me to bear up under the shame of the public admissions which were so forcibly dragged out of me in attempting to clear myself. I have already suffered every shame and humiliation possible and my burden is made heavier and yet heavier.

I am prepared to face and take whatever is coming to me, but there is so much more in my case than meets the eye, that I cannot but speak and try to let the public know further facts.

That my acquittal would have been disastrous to the War

Office and the prestige of its several departments, I need not comment upon, but that my silence should have been ensured in this manner is a matter which I hope the public will note.

My appeal to the King is being put forward both by my legal advisors and by myself, but I have the certainty of another month's captivity in the Tower before I hear of any other move in my destiny.

I have been accused (and much hangs on this) that I consorted with German agents and, although it was incredible to me that any of my friends could have been such people, I was prepared, considering the gravity of the charges, to hear that friends of mine could be *proved* as such! The 'expert' witness of the War Office came forward to give evidence and, to substantiate the expertness of his evidence, he told the court his career.

This, in itself, was simply amazing and, I venture to state, would greatly interest the British public. To come to the point. Could he tell us that Marie Louise was a Secret Service Agent? Could he tell us that Obst was? No! ! ! All he could say was that his experience made him suspect that they were! He had not seen them and knew *nothing* about either of them. When I asked this 'expert', at the taking of my summary, what grounds he had for saying that Obst was a Secret Service Agent he replied – 'That is an Official Secret!'

I challenge this witness (Major 'A') to come forward in public and state his reasons for saying that any of my friends were or are Secret Service Agents!

I hope the world will see how far suspicion and surmise alone have caused me to be convicted.

To add to my troubles, a Lieutenant-Colonel in the Judge

Advocate's Department (and also a witness for the prosecution) went round, during the time that I was giving evidence, saying that I might as well throw myself on the mercy of the court straight away!

Also, to create the necessary atmosphere, I was asked if I knew a German artillery lieutenant called Hans Reimer. Further, when a telegram, offering the assistance of another witness, was delivered to my counsel, the prosecuting officer gave out in open court that it had just been 'decoded' and made a general mystery of it.

My arrest from the start was a foregone conclusion, otherwise why would the Provost Marshal and Major 'A' have been 'standing by in case they were needed' from 2 pm until 6 pm while I was being 'interrogated', to use the Provost Marshal's own words, by Colonel Syms? Whatever explanation I gave, the result would have been the same!

I doubt if this document will ever be read by the public, but if it is I am satisfied.

The whole of this matter was started by the hotel porter, of my hotel in Berlin, reporting that I had enquired as to how to get in touch with the German Intelligence Service! This highly ridiculous and gratuitous lie has been the essential cause of my present unfortunate position. I had signed my correct name and regiment in the hotel register, which alone should give the lie to that monstrous suggestion.

From that moment, though, I was watched and every action of mine was misconstrued. I was indiscreet in many points over my affair with Marie Louise and this, of course, fed the fires. My interest in my work was interpreted in the only way possible to them. Where people live in an atmosphere of treachery and intrigue, is it not natural for them to suspect it in others?

My 'collection of information' speaks for itself. Much of it was purely elementary and my counsel has covered that point fully. That I ever gave it away or 'sold' it was and is absurd and *cannot be proved*!

There is nothing more I can say but await the inevitable consequences of such a finding as the court made. I continue to express my innocence and shall always do so. In ending, I must record the final ironical blow which Fate dealt to me. I received a letter from Marie Louise following Herr Obst's former one to my solicitor, on the morning that I heard my fate! It was too late and legally inadmissible as evidence!

My very sincere thanks are due to many kind strangers, anonymous and otherwise, who have sympathised with me and in many cases offered me help in my trouble. I am glad to say that every letter I have received has been in sympathetic and helpful strain!

With much love to you both,
From Norman

Did I get a fair deal?

The question is not directed towards the actual trial in Chelsea Barracks, but to the general circumstances: interrogations, preliminary summaries, statements in the House of Commons and to the Tower of London exhibition preceding the court-martial. On the matter of justice in the courts, John Gordon wrote in the *Sunday Express* on 24th June 1962:

Do you think justice for the citizen is so firmly based that injustice cannot be done? If you are under that delusion note the warning just given by a group of leading lawyers headed by Lord Shawcross on 'the almost insuperable difficulty of establishing the fact of a wrong conviction'.

They point out that a Home Office investigation into an

alleged wrong conviction was carried out by the police who had already been responsible for the prosecution; that a prisoner's solicitor was not informed of the reasons why new evidence was rejected and was not given the chance to rebut the police report.

Not very comforting to think about, is it?

Now, if the difficulty of establishing a wrong conviction under a police prosecution is 'almost insuperable', how much more difficult must it be when the prosecution is by military court martial, conducted largely under the aegis of the War Office?

If we assume that I was the victim of a grave miscarriage of justice, would not my chances of overcoming such an 'insuperable difficulty', as mentioned by Lord Shawcross and his colleagues, be almost impossible? For it cannot be over-emphasised that when I was tried in 1933 there was no appeal to another court as there has been since the passing of the Courts Martial Appeal Act 1951. My trial was completely in the hands of military officers with key figures from one War Office department – the Judge Advocate-General's Office. This is a very small department and was run at that time mainly by the Judge Advocate, who appeared in my case, Major Shapcott, who prosecuted, and Colonel Syms. If there had been any kind of an appeal open to me it would have been sent back to these officers. So these men would have been sitting in judgement upon themselves – an impossible situation in law!

Officers of the Judge Advocate-General's Office framed the charges, secured the appointment of the personnel of the court, collected the evidence, conducted the prosecution and provided the chief witnesses for the prosecution. And it is most extraordinary that the Judge Advocate at my trial, Mr P N Sutherland Graeme, was also the Deputy Judge Advocate-General! The

Judge Advocate, whose function it was to hold the scales equally between an accused person and the prosecution and to direct the officers of the court on points of law, went, as was the custom, into retirement with the officers of the court to consider the verdict. This is even worse than if a judge in a civil jury case adjourned with the jury to consider the verdict, because the Judge Advocate at my trial was deputy chief of the office that was instituting the prosecution. No wonder the Courts Martial Appeal Act was passed in 1951, after a Crown Commission of legal men had conducted an enquiry into procedure.

I do not suggest that the Judge Advocate in this instance was unfair to me. He merely did his duty and followed the regulations that were then in existence. In fairness to the Judge Advocate, he pointed out at the court-martial, when referring to Major 'A', that this MI 5 officer could only say that from his experience the conduct of 'Obst' and 'Marie Louise' was that of agents. The Judge Advocate added: 'Major "A" is not entitled to jump to that conclusion or to make that statement' and again: 'The prosecution had little evidence about these two persons except such as was provided in the statements made by the accused just prior to and after his arrest.'

The Judge Advocate went on: 'Major "A" is not entitled to come before you here and say he suspects a named person ("Obst") as being an intelligence agent of a foreign country. He is not entitled to say, that, from facts he knows about this case or any other case, he is confident that such a named person is a foreign agent. The prosecution alleged a sinister purpose in all that the accused was doing. The grave allegations they made were their bounden duty to prove. They must ensure that every link in their chain of testimony would stand the strain. It is not for the accused officer to establish his innocence but for the prosecution to prove his guilt.'

He added: 'The prosecution did not suggest, nor was there a shred of evidence to suggest it, that he went there [Germany] for a treacherous purpose or with an idea of doing anything deleterious to the interests of his country.'

It was recognised by the War Office that there were grave defects in court-martial procedure in Britain before the Second World War. The 1951 Act was introduced to remedy the situation. The chief defect was that a member of Britain's armed forces had no means of appealing against a conviction. The new Act provided that a convicted officer would be given the same opportunity to appeal against a conviction as is the right of any person in civilian life. I had no such opportunity. This Act also laid down, in a further effort to ensure that there was no miscarriage of justice, an appeal to the House of Lords in certain circumstances.

If such facilities had been available in 1933 when I was convicted and sentenced, I would most certainly have appealed. I am told by eminent lawyers that my appeal would have succeeded and conviction and sentence quashed. A further 'fair trial' clause in the court-martial procedure was introduced in the 1951 Act. It was that from that date the Judge Advocate would be appointed by the Lord Chancellor and not by the War Office.

Many influential people in Britain believed that I was innocent. It was stated in the House of Commons that these people included four generals, nine colonels and sixty-one other officers. Many of them expressed their convictions in public. They backed petitions to the War Office and to the Commander-in-Chief asking for a review of the case. My father and mother campaigned against my conviction until their death.

My father, in a letter published in the London *Daily Telegraph* of 13th April 1933, challenged statements made in the House

The camera reaches across the grounds of Chelsea Barracks to picture (*from left to right*) Lieutenant Eric Baillie Wright (Baillie-Stewart's brother), Baillie-Stewart, a solicitor's clerk and a Guard's Escort (*courtesy: Radio Times Hulton Picture Library*)

(*Above*) Hitler on the saluting base after the occupation of Vienna, witnessed by Baillie-Stewart. Also in this photograph are Himmler, Keitel, Milch and Seyss-Inquart. (*Below*) William Joyce, who inherited the title of 'Lord Haw-Haw' from Baillie-Stewart, at a pre-war meeting of British Fascists (*courtesy: Associated Newspapers*)

of Commons by Mr Duff Cooper, at this time the Secretary
of State for War.

He said that Mr Duff Cooper had stated in the House that I
had not complained when in the Tower, but he, my father,
asserted that the sole reason for this was that I, an inexperienced
twenty-four-year-old, did not know that I could do so. He also
pointed out that I was not aware that the War Office would
meet the expenses of the trial, which my Aldershot solicitor had
stated would be 'considerable'.

My father added:

Perhaps Mr Duff Cooper is not aware of the fact that three
distinct summaries of evidence were taken, the first starting
in January 1933 and lasting three days, and the last on 1st
March.

My son, to avoid expenses (his solicitor being in Aldershot),
attended these himself without his legal adviser being
present, a most dangerous procedure and a fatal handicap.
To my horror, I did not know of this until afterwards. In
Aldershot his messing was three shillings a day, and at the
Tower 5s 6d a day. Here again the expenses were increased.

Not until 1st March was he permitted to consult his solicitor
in privacy when preparing his defence, a great handicap. On
that date he was given a notice-board to hang on his door
in the Tower when consulting his solicitor. The giving of
this notice-board is proof of the fact that there was no
privacy previously.

Had my son realised that all the expenses were to be met
by the War Office, I feel sure that he would have had his
solicitor present during the taking of the summaries, and
would have been in a position to consult him more frequently. The solicitor being in Aldershot made it very

I

difficult and expensive. Much had to be done by telephone, an expensive business and not satisfactory.

I cannot think why there is so much animosity shown in the case of this unfortunate boy.

Right from the moment I was confronted by Colonel Syms and Captain 'B' of the Secret Services in Aldershot, irregularities occurred. They were all calculated to prejudice the prospects of a fair trial at my subsequent court martial. As a young officer, I was almost completely ignorant of the law and of my own personal rights as an accused person. My mind was confused between answering the questions in the ordinary way of my superior officers which I felt militarily bound to do, and answering questions from my superiors at an enquiry which could lead to my own conviction. I got no warning or explanation. I feel strongly that an unfair advantage was taken of my inexperience and ignorance of the law.

In Colonel Syms I had to face an experienced senior officer from the Advocate-General's office who was well versed in legal procedure and the law of evidence. Colonel Syms stated in evidence at the court martial that it was not until he was half way through the interrogation at Aldershot that he realised there might be a court martial. With the admitted fundamental facts in his possession, including copies of 'Obst's' letters and mine, it is hard to imagine the Colonel was so innocent. But even after two hours he did not stop and warn me that I need not answer the questions or incriminate myself. He went on for another two hours. On Colonel Syms' evidence alone, I am told that my conviction and sentence would have been quashed in a civil court or by a court-martial appeals court. Colonel Syms must have had a shrewd idea, however, that I was going to be arrested and charged before he started the interrogation. It will be recalled that within seconds of the departure of the Colonel and Captain 'B', the Major-General and the Provost Marshal rushed in and placed me under arrest. They had been waiting in readiness outside the room to do so. Captain Causton, the Assistant Provost Marshal, had said in evidence: 'I was told I might be required.'

It was when I was confronted by Colonel Syms at Aldershot that I took refuge in sex and blurted out the silly statement about 'Marie Louise' as a cover-up. It flashed through my mind at the time that if I gave an illicit love affair on the Continent as a reason for my silly behaviour the matter might not have been taken further.

My imprisonment in the Tower instead of Aldershot was a huge disadvantage in the conduct of my defence. From the time I was arrested on 20th January until the trial started on 20th March, I saw my solicitor only three times. One result was that I, a young and legally inexperienced officer, had to conduct my own cross-examination of witnesses during the three highly important summaries that preceded the trial. Evidence for the trial was based on those summaries and was provided by me! It is little wonder that Mr Winston Churchill and other MPs protested in the House against my imprisonment in the Tower instead of Aldershot before the court martial.

I had to wait three weeks to hear the final verdict. One afternoon, when I was sitting in my room in the Tower with Mr Parkes, the door opened and in walked the Colonel followed by the Adjutant. He had a paper in his hand and read from it the fateful words that I was sentenced by court martial to be cashiered and to five years' penal servitude.

'You will be leaving here in half an hour,' said the Colonel. 'Be ready to move. You need take nothing with you.'

With these words he left, leaving me alone with Mr Parkes.

We looked at each other in consternation and dejection.

'Well, that means five years cracking stones for me, I suppose,' I said.

'I'm afraid it does,' said Mr Parkes.

The Colonel and the Adjutant returned half an hour later.

'Well, are you ready?' asked the Colonel. 'You are going to Wormwood Scrubs Prison.'

'In this uniform?' I asked in amazement.

'Yes,' was the reply, so the final insult to the British uniform was to come from the War Office.

'But I can't go like this,' I protested.

'You will have to,' insisted the Colonel.

When I realised that the Seaforth Highlanders' uniform was not to be spared the indignity I requested that my rank badges should be taken off. The Colonel and the Adjutant then helped me to take off the gilt stars from my tunic and overcoat. But it made little difference, since my distinguishing uniform remained with badges and buttons.

As I was about to leave, the Colonel presented me with a Mess bill accumulated during my imprisonment in the Tower. It was for about £20 and the Colonel asked me to sign a form directing my bank to pay the bill. So, I had to pay for my imprisonment in the Tower, and for being held up to public ridicule and contempt!

Before stepping into a car I took a last look at the Tower of London. I was then whisked away, accompanied by the Adjutant, who sat in front with the driver. He was wearing a blue suit and bowler hat. Also in the car with us was the Regimental Sergeant-Major of the Coldstream Guards and my old friend the Provost Sergeant, both wearing blue suits and bowler hats.

As we drove through the streets of London we noticed newspaper posters all over the place announcing the result of the court martial. And that was the result of the first trial in England of an Army officer on charges under the Official Secrets Acts.

As I was received in Wormwood Scrubs I read my description in the register: 'A soldier in uniform.'

Having been stripped of my uniform, I was given a bundle of coarse prison clothing and told to have a good strong carbolic bath. I was then ushered into a room where a white-haired pleasant-looking old chaplain sat at a desk. After a few formal questions the Chaplain asked the astonishing question: 'What do you propose to do when you are released?' With the prospects of five years in prison in front of me, it was not something that I had contemplated.

'As a matter of fact,' I replied, 'I had thought of relinquishing my altruistic status and becoming a professional spy!'

If he only knew what I intended to do when I gained my freedom!

Later, after I had been moved to Maidstone Prison, I found quite a collection of colourful characters. Among them was Clarence C Hatry, a leading City of London company promoter and share manipulator. Hatry's arrest, trial and imprisonment caused one of the biggest financial sensations of the century. I remember reading about it when I was in India. Little did I think that one day I would be in prison with him in England! He was sentenced to fourteen years' penal servitude after pleading guilty to a series of appalling charges involving conspiracy, forgery and false pretences of such a magnitude that they rocked the foundations of England's financial system and big business.

I found him a very pleasant-mannered, dapper little man. He had already served more than three years in Maidstone when I arrived. We became quite friendly and for long spells we worked in the garden together. He was always kindly towards me and, as a comparatively old lag, he gave me quite a lot of useful information on prison life that helped to make things easier for me as a newcomer. Hatry always tried to be cheerful, but often he presented a picture of misery and dejection with his pale face, bald head and black moustache.

He often complained about the severity of his sentence because, he said, he had gone to the police voluntarily and later, in the Central Criminal Court, had pleaded guilty. He said he was entitled to a remission of at least two or three years.

Another character I met in Maidstone was Colonel Herman Goertz, a Hamburg solicitor. He had been sentenced to five years' imprisonment in 1933 on charges of spying on the air defences of the Home Counties.

Goertz was a personal friend of Hermann Goering and he had been tried *in camera* before being sentenced. He was released from Maidstone in time to get back to Germany before the Second World War started. Then he was parachuted into Southern Ireland. His assignment this time was to link up with the IRA and to get information about the Allied Second Front. Goertz was at large for eighteen months in Ireland before being captured. At the end of the war, after he had been told he would have to go back to Germany, he swallowed poison in Dublin Castle and died soon after.

Shadows in Europe

AT FIRST I was in no doubt about what I was going to do when
released from Maidstone Prison as March 1937 approached. I had
had four years in prison to make up my mind. I would clear out
of England as soon as arrangements could be made. Naturally,
I was feeling deeply bitter because of the treatment, the unprecedented humiliating treatment, I had received from officialdom in
Britain. In my heart I believed I had been the victim of a monstrous injustice and, on top of that, what stuck in my mind
indelibly was the limitless publicity to which I had been exposed
as 'The Officer in The Tower'.

When first imprisoned I received notification from my two
London clubs that I had been kicked out of them. Leaving
Maidstone Prison, I was, of course, an ex-convict, in itself a
ten-fold punishment for me. After actually serving my sentence,
I was a ticket-on-leave man because I had to report to the police
every week. It was at this time that I met Miss Pamela Scott
Harston and we became engaged. Under her influence and
despite my insurmountable difficulties I had thoughts at first of
remaining in England and settling down. I was offered a job of
running some piggeries near Windsor. I was prepared to accept
the job, but the local borough council announced that the
piggeries had to be closed down for sanitary reasons.

I then tried to take over an inn which I had intended to run with my fiancée. But here again I was up against a stone wall because I was informed an ex-convict could not obtain a licence.

My difficulties mounted any time I thought of trying to settle down in England as an ordinary citizen. What was I to do? What would anyone in my circumstances have done? Living in England as a ticket-of-leave man was impossible. I took stock of myself. Now twenty-eight, I had no training for any civilian occupation. Even if I could find a job I felt that life for me would be hell in England. In the eyes of the public, at any rate, I was a traitor who had 'sold his country for £50', but in my own mind I was certain I had done nothing of the kind. Still, the general public was left unconvinced. I had become known universally as 'The Officer in The Tower' and if I remained in England I would be pointed out as such, no matter where I travelled or what company I happened to be in. My photograph had appeared literally hundreds of times in the newspapers and in appearance I was well known. If I stayed in England I would be socially ostracised. The punishment and humiliation would go on because the public would not be satisfied with what I had already suffered. They would continue to point the accusing finger, hold me up to ridicule and contempt. I had been given a label that would stick to me. Like a dog with a bad name, erasing it from the public mind would be impossible.

I recalled the statement of my counsel, Mr Parkes, at the court martial: 'Any possible life he may continue outside the Army will be a life which is wholly worthless, whatever the result of this case may be.' It was only at this time that the truth and forcefulness of this comment dawned on me. My prospects in England were black indeed. In taking stock of my position, I also took into consideration the warning that had been given to me on leaving Maidstone by Hinchley Cooke – 'If it ever came to a war again between England and Germany you will be locked up immediately.'

For those reasons I decided that I had no choice other than to quit England for good. I would go to a country where I might be free from the accusing finger continually being pointed at me. I was, therefore, being driven out of England, my native land.

I had met a friend who strongly advised me to take up tourist work for Czechoslovakia or Austria. On her recommendation, I chose Austria. I went to the Austrian Embassy in London and was interviewed by Herr Kunz who gave me a letter of recommendation to the Austrian Tourist Propaganda Office in Vienna. My aunt, Mrs G Grant Smith, who had connections in Austria, wrote a letter to an Austrian major in Vienna, asking him to help me. I bought a second-hand Ford car, and as my fiancée wanted to get to her parents in Hong Kong, she decided to travel with me to Vienna.

I attempted to obtain a British passport to enable me to leave the country, but received a request in writing that I should state why I wanted a passport; where I wanted to travel and how long I wanted to stay there. I interpreted this as being further work on the part of Scotland Yard, with whose agreement I was sheltering under the false name of 'James Hope'. So I did not reply by letter but went to the Passport Office, taking an American, Robert Swinger, with me as a witness. Eventually I got my passport after a lot of difficulty.

So, in August 1937, I set off by car for the Continent. On my departure I informed Scotland Yard and I also wrote a letter to an English national newspaper stating that I was going to a country 'where my sympathies lay'. It was published.

We drove through Germany which I hardly recognised. We motored on a lovely sunny day by the banks of the Rhine and soon crossed the frontier into Austria. In Vienna I saw another 'exile' – Edward, Duke of Windsor, my former Colonel-in-Chief, with whom I had had a brief conversation during a Seaforth Highlanders' regimental dinner. In Vienna Miss Harston and I were met not by the Austrian Major but by his best friend, a Jew called Dr Kamillo Lauer. Later the Austrian Major wrote to my aunt explaining that he had reason to believe that I was receiving the attentions of the British Secret Service and, since he was serving on the Austrian Army Staff, he thought it wiser that Dr Lauer should take on the job of looking after me. My aunt sent me the letter.

Vienna appealed to me immensely. The people were natural and gay. The city was beautiful and alluring. I felt so much at home that I decided to apply at the first opportunity for Austrian citizenship. But my first objective was to get a job.

My fiancée then left with my car from Genoa, whence she shipped to Hong Kong. The Press got hold of her in Hong Kong, and she, terrified by their bulldozing, denied all knowledge of me and our engagement. I wrote to her and asked her to end the engagement because of my uncertain conditions and because I intended to stay in Europe. She protested strongly against my decision, but we remained good friends and continued to correspond.

I presented my letter of introduction to the Austrian Tourist Board. But the publicity of my past experiences had caught up with me. The circumstances of my trial had been widely reported in the Austrian newspapers and magazines. Mine was a name to remember.

In the Tourist Board Office I committed my first error. I thought it best to be open and straightforward and to tell them frankly who I was. So I was turned down. They regretted, politely, that it would be impossible to employ me because it might be regarded as 'an unfriendly act towards Britain' and they could not risk damaging their tourist industry.

Later, I got a job in partnership with two Jews in a cinema advertising business in Vienna. My chief occupation was to act as a sort of messenger boy, running around with coloured slides to various cinemas. Settling down, I felt happy when furnishing a little flat at Grinzing, a Viennese suburb. But there did not appear to be much chance of 'The Officer in The Tower' settling down to a peaceful existence. A Viennese newspaper discovered my presence in Austria and gave a big splash to my trial in London. With this the secret police were once again on my track.

All I had done since my arrival in Austria in any political sense was to apply for Austrian citizenship with the help of my Jewish friend, Lauer. In this I suffered an initial setback, for a six years' period of residence in Austria was necessary to obtain citizenship. The resourceful Dr Lauer then thought of a way out of the difficulty. He suggested that *Heimat Recht* (the equivalent of naturalisation) could be obtained.

Then came a shock. It started with a visit from a very suave English-speaking detective called Schober. He informed me that he had been the Duke of Windsor's bodyguard whilst the Duke was in Vienna.

Schober then invited me to accompany him to the Austrian Police Praesidium on the Schottengasse for a 'chat'. In the Praesidium I met Polizeirat Haslinger, the officer controlling the anti-Nazi movement in Austria.

Haslinger started by asking what my political sympathies were. I gave the wrong answer – I sympathised with the German people. This meant, according to Haslinger, that I was a Nazi, because he was including the Austrians in the generic term 'German people'.

His next remark struck me like a thunderbolt: 'You are a Nazi and we have reason to believe that you have been engaged in smuggling arms to the Nazis here in Vienna.' I could not believe he was serious. Haslinger, looking uncomfortable, told me that I could go and he would look into the matter further.

Greatly disturbed, I left and reported what had happened to my two Jewish business partners. This was early in February 1938, and they were equally alarmed because of the Hitlerite threats to Austrian independence. I was beginning to think that the whole thing had blown over when I was again summoned to the Police Praesidium.

This time I met a sterner Haslinger: 'You *are* a Nazi and you *have* been engaged in smuggling arms to the Nazis.' He sprang to a door behind his chair, and whipped it open. A man I had never seen before came in.

'This is the man,' said Haslinger, pointing dramatically to the stranger, 'who stood behind you in the post office when you posted a letter to a person called Bucher in Paris.'

'What letter?' I demanded, mystified.

'A letter arranging for arms to be sent to Vienna.'

'Have you a copy of that letter or perhaps the original?' I countered.

'That is neither here nor there.'

'But it is if I am accused of something. Apart from that, that man behind you whom I have never seen before could be lying for some purpose, or mistaken.'

'He is not mistaken and he is not lying. Please wait outside whilst the matter is being considered.'

I left the room and sat in an office where girls were typing out reports on Nazi suspects. Then I was summoned back into Haslinger's presence.

'Listen,' said Haslinger, and he then proceeded to read from a document stating that my presence in the Federal Republic of Austria was *unerwünscht* (undesirable) and that I was to leave Austria within three weeks.

'Do you hear that?' demanded Haslinger harshly.

'I hear it, but I don't understand it,' and I walked out in a rage, slamming the door behind me.

I was now in a desperate situation because my funds were getting low. However, I still possessed a British passport which guaranteed me protection.

It went terribly against the grain, but I decided to go to the British Embassy in Vienna and appeal for help and protection as a British citizen. To a young secretary I explained I was trying to earn some sort of living in Austria. I requested not only protection but an enquiry. I was informed on the spot, and without further ado, that it was regretfully impossible to assist me in any way whatsoever. Years later, William Joyce ('Lord Haw-Haw') was hanged because of similar difficulty over the possession of a British passport. A passport is a mutually binding contract between the holder and the State or the Crown. There are obligations on both sides. The State guarantees help and protection; the passport holder owes allegiance. It was William Joyce's failure to maintain this allegiance that cost him his life. But at Joyce's trial it was conceded that Joyce was an alien, having been born in the United States of America of naturalised parents. The fact that he was not British and never had been British made no difference, it was held. He owed allegiance to the Crown as a British passport holder even though he obtained the passport under false pretences.

At Joyce's trial the court was told that his passport 'placed him under the protection of the British Crown, it clothed him with the status of a British subject, and it required from him the duty of faithfulness and allegiance to the British Crown in return'.

Here, then, was the passport anomaly: Joyce was hanged for

not keeping his side of the contract, but the British Crown, through its diplomatic representative in Austria, broke the passport contract with me by refusing to help me when I was in distress.

A day before the three weeks' notice had expired I packed my belongings and left by train for Czechoslovakia, which was only a half-hour's journey from Vienna. I spent a nightmare two weeks in Pressburg, or Bratislava, where the old trouble started again – being shadowed and pestered by secret police. It seems likely that Haslinger had tipped off the Czech police, for almost from the moment I stepped off the train I was followed by detectives. They shadowed me everywhere, in the street, in restaurants, cafés and hotels.

I am a very fast walker, and this endowment permitted me to indulge in quite a lot of harmless fun – the only fun I had when in Czechoslovakia. At first, I was only followed by one detective who stood out a mile from his fellow citizens. I led him a dog's life. I took him for daily races in and out of the narrow streets of Pressburg and kept him in a permanent muck-sweat. Now and again to give him a breather I would pop into a shop, but before doing so I would signal to him and make wild signs indicating that I was about to go into the shop. Passers-by sometimes stopped to stare at this pantomime. Occasionally, when feeling irritated, I would give him the slip altogether. I was an easy thing to do.

One day a detective with a particularly ferocious and unpleasant face was put on the job of following me around. He certainly took no chances and just hung on my heels, only allowing a few paces between himself and myself. This exasperated me. I stopped dead, looked round and faced him. I said not a word, but just took up a silent position alongside him. He looked most surprised and puzzled. We must have stood beside each other some four minutes before the policeman slowly realised that I was not supposed to know that I was being shadowed. He started to shift about restlessly and looked decidedly uncomfortable.

Then, because I left him with little alternative, he began to move away. As soon as he did so, I followed him. Every few paces he looked back at me over his shoulder and his expression became intenser as he saw that I was laughing at him.

After this I always had two detectives to follow me around. The situation was quite grotesque and, although it had its humorous aspect, it was very wearing on the nerves. It rendered me unable to speak to anybody at all.

However, friends soon appeared from all sorts of unexpected quarters. First of all the lift-boy in my hotel came to inform me that I was being watched. He was a German and I thanked him. Then my chambermaid came to me and, after informing me that she belonged to the Sudetendeutsch Party, also told me that I was being watched. The information was superfluous, but I was grateful for the spirit in which it was imparted. It never ended. Detectives even enquired from newspaper boys what kind of newspapers I had bought.

Then suddenly I figured in a dramatic incident with the friendly German proprietor of a restaurant where I was lunching. I had just passed the soup stage when the German came bounding up the stairs. He gripped me excitedly by the arm and shouted: 'Hurry, hurry! Come upstairs, quick!' The German's face was beaming and he was labouring under intense emotion. We stood beside the radio and heard the sound of shouting, excitement and marching feet. The tramping sound gave place to a roar and rattle of trucks and tanks. Then there was the thunder of aircraft engines. We could hear the roar of squadron after squadron tearing across the sky.

Then came the voice of an announcer. German troops were marching into Austria. That was 12th March 1938.

In no time, I found my way to the German Consulate in Pressburg and obtained an immediate interview with the German Consul. I explained my situation and the circumstances rapidly leading up to it. Could I return now to Austria? Yes, certainly, was the answer.

I rushed out of the Consulate and into a post office. Here I wrote a pre-paid telegram to Haslinger: ANY OBJECTIONS TO MY RETURN. I received a reply within the hour: NO OBJECTIONS – HASLINGER.

I had already packed my bags and paid the hotel bill. Kissing the chambermaid (a handsome Hungarian) and shaking my lift-boy friend by the hand, I left the hotel for the railway station. I just managed to catch the train for Vienna. As the train pulled away from the station, I looked out of the window. Standing on the platform was one of the more pleasant-looking young detectives. He caught my eye and smiled. Then, as the train gathered way, he hastened towards me and called out good-humouredly: 'Why are you leaving us?'

'Because you are much too friendly and because I am going home!' I answered for lack of anything else to say. The detective waved, and Pressburg – town of horrible memories – disappeared behind me.

I returned to Vienna in time to witness indescribable scenes of jubilation. The Austrian people, despite many another tragedy that was going on behind the scenes, were crazy with delight. I took a taxi to my flat and deposited my bags.

My Jewish partners were full of fear and foreboding. I felt sorry for them. They had already taken steps to clear out of Austria, one to London, the other to Paris.

On 13th March 1938, I watched the parade of German troops

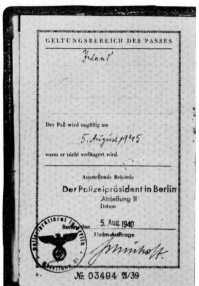

(*Above*) Page 4 of Baillie-Stewart's passport with (*right*) the translation of it used at his 1946 trial. Baillie-Stewart alleged that MI5 deliberately transposed the German word 'Inland' to read 'Ireland' (ringed on the translation, possibly by Baillie-Stewart) 'to give the impression that the Germans intended to land me in neutral Ireland as a war-time German spy'. (*Below*) Pages 2 and 3 of the passport

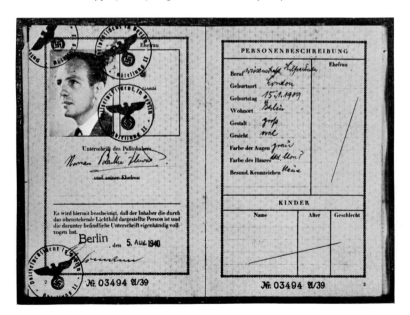

(*Below*) The receipt Baillie-Stewart received for his application for German citizenship which, as can be seen clearly from a copy of the receipt translation used in the trial (*bottom*), he made on 29th September, 1938, nearly a year before war was declared between Britain and Germany. It was his contention that he had done all in his power to obtain German citizenship and that therefore he could not be tried in a British court of law for 'assisting an enemy' country when, in fact, he was, to all intents and purposes, a citizen of that country

WIENER MAGISTRAT

Amtsstampiglie:

Aktenbezeichnung:

Name:

Gegenstand:

Eingelangt:

Aufbewahren! Sonst keine Auskunft!

A.D. Nr. 1024. - E. K. - 373. 20. - VB 1 m. - Ö.N. A 7.

TRANSLATION OF DOCUMENT REFERRED TO IN STATEMENT

BY NORMAN BAILLIE-STEWART AS ''EXHIBIT 1''

VIENNA MUNICIPALITY

Office Stamp: District Office, Döbling.

File No: B.272/56 or 58
Name: Baillie-Stewart, Norman
Re: H.R.
Handed in: - - 29.9.38.

RETAIN! Otherwise no information given!

(This is superimposed in the bottom right hand corner with the official stamp of the Döbling District Office, Vienna.)

through Vienna. It was a magnificent spectacle. Hitler was there, so were Goering and Himmler. Every German soldier was being treated like a hero. The German soldiers were surrounded by girls anxious to hear of the new Germany. Behind the scenes of rejoicing in Vienna there were tragedies; suicides occurred daily, if not hourly, among the Jews. The 'hangover' was bound to come. Following in the footsteps of the troops came the Nazi Party officials with their system of dossiers and files. German civilians came like locusts, following the luxury goods that had been scarce in Germany. Soon the Viennese shops were empty. The Saxons and Prussians, with their disagreeable manners, swarmed around Vienna and grabbed all they could.

Compulsory military service was introduced and I witnessed the last torchlight parade of the old Austrian Army in the streets of Vienna.

It was easy to get into trouble in Austria in those days and it was not long before I was in it again. This time it was because I was helping a young Jew to get out of Austria and into East Africa where he had friends. At this time I had just made my first application for German citizenship, and helping a Jew in distress was not calculated to make my application any more acceptable.

The young Jew I was trying to help was married (his second marriage) to an Aryan. One morning, after the young couple had left, I received a card ordering me to report at the Gestapo Headquarters which was now in the Hotel Metropole in Vienna. At that particular time Kurt Schuschnig, the Austrian Chancellor, was incarcerated there by the Nazis and it was with some trepidation that I entered the building. Steel gates had been erected since the arrival of the Gestapo. They clanged behind me.

I was interviewed by a Gestapo officer who came bluntly to the point: 'Why have you been assisting Jews out of the country?'

K

I remembered that I had been introducing Jews by letter to a friend of mine in East Africa. Then one day I had received a mysterious letter, which began: 'My dear Scarlet Pimpernel – please send me no more Jews . . .'

In reply to the Gestapo officer's question about helping the Jews I asked: 'What Jews?'

'You know quite well. You helped the Jews who lived in your house to get to Africa.'

Suddenly I saw a way out and I ventured: 'Surely this is backing the National Socialist policy, to get rid of the Jews.' I was doing what Germany wished.

The Gestapo officer snapped: 'That's none of your business. You leave that to others. You will get into serious trouble if you meddle in such things.'

He then smilingly changed his mood: 'I see you have applied for German nationality. You are wise to have done so. I know all about your case. But this,' he said, tapping the file in front of him with his forefinger, 'will not help you. But I will assist you if you are careful in future.'

Germany Calling

SOON AFTER MY brush with the Gestapo I got a job with the Austrian Tourist Board in Vienna. This brought me into contact with a half-English Austrian. We discussed the English-language broadcasts from Berlin that were intended for British consumption. One particular Berlin broadcast was given by an announcer with a pronounced Oxford accent. This was the chief English announcer and he sounded almost like a caricature of an Englishman with his tone of light mockery and the affectation of his accent. He ended all his announcements with a ridiculous, 'Hearty Cheerios'.

I wrote, on 14th April 1939, to a man named Frauenfeld at the Vienna branch of the German Propaganda Ministry, criticising the 'Hearty Cheerios' broadcasts. Frauenfeld called me in for a talk and I repeated my comments. He appeared very interested in what I had to say and took notes.

A few days later I received a letter from the Viennese broadcasting station, requesting me to call for a voice test. Sensing work that I might like, I went immediately. Whether I wanted to go or not did not make much difference, however, for if anyone was called to a State department under the Nazi regime there was no alternative but to go.

I continued to listen during the following months to the

Berlin broadcasts in English to hear the funny 'Hearty Cheerios' for my own amusement and entertainment.

Then, early in August 1939, I received a telegram requesting my attention at the Berlin *Rundfunkhaus* for a three-week trial as an announcer. I packed into my valise only the things that I needed immediately, for I thought I would soon be back in Vienna. In any case, if I got the job I would be able to get a few days' leave and return to Vienna for my entire belongings. But international events were to take a rapid and unexpected turn. Arriving in Berlin, I put up at the Hotel Rhineland on the corner of Wilhelmstrasse and Kochstrasse. I did not discover until later that this inexpensive hotel was a favourite meeting place for the Gestapo, whose headquarters were just round the corner in the Prinz Albrechtstrasse.

I had finished the first few days of my probationary period as an English-language broadcaster from Berlin to Britain when I met the original 'Lord Haw-Haw'. Incidentally, the first time that name is mentioned in literature, before it became probably the best-known sobriquet during the Second World War, is in Thackeray's *Vanity Fair*. So the wag who claimed to have invented it and conferred the title on William Joyce might not have been so original after all.

The *Vanity Fair* reference is:

'Little Bob Suckling . . . was talking to Fitzo of the Guards (Lord Hahaw's son) one day upon the jetty, as Betty took her walk there. Little Bobby nodded to her over his shoulder without moving his hat, and continued his conversation with the air of Hahaw.'

The first 'Lord Haw-Haw' of the Berlin *Rundfunk* was not William Joyce or myself, but handsome, six feet two inches tall,

Wolff Mittler, a man with both snobbish manners and an aristocratic voice. Mittler was a Polish-German with curly blond hair, who had received his secondary education in Britain. He was a playboy of the first order. He drove big high-powered sports cars and he was a great attraction for women.

Mittler was the chief broadcaster in English until my arrival. Immediately before, and for some months after, the start of the war the British authorities were anxious to find out who exactly was doing the English broadcasts from Berlin. There was a considerable amount of confusion during this period. The chief propaganda broadcasters from Berlin to Britain at this time were Wolff Mittler, James Clark (a son of Mrs Frances Dorothy Eckersley by her first husband), Dr Erich Hetzler and myself. There were other names on the *Rundfunk*'s English language rota, Germans who were merely technicians and stand-in men.

My last news broadcast was at three-thirty each morning and this went on for a considerable time. My health had never been good since my imprisonment in Britain and without knowing it, I had developed pernicious anaemia. Lack of sleep and bad food, due to rigorous rationing, had more or less flattened me. I was suffering from considerable nervous strain and, no doubt, this was largely due to the activities of the so-called English 'experts' in the radio station. I was worried, too, because of the war and had become irritated with my job.

Soon after the war started, the *Rundfunkhaus* was organised on a war basis. Rooms were set apart for the various speakers of foreign languages. I shared the 'English' room with Wolff Mittler, who was acting as my stand-in.

It was at this time that a very nasty individual turned up in the 'English room' with the result that I switched to the more convivial atmosphere of the 'French room', despite disapproval from above. The newcomer was none other than William Joyce.

Joyce apparently had dashed over to Germany from Britain a matter of days before the war started between Britain and Germany. It was Mrs Frances Eckersley who had introduced Joyce to the German radio station. She had broadcast on many occasions from Berlin and for some years had worked in the editorial department of the German *Rundfunk*. In addition to introducing Joyce to the German radio, she also introduced her own son James Clark. In England after the war she was sentenced to twelve months' imprisonment for her activities in Berlin.

Mrs Eckersley told me that she had met William Joyce in Berlin 'with the bottom hanging out of his trousers' and had lent him money. That was how Joyce had been able to make his celebrated début as a radio personality, whose name was to become the most hated and ridiculed in Britain.

I was standing in the short-wave station office talking to girl secretaries when a badly dressed little man with a livid scar on his face entered the room, his arm raised in Nazi fashion. He intoned a nasal 'Heil Hitler' from the corner of his mouth. He came up to me immediately, shook me warmly by the hand, and said: 'You are Baillie-Stewart, aren't you? It will give me the greatest pleasure to work with you. My name is Joyce – William Joyce.'

I was taken by surprise. I had heard nothing of an addition to the English section of the *Rundfunk* and asked Joyce what work he was going to do. Joyce replied that he was to sleep in the 'English room' at night in case anyone was needed after my last broadcast every morning at 3.30 am. So Joyce had come not merely to sleep in the 'English room' but, as it turned out, he had come to stay. At this time I was never in bed before 4.30 am. I slept badly in the daytime in the Hotel Rhineland because of the frequent heavy tread of SS boots on the stairs. It was in these circumstances, one evening, that Joyce asked me if he could do my 3.30 am broadcast. I was delighted because it meant getting to bed an hour earlier. On the following evening Joyce made a similar request and again I agreed.

On the third successive evening he asked again, but on this occasion I said I was staying on myself that night.

I was shocked at Joyce's nasal reply: 'What? Are you going to take *my* broadcast?'

That settled it as far as I was concerned. I was fed-up with broadcasting and the methods that were employed. I told Joyce to carry on.

And that 3.30 am broadcast was the beginning of William Joyce's long walk to the British gallows. It was Joyce's big chance in life to make a radio name for himself. He seized his opportunity eagerly. Vanity and ambition thrust him forward relentlessly. He was willing and ready to play the part.

From the moment we first met in the German *Rundfunkhaus*, William Joyce and I took a mutual dislike to each other. But I did not say to Joyce – as has been alleged – on our first encounter: 'I suppose you have come to take our jobs away.'

I never listened to even one of my scripts being broadcast by Joyce. I could not bear to do so. That voice, the snarl, the accent . . .

In the *Rundfunkhaus* the view was that Joyce succeeded in curdling the blood of a lot of people in Britain during certain black periods of the war when the Nazi war machine was meeting with unparalleled successes. But I warned Berlin's broadcasting chiefs that, in the long run, Joyce would merely create a war fervour in Britain that otherwise might not have been so noticeable. I warned the Nazis so often about 'Lord Haw-Haw', however, that they accused me of being 'jealous'.

When Hitler invaded Russia a propaganda paradise was created for William Joyce. Revelling in his 'Lord Haw-Haw' title, Joyce was acting as the English language mouthpiece on the German radio for Britain and the United States. At the same time, he was writing scripts for the so-called 'secret broadcasting stations'. They were purporting to be operating in England, but were actually operating from the *Reichssportfeld* in Berlin. These stations were calling on the workers of Britain to unite to throw out the capitalists and so on.

It was during the blitz on London that Joyce was at his worst. Instead of being paid to broadcast, he should have been made to pay for the 'privilege' of working off his grudge against humanity as a whole over the German radio system. Among members of the English colonies in Berlin, Joyce was regarded as having a pathological state of mind which was borne out by the fact that he had special permission from the Gestapo to carry an automatic pistol. He imagined that an attempt would be made on his life at any time. He always looked defiant and sullen, perhaps because he aroused hatred everywhere he went – even in Germany.

In the Berlin *Rundfunk* we were reasonably well informed about broadcasts to and from Britain. It was our job. We knew that monitoring stations, including those run by Scotland Yard's Special Branch and by newspapers, were very active in Britain trying to identify the speakers' voices. They were most interested, particularly, in the announcer with the aristocratic English accent.

One incident provoked a lot of English speculation about the identity of this announcer. The speaker said: 'Sir Winston Churchill recently . . .' and then realising the slip of the tongue started again: '*Ach, nein!* I mean Mr Winston Churchill . . .'

It was rightly concluded by the English monitors that I would never have made a mistake of that kind, but it was wrongly assumed that the slip had been made by Joyce. In fact the announcer was Wolff Mittler, the original 'Lord Haw-Haw'.

It was on that same day that Joyce got his title of 'Lord Haw-Haw' from Britain. The name was, of course, conferred throughout the war on Joyce for his 'Jairmany calling' broadcasts. For a few months after the start of the war the English monitors thought they were listening to Joyce when in fact the voice they heard was that of Mittler. Mittler's existence was not known in England at the time and for that reason Joyce was given credit for having a many-sided personality. Joyce's voice was, at times during the beginning of the war, confused also with mine as well as with Mittler's. For instance, all the English newspapers with their monitoring systems were speculating about Joyce's voice and mine, an Oxford accent being a major part of their 'evidence'. But neither Joyce nor I had an Oxford accent. It was Mittler who definitely had – like P G Wodehouse's Bertie Wooster. And it was not I who announced from Berlin that the clock on the public library in a South Wales town was eight minutes slow. It was Mittler – the unknown in England.

It surprised most people in the Berlin station that Mittler was not arrested and interned for his arrogance and outspoken comments. In the presence of Gestapo and Party men, for instance, he frequently expressed the view that he wished he had been born an Englishman. He was the type who made the most outrageous statements and got away with them with impunity.

I made a good impression on Dr Diettrich, who was in charge of the English broadcasts, and soon after my arrival from Vienna I became the Number One announcer on the transmissions to Britain. I thus became the second 'Lord Haw-Haw'. Wolff Mittler, the 'Hearty Cheerios' man, who had done his best to put over a Bertie Wooster and public school act, was demoted. He became my stand-in and sometimes took my place when I had a day off. It must be said in Mittler's favour, and in fact for all the English-speaking broadcasters from Berlin during the war, that they were often made to look ridiculous by the scripts they were given.

These were provided by the so-called English 'experts' in the station and their word was law. Among these was Dr Diettrich, who was half English, and his wife, who was English-born. We broadcasters were compelled to read the most ludicrous ungrammatical statements.

I had to battle on the telephone right up to the time of broadcasts in an effort to get sentences and words changed. My battles on the telephone were mainly with the English *Redaktion* (editorial department) and German 'experts' who had been in England for short periods and who could not believe that their English was not perfect. After several battles on the telephone, these English 'experts' lost patience with me and I was given an ultimatum by Diettrich who ordered me to read the scripts exactly as I received them and not to try and make changes. I pointed out that they were making a laughing stock of themselves, but Diettrich was adamant. He knew better.

One of these grammatical absurdities occurred when I was handed a script at the microphone in which it was stated that 'The German Flag had been hissed at Danzig'. This was caused by confusion between the French verb *hisser* and the English word 'hoist'. On another occasion I had to announce that a certain German airman had 'made an emergency watering on the sea' – presumably for want of a public convenience!

A further example of the nonsense I had to broadcast under orders was a sentence to the effect that a battleship had been sunk 'after being hit in its kettles'. The German word for kettle also means 'boiler'. What the script writer really meant was that the ship had been hit in its engine room.

I had taken a couple of hours off between newscasts on 3rd September, and was lying in the sun at Lake Halensee when a newspaper seller came along, stepping over the bodies of sunbathers to distribute an abbreviated news sheet. But he had run out of papers long before he reached me. However, one of the news sheets was floating in the water so I fished it out with my foot – to read of Britain's declaration of war.

I looked along the long line of sunbathers reading the news sheet. I was amazed to see that there was practically no reaction or comment. The men just lay back after reading, closed their eyes and continued their relaxation. Doubtless they were busy with their own thoughts, but they gave no sign of any emotion or the slightest interest. Gone were the days of flag-waving, patriotic demonstrations and war hysteria.

I sprang up from the lakeside and ran to a dressing cubicle. Having dressed hurriedly, I rushed back to the *Rundfunk* to find out what was going on. There was no excitement! The time had come for the next news broadcast and the usual record of *Auld Lang Syne* was played. I read through the news script, which included a progress report on the campaign in Poland and Britain's declaration of war. At the end of the broadcast *Auld Lang Syne* was played again.

After the broadcast I ran up to Diettrich's office in the short-wave station and suggested that, in the new circumstances, after the declaration of war the continued playing of *Auld Lang Syne* was entirely out of place. Diettrich did not appear to understand the significance of the tune, but said he would consider the matter.

Apparently, being a good Nazi official, he was afraid to do something on his own initiative. He must have been given instructions by a superior official soon afterwards, because from that time the familiar *Auld Lang Syne* was dropped from the programme. It seems that the purpose of playing the tune was to remind English listeners of the ties of blood and friendship between Germany and England.

At the short-wave station on the Kaiserdamm, from which William Joyce, the other English broadcasters and I operated in Berlin, were a number of American journalists and radio commentators. According to the Americans, they went in peril of their lives whilst shooting their respective lines over the German radio to America. They were, in fact, in little or no danger. They were given a latitude which surprised me and the other English broadcasters. The broadcasts by the Americans were largely unfavourable to Germany. Not only that, but some of the Americans acted as official or unofficial intelligence agents, right under the very noses of the Gestapo! Diettrich himself seemed to encourage them. They wandered around the radio station just as they liked and mixed freely with the German foreign language broadcasters whose identities were soon disclosed.

One American radio man even went so far as to enquire openly for the names of the various broadcasters. Not obtaining a satisfactory reply, he stopped the 'foreigners' in the street and outright asked them their names.

Among these Americans was William Shirer, author of *Berlin Diary* and *The Rise and Fall of the Third Reich*. As a result of all this cross-questioning by the Americans, Diettrich ordered the 'foreigners' to take on assumed names. Joyce's name became Wilhelm Fröhlich, which means jollity in German, and I took on the name Manfred von Krause, the name of an ancestor of mine. But these changes really meant very little because Joyce and I were personally known to the American newsmen and broadcasters. I, in particular, drank frequently with the Americans at the *Rundfunk*'s local. To the English broadcasters, in particular, at the *Rundfunk* the Americans were regarded as a nuisance. They received favourable treatment in Berlin and, relatively, they had the time of their lives. That was, of course, before America entered the war. When I complained to Diettrich I got an angry retort that I drank with the Americans in the local pubs, so what could I expect?

It was part of the American radio men's job to report the bombing of Berlin by the British Air Force. Cars were placed at their disposal to enable them to view any damage they might like to see.

Occasional propaganda successes were inevitable on both sides, German and Allied, during the war. Joyce and I took a leading part in one of these successes which was later hailed, although we did not know it at the time, as one of the propaganda coups of the war. Two American 'diplomats' had had a telephone conversation with each other. This telephone conversation was tapped by the Gestapo's Secret Service men and taken down word for word. It made interesting reading, constituting, as it did, a particularly blatant bit of underhand intrigue. Joyce and I were ordered by Diettrich to reproduce this telephone conversation for a radio broadcast.

My American accent was not too good, but Joyce was brilliant and, after some rehearsing, we managed to put over on our unsuspecting listeners a very natural performance.

For us in the Berlin *Rundfunkhaus* one of the most dramatic incidents in the early part of the war happened on 27th September 1939 when Warsaw capitulated. For Germany, the war appeared to be going without a hitch in a series of unbroken triumphs against Poland. The Polish armies were being smashed and pulverised by the German forces on land and in the air. In the *Rundfunkhaus* there was an air of expectancy and excitement, for we all knew that soon an announcement of major importance would be made to the nations of the world.

I remember I was having a drink in the canteen with Mrs Eckersley, and an American commentator who went under the name of Anders, when a loudspeaker announcement went through the building ordering us to stand by for duty. The broadcast was to go out on the entire world networks. This meant that native speakers of all the major languages in the world would be required, about twenty of us in all. We were ordered to be ready in ten minutes. These were the Fuehrer's orders. We had gone through rehearsals for this sort of thing and we had to carry out our orders with military precision.

We were wondering if the announcement was going to be the end of the war, for the German public were told very little in advance about the international situation. We were all left guessing as we dashed down our drinks. Then, dramatically, our orders came over the loudspeaker. Warsaw had surrendered.

About twenty of us dashed for the microphone and got into a queue immediately. One after the other we stepped up to the microphone and said our piece. It was brief and simple: 'Warsaw has fallen!' That was that and we felt certain that the war would be over within days.

When the war started I had been living under German jurisdiction for eighteen months since Hitler had annexed Austria. I had been out of England for more than two years. I did not see how my situation could have been affected by the war. I regarded myself as a German citizen and in 1938 I had registered for service with the German Army. There could, therefore, have been no return to England for me in September 1939, even if I had wished. Whether I liked it or not, I was trapped in Germany when the war started. Had I tried to leave Germany I would have been interned immediately, and if I had succeeded in reaching England I would also have been imprisoned, as Mr Hinchley

Cooke had warned in 1937. So I had to remain at my broadcasting post, whether I liked it or not.

There was no doubt in my own mind that I was a German citizen. I was even taxed and rationed as a German before the war started. In October 1938 I had written to the British Foreign Secretary in London informing him of the fact that I considered myself at that time to be a German and asked him what he wished me to do with my British passport. I received no reply to this letter and, therefore, assumed that due official notice had been taken of my intimation. It may be remembered that when I was in difficulties in Vienna I went to the British Embassy and sought help after producing my British passport. This was refused despite the fact that the holder of every British passport is guaranteed protection and help when in difficulties abroad.

Under the German Labour Laws listed in my 'Labour Book' I was bound to stay in the position I held and to obey all orders 'under pain of death'. The cost of disobedience would have been my life – either from a firing squad or, more slowly, in a concentration camp.

Some months after the clash between Joyce and myself, Hitler appeared to have the Continent of Europe at his mercy. His armed forces had smashed through France, Holland and Belgium with bewildering speed. Then Hitler was poised for the final knock-out blow – the invasion of England.

It was at this time that Professor Haferkorn, the leading man in the English Department of Germany's Foreign Office, started looking for recruits among the English-speaking staff of the Berlin *Rundfunk* to help in the government of Britain after the final conquest. I was asked to enrol for a high-ranking post in London, but I declined, saying that I would only go under strict orders. Among others, Joyce was enrolled. Everyone in the *Rundfunk* and in the English-speaking department of the Foreign

Office understood that Joyce was to fill the post of Deputy Nazi Gauleiter of Britain. Joyce was also earmarked to be my London boss on the staff of Dr Hesse. One day I was called into Department Two of the Police. There I was requested by Professor Sics of Berlin University to prepare a list of historical and artistically valuable buildings in London that were to be spared during the German invasion. For this purpose I used travel guides, and prepared a long list of historical and other places which the German forces were to avoid. I took the opportunity of requesting that I should not be included in any force invading England.

When Hitler was preparing his invasion of Britain, Joyce was at the height of his career as 'Lord Haw-Haw' in the eyes of the Nazi bosses. He was looked upon as a person with considerable influence and he was on friendly terms with Goebbels, the Nazi Propaganda Minister. It seemed natural that he should have been chosen Deputy Gauleiter of Britain, as a leading British Fascist and ardent National Socialist. If the information of the *Rundfunkhaus* staff was right, it was an indication of the profound ignorance of the leading Nazis in choosing a swashbuckling character like Joyce for such an exalted position in London. But then most of the top-ranking Nazis, from Hitler down, were men who had no personal knowledge of either foreign countries or foreign languages. Goebbels, for instance, like Hitler, had never even travelled outside his own country although he was, from the German point of view, a good foreign Propaganda Minister. The Nazis would obviously have needed the services of such a faithful follower as their new-found friend and broadcaster William Joyce. I was getting increasingly disgruntled with the entire set-up in the *Rundfunk*. I longed to go back to Vienna and to meet the friends I knew there.

It was at this time that one of the French announcers, who happened to be a brilliant cartoonist, did a caricature of me. I was depicted turning my back on the German radio station and walking along a road signposted 'To Vienna', whilst pulling a small pantechnicon van with my luggage in it. From this time on, I decided to take an indifferent interest in my work, so that I might possibly be released from my broadcasting duties. I went to Professor Hauer on the Kaiserdamm and obtained a medical certificate recommending treatment and a complete rest. I approached Diettrich with the medical certificate, but the radio boss merely sneered: 'You will have to continue.'

At this time the *Rundfunk* was completely militarised. Day and night, steel-helmeted armed guards patrolled the precincts of the radio station. And a Gestapo man, Dr Hetzler, was introduced into the station to do censuring and to keep an eye on 'unreliable foreigners'.

But armed SS guards had a dual purpose because they were on duty more for the purpose of preventing German Foreign Office officials entering the *Rundfunkhaus* than to keep an eye on the foreign broadcasters. The reason for this was the perpetual war of jealousy and intrigue going on between the German Foreign Office and the Propaganda Ministry.

Dr Goebbels' men insisted that high-ranking officials from the German Foreign Office had no right to enter the radio station. Goebbels and Foreign Minister Ribbentrop were perpetually at each other's throats over the use of the broadcasting station.

I, of course, had no alternative but to continue my work in the broadcasting station. Not only did I do announcing, but I had to provide commentaries as well. At first, I broadcast these but later they were used as scripts by Joyce. At this time I rarely spoke to Joyce, as I had taken permanent refuge in the 'French room', and when I did the conversation was strictly limited to business.

Then, one day, I was summoned unexpectedly by Diettrich

L

who told me bluntly, 'Your nerves are getting bad and I think it would be better if Fröhlich took over your broadcasts. You can take the morning and early afternoon broadcasts.'

I thanked Diettrich and left rejoicing.

The Foreign Office

JOYCE BY NOW had got thoroughly into his stride as a broad-casting personality. His confidence was superb. As reports came in to the *Rundfunkhaus* of his radio 'successes' in Britain, he strutted around as proud as a peacock. He was a great man for the bottle. I often stayed late in the evenings to watch him broadcast through the glass panel of neighbouring boxes. Joyce not only gesticulated violently whilst broadcasting, but he also gave the impression that he was going to eat the microphone. His alcoholic breath could be heard if not smelt. At times his breathing was positively stertorous and his accent was at all times sublime. Joyce was at his best nasalling: 'Where is the *Ark Royal*?' I, too, had also to repeat the question continuously over a period of days. They hadn't a clue as to the whereabouts of the British aircraft carrier. I knew that they were making fools of themselves with the same asinine chant, 'Where is the *Ark Royal*'? – 'Where *is* the *Ark Royal*?'

In retrospect, I was glad that I stepped back to let William Joyce take the limelight which he craved so much. Otherwise, I, too, might have shared the same fate, at the end of the hangman's rope. Incidentally, it was stated by the British Attorney-General in the London Central Criminal Court in 1946 when I was in the dock that (the quotation is from the official transcript of the trial) my 'broadcasts were not couched in such vicious or vitu-perative language as some of those which were disseminated over the German Wireless System'.

Joyce had become a close friend of Hetzler, the *Rundfunk*'s Gestapo man, and Diettrich. The alliance meant trouble for me.

Hetzler was a fanatical Nazi and always wore his black SS uniform in the broadcasting station. He was never known not to have worn his uniform, even when he was doing occasional broadcasts to Britain. He strutted around the station not merely in his impressive uniform but wearing his sword as well.

Trouble for me came over the sinking of the German battleship *Graf Spee* by British Naval forces at the battle of the River Plate. When the news broke, the Berlin evening newspapers came out with enormous headlines to the effect that the British had used gas shells in the battle between the solitary German warship and superior British forces. In the presence of witnesses in the radio station, I was indiscreet enough to state that I did not believe the British Navy had used gas. I also pointed out the technical absurdity of such behaviour. How, I argued, could a battleship be sunk with gas shells? And how would gas remain on a ship that was speeding at probably thirty knots into the wind?

I did not know until weeks later, and then only by chance, that my remarks had been reported by an informer to Diettrich. The radio boss in turn informed the Gestapo through the SS man, Hetzler. A report immediately came out that I had made a *Staatsfeindliche Ausserung* (a remark hostile to the State) and was 'politically unreliable'.

Despite this unfavourable report, and whilst Diettrich was presumably waiting for the official machine to take action, I was still allowed to broadcast into the live microphone. I was dis-gusted with the amount of rubbish and nonsensical statements that were being put over the air. I also wanted to go over the head of Diettrich and I contacted a friend in the English section of the Propaganda Ministry. This official was the usual German 'doctor' and he was supposed to be an English expert. English books, mostly political works, lined the shelves of his office, but when I started talking to him in English he switched immediately to German. He failed to grasp the points that I was trying to stress about the persistent errors that were being made in English broadcasts from Berlin. Failing to make an impression with these complaints, I then got on to the subject of William Joyce.

I asked the Doctor if he thought Joyce was doing Germany any good by his sneers and objectionable delivery. At this the Doctor's face flushed almost with triumph and exclaimed: 'He has made a great hit. The English call him "Lord Haw-Haw – Lord Haw-Haw"!'

The Doctor expressed the general view of Germans, particularly the high-ranking Nazis, towards English lords and the upper classes in Britain. They had the greatest respect for British aristocracy. They were still living in the England of Edward VII when the rich English flooded German spas. I found that the northern Germans in particular adored titles; titles seemed to take precedence over frontiers. Uniformed Nazi officials looked upon an English lord as a person possessing exceptional influence in Britain and one very close to the Monarchy. In this respect Nazi officials were not as men of the world; few of them had been outside their own country.

Although Rudolf Hess had in fact travelled a little outside Germany, which was more than his leading Nazi colleagues, he too possessed the 'lord' mentality. It was as a result of this that Hess made his historic flight to Britain in 1940.

He went to contact the Duke of Hamilton, who, he believed, had immense influence with the King and could have stopped the war. It was against this background that William Joyce made such a hit as a radio propagandist with the National Socialists in Germany. They were delighted that the English had conferred the title of 'Lord Haw-Haw' on their leading broadcaster in English. They did not understand that this title was not one of respect and that it ranked, in this instance, as buffoonery. I pointed out to the Doctor that the term indicated a failure to register as a 'lord' and did not indicate success. But my remarks were lost on the Doctor.

I then wrote an official letter to Diettrich, asking for permission to resign from my broadcasting job although I knew that that was an impossibility in wartime. I gave my reasons. Without waiting for a reply, I went to Fritz Spitta, a much travelled man, who had lived in China and in British colonies for many years. I outlined to Spitta the various broadcasting absurdities that had gone out from Berlin.

Spitta introduced me to Walter Hewel who was then liaison officer between the German Foreign Office and Hitler's own personal headquarters. I went to see Hewel in his office and he appeared to grasp the points that I had stressed about the absurdities of English grammar and the 'news' items that had gone out on the instructions of Diettrich. On Hewel's advice I withdrew my letter of resignation and Hewel rapidly got the English editorial department of the radio station reorganised.

Near Christmas 1939, I noticed that my name did not appear on the staff rota for broadcasting on the days following Christmas. Instead there was the name of James Clark, son of Mrs Eckersley. Curious to know what was going on, I asked to see Diettrich who informed me forthwith that my work at the radio station had ceased. I had no doubt that Diettrich and Hetzler had been putting their heads together and I assumed that this would now leave me free to return to Vienna.

Returning to the Hotel Rhineland, I packed a few things and

went over to the local police station to notify my change of address, as all Germans were bound to do by law. The police official was friendly, but informed me that I would be unable to leave Berlin without approval of police headquarters. Mystified, I went to the police headquarters, where I met two plain-clothes officers who seemed to know all about me. This visit probably saved me from a concentration camp. They told me that I would have to report to the police station every day until further notice and they added that Diettrich had informed against me. One of the officers offered: 'We would help you if we could, but there is nothing we can do.'

As I left the office, one of them remarked: 'If you have influence, it might not be too late.'

I left the police headquarters shocked by what had happened. I decided immediately to report to Fritz Spitta, but he was not in Berlin and it took some days to contact him. Meanwhile, I reported every day to the police and almost hourly expected a call from the Gestapo.

Help came unexpectedly. I was walking in the corridor of the Hotel Rhineland when I was stopped by an enormous man in the new field-grey Gestapo uniform, wearing the usual skull and crossbones in his cap. Good-humouredly, the Gestapo officer playfully tapped me on the shoulder and said: 'Ha! You are the English-speaking man in this hotel! I know all about you. You are now a German, aren't you?'

'I believe so,' I said, 'but it would seem that I am not likely to remain one for long.'

I then told the whole story.

'Wait a minute,' said this large and imposing man, 'I'm off to the Prinz Albrechtstrasse [the Gestapo HQ] and I'll send someone to you.' He left immediately and I sat down to wait in my bare, cold room. About half an hour later there was a knock at the door and a highly presentable young man in a well-cut civilian suit came in. Speaking in faultless English, he said, with his hand outstretched: 'Hello, how are you, Mr Baillie-Stewart? My name is Daufeld – Sturmbannfuehrer Daufeld. I am sorry to hear about your troubles; we must see what we can do.

'I have just been looking at your dossier and things don't look too good. Diettrich's report on you is there. Apart from that, I see that you once had a little affair over some Jew. However, we won't worry much about that.'

We sat down on the bed and once again I told my story, including the *Graf Spee* episode.

'Ha! That is where Diettrich got you. He reported you as having made a remark hostile to the State over the sinking of the *Graf Spee*. He says that you are politically unreliable.'

I said I did not think that the remark about the *Graf Spee* was intended to be harmful to Germany.

'But you must remember where you are,' said Daufeld, as he left with a promise to help.

Meanwhile I continued to report daily to the police. Then a letter arrived from Fritz Spitta instructing me to report to his friend Legationsrat Dr Schernier of the German Foreign Office. Spitta had already written to Dr Schernier explaining the situation.

Dr Schernier was a pipe-smoking individual clad in tweeds and looking like an English country gentleman. Before I had finished my story, the Doctor was dialling Glasmeier, the supreme head of the German *Rundfunk*, a prominent SS man. In the conversation I was in the role of a ping-pong ball. Schernier told Glasmeier bluntly that there was intrigue going on at the short-wave station and Diettrich was at the bottom of it. He demanded my immediate reinstatement as a radio speaker and a ban on Diettrich making any more reports on me to any State authority.

Schernier's word appeared to carry weight with Glasmeier because he too was a prominent SS man. During a pause, Glasmeier left to telephone Diettrich. After a while he was back – Diettrich had moved William Joyce into my place and there were no vacancies left.

'There,' Schernier said, 'Diettrich has been doing some covering up. Never mind, from this moment you are employed by the Foreign Office. You will stand under our protection. What was your salary at the radio station?'

'Five hundred marks a month.'

'You're employed at the same salary here.'

I was bewildered at the speed of events. Again I was under orders by a State department and I could no longer make decisions myself.

In the constant struggle that went on between the Foreign Office and the Propaganda Ministry, Schernier lacked neither moral nor physical courage. An instance of this occurred when the Propaganda Ministry officials at the short-wave station decided to get rid of a Foreign Office man employed there. They resented his presence in what they regarded as a purely Propaganda Ministry sphere. When the Foreign Office man refused to go, his telephone was disconnected and all his books and papers were taken out of his office and dumped in a corridor by the SS guards.

Hearing of this rumpus, Schernier immediately put on his SS uniform and drove straight to the radio station. Under the eyes of the armed SS guards, he picked up all the papers himself and carried them back into the room from which they had been taken. He did not leave until he had secured an order from Glasmeier cancelling the eviction.

Soon after Schernier informed me that I was on the staff of the Foreign Office he telephoned police headquarters and had my order to report daily cancelled. Then he got on to another official of the Foreign Office, Legationsrat Dr Fritz Hesse, and told him that he was sending me over to him. I was just the man Dr Hesse was looking for, said Schernier.

I reported to the 'Dienststelle Ribbentrop' (Ribbentrop Office) in the Wilhelmstrasse and there met Dr Hesse, a rotund little man, like Buddha himself, sitting in a luxurious office suite. Dr Hesse, in spite of a rather shabby attitude he displayed at times, had a good heart. He divided his colleagues between blacks and whites – those who were his friends and those who were his 'enemies'. This followed the usual German pattern of bad team-work and unwilling co-operation.

After Hesse had had interviews with Ribbentrop he sometimes looked as if he had been pole-axed at his desk. Ribbentrop had a habit of bellowing at his subordinates and this had a very demoralising effect upon them. Hesse often took the full brunt of Ribbentrop's ill-humour and Prussianism.

On Hesse's instructions I was installed in a double room at the Hotel Adlon on the Unter den Linden. This room served the sole purpose of an office and was necessary because of the immense expansion which the Foreign Office had undergone under the National Socialist regime. The Nazis believed in over-staffing all Government offices which overlapped each other. This kept them quarrelling amongst each other.

A lot of my work was translating and when Dr Hesse promised that none of his work would go through the hands or pass from the lips of William Joyce, I agreed to write occasional broadcast talks. As a rule, I did not listen to Joyce, but on a couple of occasions when I happened to tune in I discovered that in fact my scripts were being used by Joyce. So Hesse had played a trick on me.

When I questioned him, Hesse merely shrugged his shoulders

and told me to continue writing scripts. I did not remain long in his luxurious room at the Adlon. The Foreign Office had taken over the whole block of one of the less reputable hotels in the Saarlandstrasse and this section of the Foreign Office was given the name of 'Kult R'. There I was installed in a small room and, as a German citizen, I was compelled to take the formal oath of allegiance to Adolf Hitler and to swear to secrecy. But my work was not particularly secret.

Shortly after my appointment to the Foreign Office, I met Daufeld again. On this occasion, Daufeld handed me a document of considerable value – as far as protection was concerned. It was typed on Gestapo notepaper, stating that I had left my job at the radio station of my own free will. At the same time, I mentioned to him that I had not yet received my certificate of naturalisation. Daufeld cursed the German bureaucrats for their slowness and told me that a car would come and fetch me at the Hotel Rhineland on the following day.

I told Daufeld that my now worthless British passport had been withdrawn from me by the German police many months previously. I asked for a German passport in addition to my long-awaited naturalisation certificate. Daufeld said this would be difficult because passports were only issued in wartime for the sole purpose of foreign travel, but he would see what he could do.

On the following day a big black SS car drove up to the Hotel Rhineland, driven by Daufeld's assistant, an SS officer named Macivald. We drove straight to the police station where everything had been arranged. I was handed my naturalisation certificate with an apology for the delay, then got a passport made out with permission to travel abroad for three weeks. I left the police headquarters feeling at last properly equipped as a German citizen.

MI 5 have maintained throughout the years that they have

never seen my naturalisation papers which I left with my other papers at my residence in Austria after the war. I had been promised full access to all my papers, and I could not know at this time what significance this would all have until much later.

One day a car came to fetch me from the Saarlandstrasse. I did not know what was going on or why I was wanted. I simply got into the car as instructed and was driven to the Wilhelm-strasse. There I met Dr Hesse who, warning me to maintain absolute and utter secrecy, handed me some sheets of paper type-written in German. I was instructed to translate them, not literally, but in good, flowing, colloquial English. Believing that I was to go back to the Saarlandstrasse to translate the documents, I got up to leave but was promptly stopped.

'No, sit down,' said Dr Hesse, 'you are to translate them here and now at this writing desk. Hurry up with them. An airplane is waiting.'

I sat down again. As I read, I gasped with surprise. The papers were proclamations to formations of the British Army in France, informing them that they were surrounded, that certain forces were on their flanks and that they should lay down their arms and surrender!

It was not for me to question or even query the order that had been given to me. I translated the proclamations in natural English. They were then typed on the spot by a girl secretary using one of the special Foreign Office typewriters with large lettering. I then checked through the typewritten sheets which were handed to a German officer who came to fetch them.

I returned to the Saarlandstrasse after having received fresh, stringent instructions to 'Hold my tongue'.

I waited in some suspense to discover the meaning of the extraordinary proclamations. It was some time later that the sensational news came through of the German blow in the West.

I then realised the importance of the proclamations I had been ordered to translate: they had been dropped by air over the disintegrating British forces in France just prior to the Dunkirk evacuation.

Call-up Papers

DURING A TRIP of a few days to Vienna where I went to see some old friends and to collect belongings that I had left behind, I was called back to Berlin.

Almost immediately on my return I received my call-up papers for military service ordering me to report for 'Musterung' at 9 am two days later. Fearing to be late for work at the Foreign Office, I reported at 8.30 am, hoping I would be finished earlier. To my surprise, I found the whole place packed with men who had been there since 8 am, and they were not due to finish until ten.

After waiting around until my 9 am batch had arrived to swell the seething throng, I decided to act boldly and ask for priority. I had a lot to do in the Foreign Office that morning and the work could not wait.

I approached the German Sergeant-Major and asked respectfully if I might, owing to pressure of work, receive a very necessary priority. 'I'm in the Foreign Office,' I explained. The effect was startling.

The Sergeant-Major whipped round and bellowed 'You are not in the Foreign Office now; you are in the Army! Understand that? Go and fall in over there with your batch!'

I was now beginning to appreciate the humour of the situation.

I walked softly across the room and joined my batch. After being made to take our dressing and some drilling, we were called to attention whilst the Sergeant-Major came over to us with a glinting, beady eye fixed on me personally.

It was unfortunate for me that I was so tall because I towered above the two ranks in front of me. I met the Sergeant-Major's eye and was compelled to listen to his snarling tones: 'Some of you here' – the Sergeant-Major's eyes bulged – 'some of you here may have been so big' – he raised his hand to about my height of six feet two – 'when you came here, but now you are just little bits of dirt!'

He cracked his fingers with a snap as if to emphasise the point and looked fiercely at me. It reminded me of my days at Sandhurst.

We were told that if we were asked questions by the Major we were to stand rigidly to attention and answer: '*Jawohl, Herr Major,*' or '*Nein, Herr Major!*' as the case might be. These were answers to be barked out. We were then dismissed to await our turn.

As the ranks broke up, the Sergeant-Major beckoned me towards him. Realising, perhaps, that I, too, was a Government servant and maybe an important official, he said, 'Follow me!' He led me me over to an open telephone. Standing over me at the telephone, the Sergeant-Major rattled in a harsh northern German accent: 'You can phone your Foreign Office and tell them that you won't be coming – because you are now in the Army!'

The last words were barked out. I smiled, clicked my heels, bowed and lifted the receiver, whilst the Sergeant-Major stood close to hear what was being said.

'Good morning, Fräulein Rost,' I said to my secretary. 'I'm afraid I can't come along this morning. You see, I'm in the Army.'

'What?' came the astonished reply from Fräulein Rost over the phone.

'Yes, Fräulein Rost,' I replied, 'I have just been informed that I am now in the Army. The gentleman who says so is standing beside me now.'

The Sergeant-Major looked uncertain; could I possibly be pulling his leg? Then came Gisela Rost's voice again.

'Where are you speaking from now?' she asked.

She was an intelligent, quick-witted girl.

The Sergeant-Major walked away with an air of disappointment – perhaps he didn't believe that I was in the Foreign Office. After I had managed to convince Fräulein Rost that I was in the Army, I had to strip to go through all the little antics required by a medical examination. Then – still undressed – I had to go before the Board.

At a long table sat the five members of the Board. On entering each recruit had to begin at the end of the table nearest to the door and, standing to attention, move from one member of the Board to the next by the simple process of 'right closing'. As each recruit came before each member of the Board, questions were put and notes taken by the President – a very dapper and smart Prussian Major of the better 'old school'.

When I entered I was indifferent to my fate. I hated the war, but felt, in the circumstances, I would be better in the Army, where at least there would be little responsibility. Furthermore, in the Army I could be free from political victimisation.

Having moved along the line, I landed up in front of the President. All that I was wearing was a Catholic medal from a famous Austrian place of pilgrimage – Mariazell. This hung from my neck on a thin silver chain and it immediately attracted the attention of the jovial President.

'What's that you've got around your neck?' he asked. The

Senior Medical Officer on the Board got up and walked over to examine the medal.

I explained that it was from Mariazell.

'Where from?' the President persisted, apparently not having heard of Mariazell.

'From Gibraltar, Herr Major,' answered the Senior Medical Officer, who must have been examining the medal upside down.

'Now,' said the President smiling, 'have you any particular preference as to which branch of the services you would like to join?'

This was an old question for me. A man expressing preference for the Air Force would be put into the Pioneers; a man asking to serve with the U-boats would be sent to the Air Force, and so on.

I said I would like, if possible, to serve in a mounted cavalry regiment.

'Ah! a mounted cavalry regiment. And why do you choose the cavalry?' asked the Major.

'Because I like riding and horses, Herr Major.'

'But,' put in the Major, looking me up and down, 'I think you would do much better in the heavy artillery. However, I note your wish.'

I thanked the Major, hoping that the worst was over. But the President leaned forward: 'Have you had any previous military experience?'

This was it, I thought to myself. Despite my name, no one had thought of the possibility that I might have originated from that unfriendly island across the water. Strange names were common in Germany, where Poles, Czechs and all nationalities mixed freely with one another. My name had clearly aroused no interest or curiosity. I answered, '*Jawohl, Herr Major!*'

'Good, and in what regiment did you serve?'

M

'In the infantry, Herr Major.'

'Yes, and what was your rank?'

I was now beginning to get a bit hot under the collar I wasn't wearing, but there was no escape.

'Lieutenant, Herr Major,' I answered.

'Ah!' breathed the Major, and then he popped the question that I had been fearing all along. 'In what army?'

'The British Army, Herr Major,' came my reluctant reply.

At the mention of the word 'British' the whole Board shot upright in their chairs as if stung by wasps. I, as an ex-British officer, became the immediate centre of lively interest. The Major, enjoying himself, leaned forward and said: 'That makes things very different, very different. We will, of course, not expect you to serve in the ranks. Let me see now; I'll tell you what: report to me at the Wehrbezirkskommando [District Military Office] in the Krausenstrasse in two days' time. We will talk things over. How would that do?'

'*Zu Befehl, Herr Major,*' I replied and marched out of the room.

On the following Wednesday I reported to the officer who was a Major Ritter. The Major was kindly and courteous and invited me to sit down.

The Major said he had been checking up on me and I would get my rank back in the German Army. With a smile, he said: 'You will, of course, not be required to fight against the British.'

I thanked him and said I could make no voluntary decision without consulting my chief, Dr Hesse, at the Foreign Office. The Major then made a surprising suggestion – that I should put in an official application to join the Army and ante-date it. This, he suggested, might be a way of getting around the Foreign Office.

On the following day I went to the Wilhelmstrasse and informed Dr Hesse of my interview with Major Ritter and the promise of a commission. Dr Hesse exploded.

'You will *not* join the Army!' the Doctor shouted in Ribbentrop style. 'Ours is a gentleman's agreement and you will not leave my service. You have nothing whatsoever to do with the Army and I warn you that if you attempt to go on with this idea on your own I shall personally guarantee that you do not get a commission.'

These words got my back up. I knew that once I was in the Army Hesse would have no control over me and could not order the withholding of a commission. I consulted another friend who advised me that I would probably be given some indoor job in the Army and I would thus be merely exchanging one writing desk for another. In the Army discipline would be much more strict. These were sobering words and I agreed that my friend should have a talk with Major Ritter. No call-up papers came on this occasion, but on four subsequent occasions they did arrive and each time Dr Hesse claimed me as 'indispensable' in the Foreign Office.

Ironically, if I had gone into the German Army I could not have been captured and sent to London for trial as a 'traitor', as I was to be in 1945.

Shortly after Dr Hesse took steps to ensure that I would be permanently on his Foreign Office staff, I was persuaded to become a lecturer in English at Berlin University, each day after I had finished work at the Foreign Office. It was with fear and trepidation that I did so on being pressed by Dr Schobert, head of the English Faculty. At first, I was as nervous as a kitten, but I got to like my work so much that I stayed on for two years.

In fact, one of my students, a girl called Christa Liez, wrote, in my support, a letter to Bow Street Magistrates Court when I was on trial at the Old Bailey under the Official Secrets Act. It read:

'He opened up his mother country before our eyes, told us about its people in a very favourable way for the English, their way of living, their honesty and high principles of life.

'We learned about England and Germany as brother nations which, only through rather unlucky and unfavourable circumstances, had to go to war with one another. . . . If some problem causing the war were touched, he always showed a very upright standpoint, never without trying to make clear the English point of view so as to understand also the other side. A nation that has fought for a free democracy with free expression of opinion should always stand for its principles and not condemn a man who did not hide his opinion.'

As the war progressed in Hitler's favour, the various internment camps in Germany for Britons released on an average five or six internees a week on condition that they worked for Germany. Most of the internees were servicemen who had succumbed to the seduction of John Amery's drive to establish a British Free Corps in Germany. But many others drifted into German Government departments in Berlin and at the end of the war I estimated that there were several hundred. Only a mere handful of them were later tried.

One of my 'protectors' in the Foreign Office was Dr Schernier, whose weakness was snobbery. Two of his playboys were Werner Plack and Kark Schwedler who were permitted to do almost anything they liked in the name of Germany and the Nazis throughout the war. They were both given every facility to travel to neutral countries. There they stocked up with every conceivable commodity that was scarce or rationed in Germany – silk stockings, liquor, soap, chocolates, cigarettes, and so on.

Schwedler was perhaps the most colourful character of the two. He was, amongst other things, a crooner and his voice was often heard on musical broadcasts to England. His trips to neutral countries and to countries that had been recently occupied were for the alleged purpose of collecting the latest English dance music for his broadcasts. When in Switzerland, he told me, he used to pose as an unfortunate Austrian who had been deprived of his estates by the wicked Nazis. That line of talk went down well. In fact he had received unprecedented benefits from the Nazis and both he and Werner Plack were permanently exempt from military service. Dr Schernier was a great admirer of these two colourful characters. He used to throw parties for them and they gave him judicious gifts of silk stockings and the like to silence criticism.

On the left breast of Schwedler's superlative silk shirts was a finely stitched coronet with the initials 'SS' underneath. On a finger of his left hand was a massive signet ring engraved with a bogus coat-of-arms. At times he even sported the Old Etonian tie until I mentioned the fact.

On one occasion Schwedler advertised for a flat in a German newspaper, claiming that he was a German refugee from foreign oppression! In the advertisement he even included the Foreign Office telephone number. He got his flat.

Schwedler and Plack possessed charm and cheek that prevented anyone disliking them despite their scandalous behaviour. Both spoke excellent English. One of Schwedler's sidelines was the manufacture of gramophone records sung by himself. They included such hits as *St Louis Blues*, *She's Funny that Way*, and *Dinah*. But if one listened carefully to the words, it became obvious that they had been tampered with and that the records were intended to be amusing skits on British wartime policy and personalities. Most of them were distributed in neutral countries. The words, I found out, were written by an American girl in New York, but Schwedler got the credit for that.

One day he came to me in great haste. Would I write a straight text in English for the song that was then sweeping Germany and Europe – *Lili Marlene*? I never liked the song and could never stand the whining voice of the singer Lale Andersen.

However, I consented and immediately wrote a new English text. I was later present at the recording of it with Lale Andersen as the singer again. The record was an astonishing success; many hundreds of copies of it were signed by Lale and sold at outrageous prices, the proceeds going towards providing sports kit and other such equipment for the British prisoners of war in Germany.

This record, with my text, was broadcast constantly to the British troops in North Africa and was later played over all the German radio stations. A British version, incorporating most of my words, came out subsequently and was an immediate 'hit'.

After my first meeting with Lale Andersen, who was no glamour girl, and had a grown-up family of three, we worked together in my spare time. We collaborated on many German songs with English words, all were recorded and most of them became 'hits'.

When I first met Lale Andersen she had been banned from broadcasting by Goebbels and had also been forbidden to entertain the German troops. The reason came from Lale herself. She had first started cabaret work in Zürich where her manager had been a Jew. In a letter to him from Germany, written after her success with *Lili Marlene*, she had spoken of the 'good old days'. This was a reference to their work together in Switzerland and the fact that she longed to be back with him. This letter was, of course, intercepted by the German censor and passed on to Goebbels under whose jurisdiction came actors, singers and entertainers. Goebbels got on his high horse and punished her with the ban. But it must be said that Lale Andersen was never interned in a German concentration camp.

Werner Plack, the other playboy, was installed in a delightful flat in one of the best residential quarters in Berlin, near the Zoological Gardens. Plack was chosen to entertain important Foreign Office guests. It was at Plack's flat that I met Count and Countess Bernadotte from Sweden. It may be remembered that the Count, a member of the Swedish royal family, and the United Nations mediator for Palestine, was assassinated by Jewish terrorists in 1947. And it was Plack who brought John Amery to Berlin.

My immediate superior in the Foreign Office in the Saarlandstrasse was Professor Harold Haferkorn, who had drawn up the list of names of native English speakers in Berlin at the time Hitler was planning his invasion of Britain. He was a lecturer in English at the German University of Greifswald, and was a Party member with the rank of SA (Stormtrooper).

It was Haferkorn who, when entrusted with the task of making an *Erfolgsbericht* (report on the impression made on the outside world) on William Joyce, deliberately suppressed the unfavourable newspaper reports which I had supplied. He produced a printed report containing no single word of adverse criticism.

This was placed before Foreign Minister Ribbentrop who then continued to live in a fool's paradise and to remain uninformed about the effect of 'Lord Haw-Haw' on wartime Britain. It was known in Berlin that Germany suffered directly from the fact that the yes-men surrounding Hitler continuously withheld criticism and adverse reports from him.

One day I was sitting in my office and had occasion to ring Haferkorn on the internal line. To my surprise Haferkorn picked up the phone and said, in accusing accents: '*Der Führer spricht!*' He then hung up before I could say another word. I had forgotten that Hitler was making one of his periodic speeches on the radio, but even so, these speeches were always repeated three or four times and were reprinted in full in the newspapers. I became furious at this snub and rang up Haferkorn again, asking him bluntly what he thought would be the result if everyone in Germany stopped work because Hitler was speaking. And I then gave measure for measure by hanging up abruptly as the Professor had done with me.

It was not long before the reaction came. I was summoned to visit Dr Hesse in the Wilhelmstrasse. He was sitting at his desk as if he was ready to erupt like a volcano. He took a deep breath and then bellowed: 'Do you know where you are? You are in Germany!' Then there was another deep breath and a roar: 'Do you know what would happen if the Gestapo were to hear of your behaviour? Perhaps you don't know, but I can assure you it would be very unpleasant – very unpleasant indeed. You are to apologise to Professor Haferkorn immediately.'

I was not intimidated by roars or threats. I told Hesse I would not apologise and that I considered Haferkorn was wrong. This brought on another eruption. Was I trying to defy my superiors? If that was the case, I would soon be dealt with. Professor Haferkorn, moreover, had complained that I was sabotaging the work by conducting a go-slow campaign and evading orders.

All this was unfortunately true and I began to see dark clouds on the horizon.

'Do you intend to report this to the Gestapo?' I asked.

'No,' said Hesse grudgingly, for he was not bad at heart.

'In that case,' I said, 'and in view of the fact that I cannot see my way to apologise to Professor Haferkorn, I shall have to accept my dismissal and volunteer for the Army – as a private soldier.'

I had said the right thing this time.

'I respect you for that,' said Hesse softly. 'It is noble and honourable of you, but, none the less, you will not leave my service. I regard you purely and simply as a gifted instrument and if you refuse to apologise to Professor Haferkorn I shall tie you down to obeying every order he gives you. You will sign an undertaking to obey *every* order – regardless of what it is – that Professor Haferkorn sees fit to give you. You may go now.'

As I left Hesse's office, I noticed that the girl secretaries had been standing in the corridor listening to the uproar going on inside.

Some hours later a typewritten document was brought to me for signature. It delivered me into the hands of Professor Haferkorn lock, stock and barrel. I then took my girl secretary's advice: 'For heaven's sake sign. It will make no difference and you can carry on as before.'

It was not long before the next move came. Haferkorn, who knew my aversion to broadcasting, came to me and said: 'It is intended that the Foreign Office shall have a spokesman on the wireless. The Minister has decided that the Foreign Office point of view is not being represented. You will have to undertake the broadcasts.'

I protested that I did not wish to broadcast, but the Professor was adamant. It was an order. From that time on, I had to proceed to the radio station twice a week and have my talks recorded. I was no longer trusted by the *Rundfunk* authorities to speak direct into the microphone. The only condition I was able to extract from Haferkorn was that I was to remain anonymous. For this reason he chose the pen name, or *nom de plume*, of 'Lancer'.

Another aspect of my work was contributions towards entertaining the British prisoners of war in Germany. This included the publishing of a weekly paper called *The Camp*. I planned the layout of the first edition, after which the editorship was taken over by an English-speaking German named Axel Seeberg.

Seeberg was a Nazi and, oddly enough, could not speak anything but a few sentences of broken English. Some kind of influence had got him the job. I had many a tussle with him over the pompous military reports which always made the front-page news. These reports were provided by somebody in the War Office and had to be translated into English.

When I had to do the translating, I always toned down the wording and often even changed it. I did this especially when I was asked to translate absurd military wireless talks by such nincompoops as Admiral Lutzow and Captain Blei whose voices were familiar to the British public. Scripts from these two were both illogical and unmilitary. On one occasion, Captain Blei complained that he could not recognise his talk after it had been doctored by me for the better. As a result I was forbidden to do any more translation and the job was handed over to Mrs Eckersley. She had a very good sense of humour and cared nothing what kind of rubbish she translated. They asked for a literal translation and they got it.

I supplied the entertainment articles for *The Camp* and through this befriended several British prisoners of war. Some of them wrote to me under my *nom de plume* to thank me for my articles, not knowing that they were writing to 'The Officer in The Tower'. My articles were mostly about model aircraft, riding, motor cycles, the German 'People's Car', scientific subjects and sport.

These articles were mentioned in a book by a Pole, S Leszczyc, entitled *Prisoner of War*. On page 71, it reads: 'The third edition of the illustrated weekly is printed in English and called *The Camp*. It contains little propaganda apart from doctored political news.

'Anxious to please the British soldiers, *The Camp* gives in every issue the results of all the Saturday League matches played in Britain.'

On one occasion I took a trip down to a British POW camp near Munich with the object of reporting on the inter-camp boxing contest that was being held there. This report was published in *The Camp* and later broadcast to British Home and Overseas forces.

I had a ringside seat where I was surrounded by British troops, but none seemed to recognise me as 'ex-Lieutenant Norman Baillie-Stewart, The Officer in The Tower'. They all seemed to be too absorbed in the boxing contests. In the hut where the boxing took place there was no escort and no guards. The German camp commandant sat opposite me on the other side of the ring. Before each contest a massive, tough-looking Australian padre spoke to the contestants like a brother. He said he wanted to see blows and blood, but the fighting would have to be clean.

Well, they took the padre's advice. There was enough walloping and blood to satisfy even a Roman audience in an amphitheatre.

During the fighting I chatted to the prisoners all around me. They were quick to help with the names of the boxers for *The Camp* and for broadcasting.

I was sometimes amused and sometimes alarmed by the conjectures in Britain and America as to what I was supposed to be doing in Germany, my presence having been revealed by American radio reporters. One report was that I was operating a secret Scottish Freedom broadcasting station in the Black Forest. I was particularly alarmed by a statement in a book called *Siegfried Spy*. For the purpose of the book, I was given the name Cranby-Mackintosh and was described as a spy for Britain's MI 5 operating in Germany. Such was the circumstantial nature of the book that had it reached the Gestapo I might have found myself in a concentration camp or facing a firing squad.

In connection with my work with British POWs, I would like to state that I did not join the 'British Free Corps' in Germany and, furthermore, that I advised British NCOs in PoW camps not to have anything to do with it.

In the Foreign Office I continued to 'dodge the column', but this did not mean that I had any lingering sympathy for Britain. The truth was that I was fed up with both sides; and with the war and the incompetence and unreliability of Nazi officials who staffed the Foreign Office. The impression was that the war was being waged by the Nazis for the Nazis. They cared little for the fate of the German soldier or for the civilian population who were being bombed incessantly towards the end by the Allied air forces. In 'dodging the column' I was not trying to sabotage the German war effort. I merely refrained from doing useless work.

My anxiety for the fate of Germany in the last year of the war was very real. Like millions of Germans, I supported the Nazis because I felt that to do otherwise would have been to stab Germany in the back.

But there were many Germans who did so. They were in the most responsible positions, particularly in the *Abwehr* – German Intelligence. From my reading through the *Abhorbericht* (daily report on the BBC), it was quite clear to me, to the staffs of the *Rundfunkhaus* and to the German Foreign Office that some kind of a major military plot was being planned against Hitler. The German General Staff was specifically mentioned as the most likely body to attempt his overthrow. I tore out the relevant sheets of the *Abhorbericht* and put them aside in a file for future reference. They had also, of course, been scrutinised by the Gestapo. Altogether, it is claimed, there were three cryptic references to the German General Staff in an intended plot 'to put Hitler aside'. And these messages, a coincidence or otherwise, preceded the plot of 20th July on the life of Hitler. They involved Rommel, Count Moltke – a member of a celebrated old German family – Field Marshal von Rundstedt, Count von Stauffenberg – the man who placed the bomb beside Hitler – and other German generals.

The failure of the plot led to a state of terror among top-ranking heads of State departments, the Gestapo and military. Wide-scale arrests were swift, as were the executions.

One of the big problems for civilian life in Germany was, of course, the British bombing. I used to listen to the BBC broadcasts and I heard frequent mention of the RAF's precision bombing. There was frequent mentioning of 'Block Busters', 'Obliteration Bombing' and 'Carpet Bombing'. I experienced it all at first hand because I lived in a residential district of Berlin for the last half of the war before I left for Vienna. This was the district between Steglitz and Dahlem which experienced an unmerciful pounding. Many a time I thought it was my last hour.

In my residence there was no cellar or protection and the little modern house where I lived was twice blasted and finally knocked sideways. But I continued to live in it. Soldiers that I spoke to preferred the front line to living in German cities.

Berlin women, in particular, showed extraordinary courage, and bravely tackled the incendiaries and fire bombs that were hailed down like pepper. My own job was to patrol the house from top to bottom during the lulls in the bombardment.

In 1944 I obtained a medical certificate enabling me to return to Vienna for health reasons. At the same time I was to take up a job in the Foreign Office there. I spent the first three weeks in the Viennese General Hospital suffering from pernicious anaemia and hepatitis.

During this visit to Vienna I made the acquaintance of a young Rumanian student of music, Carola Rulescu, and we became inseparable. She was an extremely beautiful and attractive girl with marked Slav features and the accompanying almond eyes. The language we conversed in was German, which to neither of us was a native language and which she could speak but haltingly. Her command of other languages was immense. She could speak

Rumanian, Hungarian and French fluently and her German wasn't really too bad. The way she spoke it was, at least, very attractive.

We got on so well together that we became engaged, an unpopular action in Berlin, I discovered, when I was called back over the 'Charlie Kunz' affair.

Before I left for Vienna I had met a German officer on leave from the Crimea in Berlin. This officer – like me – was a Charlie Kunz ('the old rocking horse' as a BBC announcer described him) fan and he had quite a collection of Charlie Kunz records.

One day when he was playing them to me in his mother's flat he said to me: 'You know, Charlie Kunz is down in the Crimea serving with a heavy machine-gun company. His real name is Joachim Behnke.'

'But that's impossible,' I said, 'Charlie Kunz is an oldish man and is still playing for the BBC.'

My friend laughed. 'That's not the real Charlie Kunz,' he said. 'The real Charlie Kunz of the original pre-war recordings is a young man. The Charlie Kunz now in England is merely using the same stage name.'

This of course interested me very much. The German wireless was looking for entertainers and this would be something sensational. I made further enquiries and learned that the 'Charlie Kunz' down in the Crimea – Crimean Charlie as I began to call him – was used extensively for troops' concerts and did allegedly play in the Charlie Kunz style. I obtained his name, regimental number and unit.

All this information I submitted to the Foreign Office authorities and demanded Crimean Charlie's immediate recall and reclamation from military service. The idea caught up, but the Army brought up all sorts of difficulties about letting him go. It all took so long that I gave up hope and when I left for Vienna I had forgotten all about it.

After I had been in Vienna a while, I was informed that Crimean Charlie had arrived in Berlin and I was asked to come up and meet him in order to arrange things. So I went to Berlin and put up in what was left of the Eden Hotel. I hadn't been there long before Crimean Charlie arrived and presented himself.

He was a young man – far too young, I thought, to have been playing in England before the war. His English was rudimentary. We had lunch together and I proceeded to question him. He seemed, however, to be quite genuine and his story was at least plausible. He had, he said, done his 'Rex' recordings when he was seventeen or eighteen. He had been a youthful genius, I presumed.

I suppose Crimean Charlie was not to be blamed. He was probably very glad to leave the Crimea and to enjoy a holiday from the Army. I was not quite satisfied with all the details supplied to me, but quickly wrote some scripts to be used in the event of Crimean Charlie coming up to the mark. With these scripts I then went to the radio station and introduced, as a Foreign Office surprise, the original 'Charlie Kunz'.

Great was the surprise and even consternation that the Foreign Office should have put one over on the Propaganda Ministry. My main concern was to hear Crimean Charlie play. I knew that I would immediately spot the authentic Charlie as soon as I heard him.

With Crimean Charlie I dashed from one broadcasting studio to another, trying to find an unoccupied piano. All the while Crimean Charlie was explaining that he was a little rusty but that he would soon get into it. My luck was out, though. There wasn't a piano free in any of the studios. I therefore left Crimean Charlie with the music director of the foreign programmes while I delivered my scripts.

When I met the music director again he was looking a trifle glum and serious. 'He's no good,' he said.

'But with a bit of practice he'll be all right,' I suggested.

'I don't think so,' came the discouraging reply. 'I have given him a try-out.'

This set me back quite a bit. Having had the man fetched all the way from the Crimea and got him away from the Army, I *had* to be right. This was the first thing for which I had felt any enthusiasm for a long time. What was I to do? I could only leave him to the wireless people and hope for the best.

The worst, however, followed. They bungled everything. In spite of their doubts as to whether Crimean Charlie was 'the genuine article' or not, they broadcast my scripts heralding the original, and one and only, Charlie Kunz.

The scripts should, of course, have been broadcast with accompanying music from Crimean Charlie. Instead of this, they never dared to put him on and, from start to finish, he never played a note before the microphone.

It was all, of course, a gift for the real Charlie Kunz in England. He came on the air and played back at us. A great time was had by all – except by me and the rest of us who had made fools of ourselves!

I never saw Crimean Charlie again and don't know what happened to him. Perhaps he was returned to the Crimea. After this fiasco, I went to Dr Hesse and told him, as in duty bound, I wished to marry.

'Whom do you wish to marry?' he asked. I told him that my fiancée was a Rumanian.

As soon as I said this, I met with immediate opposition. If I were a British citizen, Dr Hesse explained, I could marry whom I liked, but as I was now a German I could not marry a Rumanian. This followed the Nazi racial precepts which were particularly applicable to members of Government departments. I argued, but was told that it was impossible. The usually humane Dr Hesse was adamant on this point.

By no means satisfied, I returned to Vienna intent on marrying at any cost. Vienna was an easy-going city and I would certainly find someone who would 'fix things'. Nothing would be easier, and damn the consequences!

Back in Vienna I met Carola and explained the situation. We did not feel discouraged – merely annoyed and disgusted – and went ahead with our arrangements. I already had a flat, my own furniture and everything necessary down to the last teaspoon. Before marrying and settling in Austria, Carola wanted to see her parents in Bucharest. She was to go for a month and settle all her affairs.

Leaving her things behind her, she left for Bucharest. I went with her to the station and that was the last I ever saw of her.

We had agreed not to write to one another during the month of her absence because we thought the time would go quicker that way. The month dragged by on leaden feet. She was to have returned in time for her birthday and I had ordered flowers – her favourite ones – and bought presents. Then came the blow.

The Russians swept into Rumania. The situation grew desperate, as I did, too. The month had passed and I saw that there was no time to lose. I had one friend left in Berlin to whom I would go over Dr Hesse's head. This friend was Paul Schmidt, Hitler's personal interpreter and the man who had interpreted at the Chamberlain-Hitler meetings. I had met him on several occasions and had always found him helpful and sympathetic.

I took a plane to Berlin and obtained an immediate interview with Schmidt. Being no Nazi, he listened with sympathy to my story and then asked me what he could do to help me. I suggested that I should be sent to Bucharest as Foreign Office observer

N

and would then write scripts for broadcasting on my impressions. At the same time I would be able to contact my fiancée in Bucharest.

Schmidt was agreeable in principle. I could have fallen on his neck and hugged him out of gratitude. Yes, he said he would arrange things. I was to see him on the following day and he would let me know how it could all be done. Now there was decency and humanity! There could be a row about it, but Paul Schmidt didn't mind.

I slept badly that night, knowing that every hour counted. On the next day I went to see Schmidt. He looked grave.

'I am very sorry to tell you,' he said, 'but it is now impossible. The Rumanians have turned on us and are even now our enemies. We are fighting our way out as best we can.'

The bottom dropped out of my world. Carola had meant a lot to me, more in fact than the whole war itself. Schmidt shook my hand sympathetically and I left him to return by plane again to Vienna.

Daily I watched the progress of events in Rumania but as each day passed, my hopes sank lower. Perhaps Carola would manage to break through somehow to Vienna, but I knew that this, too, was a forlorn hope. How could a young girl manage such an adventure on her own?

I never heard of her again. I wonder what happened to her.

Alt Aussee

AT THIS TIME the beginning of the end of the war was in sight and there were many and repeated American Air Force raids over Vienna in broad daylight. I helped at the hospital carrying the most seriously ill patients to air-raid shelters in the cellars. It was during one of these American daylight raids that I again found myself in trouble. During this particular raid, a stick of bombs, which passed just over my house with a roaring whistle, caused a lot of devastation. After the 'all-clear' I joined an idle throng inspecting the damage.

As I stood on the outskirts of the crowd I suddenly met the beady-eyed gaze of the local Party 'Block Leiter', a man whom I had not seen since before the war. I was surprised to see this man going over to a policeman and whispering earnestly in his ear. Apparently the 'Block Leiter' had told the policeman that I was an Englishman and was inspecting the bomb damage. After a lengthy rumpus the tables were turned on the 'Block Leiter'. I produced my Foreign Office identity and insisted that the 'Block Leiter' be reported officially for exceeding his duties on the one hand and neglecting them on the other. This particular 'Block Leiter' was the man who had some dealings with the file in which I had been reported for getting a Jewish family to Africa.

A peculiar aspect of the air-raid precautions in the city was the novel Viennese method of warning the populace of approaching bombers. One could be listening to music on the radio when a sudden urgent, but melodious, call of the cuckoo would break into the music. After this the music would continue, before being briefly interrupted, though not stopped, some minutes later by a second call from the cuckoo. After the third call, the music would cease and a girl's voice would inform the listeners that enemy bombers had reached square so-and-so (everybody had city maps marked out in squares) and were flying in a particular direction. Everybody was able to follow the approach of the bombers from square to square as we used to do in pre-war radio reports of football matches. Often as not the target was Vienna, but sometimes targets in Czechoslovakia were chosen in which case the Viennese breathed again. The air-raid alarms were only sounded when it became certain that Vienna was the target. Even then there was plenty of time to get to the shelters.

Whether I continued to 'work' in Vienna or elsewhere was immaterial. Because of war damage and the destruction of communications my work had now taken on the form of a postal correspondence. With the help of a fresh medical certificate I had no difficulty in getting permission for a change of air to the mountains. I was intent in getting back to Alt Aussee (not far from the famous 'Salzkammergut') where I had spent a most enjoyable holiday and where I had some good friends.

I had to leave many of my belongings behind in my flat in Vienna. I was told subsequently by MI 5 that the Russians had plundered my flat but I had my doubts.

The journey to the mountains was not easy. Damage done to German rolling stock by the constant air-raids had been heavy and in most of the compartments of my train the glass was missing from the windows. Little did I know that my destination, Alt

Aussee in the mountains, was a place where important events were taking place and where more were to be held.

Alt Aussee was not far from Berchtesgaden, Hitler's fortified mountain retreat where so many historic meetings were held, secret and otherwise, and where Hitler planned much of his war strategy. This area was in fact the last pocket in Germany and Austria to be occupied as it was an ideal location for a last Nazi stand against the invading Allied forces. When I first visited Alt Aussee, it was a sleepy little Austrian lakeside village occupied mainly by Austrian and Bavarian aristocrats.

In the old days of the Austro-Hungarian Empire it had even attracted for a time that extraordinary and beautiful woman, the Empress Elizabeth of Austria.

Alt Aussee was a rail cul-de-sac in the mountains. Approach was possible only from one side, unless the difficult task of crossing the mountains was accomplished. It was an ideal spot, but the Alt Aussee that I returned to after two years' absence was by no means ideal. There was no more dangerous a trap in Europe.

As I entered the village on a lorry, my cases beside me, I could see standing in front of the village post office two White Russians attached to the Berlin Foreign Office and the Saarlandstrasse Department. I was soon to learn that a complete section of the Foreign Office had been installed in the town. I also discovered that two 'exile' governments – Rumanian and Bulgarian – held their 'cabinet' meetings in the village inn. All of the 'Ministers', I understood, were armed with pistols.

Another resident was the infamous Ernst Kaltenbrunner, one of the Gestapo bosses, who had himself accommodated in the house of Prince Max von Hohenlohe, a friend of mine. Kaltenbrunner, who succeeded the notorious war criminal Heydrich, ordered the execution of fifteen members of an Anglo-American mission which had parachuted into Slovakia in January 1945. He was later hanged at Nuremberg.

A short distance up the mountainside from the town there was a large villa occupied by the worst type of Gestapo and SS guards. They had a radio transmitter and receiving set and much villainy emanated from this particular villa. The atmosphere was made even more electric by the fact that these Nazis were, at this stage, opposed to Kaltenbrunner.

In the village itself there was also quite a strong Communist element. With these highly volatile ingredients, Alt Aussee was pure dynamite and I had chosen it as my last refuge!

Added to all this was the presence of the nearby 'Salzberg' just outside the village. The 'Salzberg' was a salt mine that contained a labyrinth of subterranean passages where a large number of the art treasures of Europe had been stored by the Nazis. It had, in fact, become not a salt mine but a gold mine; the treasures it contained must have been worth several millions of pounds. Alt Aussee should have been occupied by the Russians because it came within their 'Yalta' Zone, but the Americans – always the smart business men – rushed to get in and got there first. This meant that the Nazi treasure went west instead of east.

At that particular time, when the war in Europe had practically ended, this little mountain village was one of the most fantastic spots in Europe. In it, politics of every kind were rampant. With the scales tipping heavily against Germany, self-appointed Allied and Russian agents suddenly appeared from everywhere. One could never know with whom one was talking. As the invading armies swept closer, even the Gestapo ceased to function except as splinter parties opposed, for the most part, to each other.

Incredible things were happening in the area. I spent hours watching SS cars, laden with gold bullion and coinage, sweep through the district on their way to secret destinations. Some may have made their way to the Swiss frontier, an easy way for the gold to be smuggled into Switzerland.

The food situation in Alt Aussee became catastrophic. The bombing seemed to have cut the village off from all sources of supplies. We had no meat, butter, sugar or bread. I subsisted on an issue of nearly black seed potatoes and a few beans, and what stinging nettles I could find.

There was now nothing to do but wait until occupying troops came from the East or West. From the ridge of mountains behind Alt Aussee we could hear the sound of Russian gunfire, but the Americans, with an eye on the 'Salzberg' treasures, pushed on faster. On the instructions of Eigruber, a local Gestapo man, the 'Salzberg' had already been prepared for demolition. It only needed to be touched off and an art heritage of centuries would have subsided into crushed pulp and torn canvas.

The 'Salzberg' was guarded by local Gendarmerie who had been instructed to blow it up on the advance of occupying troops. But when that time came they refused to obey their orders.

There was a deathly calm in the village during the few days before the arrival of the Americans. Hitler was allegedly dead and Germany was left without a rudder. The Gestapo and SS men in the radio villa on the mountainside were having a final fling. Vast reserves of alcohol suddenly appeared and the SS guards made full use of it. There was much noise and activity at the villa.

Then suddenly, overnight, they were all gone with their police cars and lorries. The German Foreign Office Staff and the Rumanian and Bulgarian 'Governments' fled, too, probably through Switzerland. The villa was left empty except for two women (Gestapo wives), who, on the approach of the American troops, hoisted the Austrian national colours over the villa.

I soon learned where the 'radio villa' Gestapo men had gone. I met a peasant who had followed their trail to pick up what was dropped by the fleeing Nazis.

They had struck out into the mountains and pine forests, leaving two wrecked vehicles behind on the way. They had formed a complete encampment high up in the mountains. They had many boxes of ammunition and SS guards were posted all around the camp. Here they had decided to make a last stand. But they surrendered later without firing a shot.

The next to disappear was the SS leader Ernst Kaltenbrunner, who had the reputation of being a killer. He disappeared into the mountains behind Alt Aussee and evaded the Americans for a long time, in spite of all the patrols and search parties that hunted him. He finally gave himself up.

As it became clear that liberation was to come from the Americans, people in Alt Aussee began to show their colours – or rather their new colours. The first to appear openly were the Austrian Nationalists (Austrian Freedom Movement) who produced red-white-red armbands and strutted about with them. Many German nationals wore these arm bands, including even Prince Max von Hohenlohe who, a couple of days previously, had had as a guest in his villa, although an unwelcome one, the SS leader Kaltenbrunner.

While all this superficial change of allegiance was going on, the Nazi Party continued to function; the Party badge was still seen everywhere and the local Nazi Burgermeister still held office. People who for years had been servile Nazis now stepped forward and asserted that they had been working for the Allies all along. This tale became the fashion and was hard to disprove. Out of sheer necessity, I had to have recourse to it myself on occasions, although I confessed later that I was ashamed of having done so. It was a case of sink or swim and I found that there was always someone ready to jump on your back to sink you. Many good German Nationalists have survived by such methods.

In order to justify their existence and to cover up their own tracks, the Austrian capitalists began to prepare denunciations of various people in the village for the benefit of the Americans. They formed a committee and prepared protests in English against the Nazi concentration camps. These protests called for a new 'bloodbath' – this time with the Nazis as victims. The Americans, with their limited knowledge of the Continent and its ways, were to be faced with a big problem.

'Himmler's Killers'

I COULD HAVE walked away from the Western Powers a hundred times. I had every opportunity to do so. I could have walked a few miles to the Russian zone, or could quite simply have 'gone underground' and remained hidden for a while before making the next move. Nothing would have been easier. Unfortunately for me I remained, believing that as a legitimate German and as a man who was no 'war criminal' and had only done my bounden duty, I could scarcely be prosecuted or troubled – much less escorted to England and put on trial as a 'traitor'.

Even good friends of mine whose past history I knew, now seriously tried to tell me that they were anti-Nazis. I had to listen to it all and began to fear them as well. There was no knowing from what quarter a stab in the back could come. Other friends advised me to stay in Alt Aussee and offered their 'protection'.

Then suddenly all fighting ceased. We heard over the radio the news of Germany's 'unconditional surrender'.

It was not long before the first American tanks appeared in Alt Aussee. The villagers watched their entry with mixed feelings. The Americans lounged on top of their tanks and distributed silk stockings to the women who gave them the warmest welcome. Here and there an uneasy 'Austrian Freedom Movement' man stood, displaying his armband and probably wondering if it quite covered up all his sins of the past years. In most cases it did. The Americans had so many prisoners on their hands that their confusion became lamentable. In the end they had to release many.

It was inevitable that I should come into contact with the American military authorities because I was always in demand as an interpreter. On these occasions, the Americans never seemed to question my good English or my name which I did not hide. I did many necessary jobs of interpreting on behalf of the refugees, the Red Cross, and individuals requiring repatriation.

I found my contact with the American authorities interesting. It enabled me to size up things and to keep in touch with developments. Apart from anything else, I found the Americans to be strongly anti-Russian and anti-Communist, and this while they were still comrades-in-arms with the Russians.

At a friend's request I arranged for an interview with the American Commandant, Major Ralph Pierson. I acted as interpreter at the interview which lasted over one hour during which we gave Major Pierson a detailed review of the political situation – particularly concerning Nazi plans for the future. It was we who gave the Allies the very first news of the secret meeting of the Nazi chiefs in the Chancellery in Berlin in April and the preparations which had been made for the Nazi Party to go underground. The information we gave the American Commandant was so vital that it was immediately forwarded to Army HQ.

The Americans worked to a great extent on denunciations, and these poured in with such profusion that even the Americans were disgusted. Several asked me outright what kind of people lived in this country of Austria. But the same thing was going on in Germany.

A most embarrassing situation for me developed during a

dancing and drinking party in an Alt Aussee villa. It had, however, its humorous side. In response to a call from the hostess, I went over to her and found her together with the somewhat inflamed American Major. There was something wrong.

'Will you please translate the term *andere lander, andere sitten* to this gentleman here?' the hostess requested, glaring.

This was said in German and I looked at the Major who seemed anxious to know what it was all about. It seemed that he had made a 'pass' at the hostess. Now this was rather embarrassing. The term *andere lander, andere sitten* means 'other countries, other customs' and on this occasion it had only one meaning and that was an unpleasant one.

'Will you please translate that expression!' called the hostess once more, this time somewhat imperiously.

There was nothing else for it. I translated it with an expressionless face. The meaning dawned upon him very quickly, in spite of his heated condition, and he shut up. He remained subdued and moody for the rest of the evening.

I met the Major the next day when he was again his old courteous self. Perhaps he remembered the incident of the night before because, as if to make up for it, he asked me if I would like to take a ride in his jeep with him and visit the famous 'Salzberg'. It had been saved from demolition by the presence of mind of our gendarmerie and I accepted the offer with enthusiasm.

We duly arrived at the salt mine, which housed all the art treasures collected from so many parts of Europe. The inside of the mine was guarded by American sentries with tommy-guns. Locked steel gates barred the way down into the shafts. Unfortunately no one was allowed to enter the shafts so that we did not see much of the inside. Apparently not even the Major was privileged in this respect, so we could only return, having seen very little.

We drove back into the town and stood talking for a while at the side of the road. As we talked, we saw a sad sight.

A pitiful procession moved slowly towards us – a tattered, gaunt and bare-footed section of Austrian Alpine troops. A mule which had once carried a gun was with them, and it would have been possible to hang one's hat on its skeleton flanks. The men seemed to be walking in a dream. They were unshaven, starving and utterly exhausted. The picture of this mournful, desperate-looking straggling line of men was the epitome of a lost war. Napoleon's troops must have looked like this on their return from Moscow.

The Major shouted at them harshly: 'You can't come along here,' he roared. 'Get back! Get back to where you came from!'

The Austrian troops, not understanding a word, continued to lurch along the road towards us. They had clearly come all the way up from Bad Aussee following the only road. It was inconceivable that in their state they should be sent back again.

As they came up to the Major and me, they stopped and stood, swaying, looking out from glassy and uncomprehending eyes.

I went up to the leader of the section and asked him where it was he wanted to go. He said they wished to cut across the mountains. Cut across the mountains! I looked at them and saw that none of them had any provisions, equipment or covering for a night's sleep. And yet they wanted to go on and cut across the mountains!

I didn't ask them where they wanted to go, it was none of my business. I could only attempt to pass them off to the Major as quite harmless and tell him they were only going to take a short cut across the mountains.

'A short cut across the mountains!' exclaimed the Major. 'We don't want anybody in the mountains – much less people like this. These men ought to have been rounded up long ago.'

With this he again started shouting at them, calling upon them to get back where they had come from and to stay on the road. I was told to translate this.

Horrified at having to pass on such an order, I walked up to the leader of the section and kept my back turned towards the Major. I then quietly told the section leader what the Major had said, but advised him that if he turned and walked back until he was out of sight he could branch off down to the lake and then proceed along its far shores until he could find a way through the mountains.

He accepted this and the skeleton section turned round and retraced its steps. I then hurriedly took leave of the Major and followed the cortège with a friend who knew the district well.

We caught up with them, had a hurried consultation with the section leader and my companion pointed out their best way over the mountains.

About this time I met a Dutchman called Schilz who had been on the staff of a Dutch newspaper when the Germans occupied Holland. He continued to work for the newspaper in a leading capacity under the Germans, making several visits to Germany. He had been a collaborator, and apparently knew how to talk himself out of difficulties with the American authorities.

Looking back, I believe that this Dutchman was the price of my own personal freedom. We talked a lot and I told him my story, including my incarceration as 'The Officer in The Tower'.

Schilz came to me with a very sad story. He had some five or six children and it was essential that he should get back to Holland to be with them.

In order to do this, he said he needed papers from the American CIC post in Alt Aussee. Would I go with him and interpret for him?

I replied that I would gladly do anything to help, but that by going to the CIC, I would be putting my head into the lion's mouth. I explained that my own situation was none too secure.

Schilz pooh-poohed all this. He said that not only had I nothing to fear but that he would guarantee my safety. He added that he knew the head of the Dutch Secret Service personally and that in the event of any difficulty he would communicate with him directly through the American authorities. He even mentioned the name of the Dutch Secret Service chief.

The talk about the Dutch Secret Service man did not impress me, but I rashly decided to help Schilz. Next morning I went with him to the American CIC post and obtained an interview with a Swedish-looking American Intelligence officer. The three of us sat around a table and I started to interpret Schilz's needs.

The American appeared to become suspicious of Schilz and spoke to him sharply. Schilz then began to stutter in Dutch which I could not translate. I told Schilz to speak German and we continued.

Suddenly the American banged on the table and said to Schilz, without giving any reason: 'You are under arrest! Put all your papers on the table.'

He then turned to me and barked: 'And who are you? Show me your papers.'

I produced my Foreign Office identity card and German passport. The American glanced at them and then said: 'You are under arrest too. Put your papers and the contents of your pockets on the table.'

There was nothing to do but to comply. We were deprived of all our possessions and locked in an upstairs room. Schilz did not seem at all perturbed.

Soon Schilz was taken away for what the sentry called, 'interrogation'. I remained at the window looking out mournfully and wondering what would happen next. I saw a girl friend of mine walking down the street and called to her softly. I explained my situation and asked her to let my friends know. This she did immediately with the result that two of the leading members of the 'Austrian Freedom Movement' later arrived and pleaded fruitlessly for my release.

I was still standing at the window when I saw Schilz smilingly depart – a free man. The Dutchman did not look up at the window and made his way rapidly up the road. This was the last I ever saw of him and the typewriter I had lent him.

I was then called for interrogation and this time the American and a Jewish Intelligence officer faced me across a table.

I was to learn later that they had already been on the phone to the British military authorities who were undoubtedly delighted at the idea of my 'capture'. I was also to learn later, when in a British prison, that the British Intelligence section had received instructions to look for me in northern Italy.

The interrogation began. The Jewish officer left the table and the American took up the questioning. He was greatly excited by my story and described it as 'the story of the century'.

However, he had a Hollywood mind, as it transpired, because he noted in his report that I was in the German Intelligence Service, was a member of the Propaganda Ministry and also a member of the Foreign Office. He also put me on the SS list for the classification of prisoners. Such prisoners were singled out for a particularly bad time.

After this interrogation I was taken back to the bare room at the top of the house and stationed myself at the window again.

Later I asked the American why I was being held. He replied that I had nothing to worry about; I would be taken away from Alt Aussee for three days for an interrogation and returned.

The man was lying, as I was soon to discover. However, I

asked permission to obtain my shaving and washing kit, and pyjamas. I received permission promptly and then, looking out of the window, saw my girl friend outside watching the building.

'There's a friend of mine,' I told the American. 'May I ask her to fetch my things?'

'Certainly,' was the reply and the American peered out admiringly at the trim figure of the girl.

Calling out in German, I asked her to fetch the required kit and to bury my pistol (which I had obtained for my protection during my stay in Alt Aussee). I told her we would have a chance to talk when she returned.

It all worked very well. In a short time she was back with all the American soldiers wolf-whistling after her. With my American interrogator and a sentry standing around we spoke to each other in German.

My girl friend was much concerned for my safety, but I assured her that I would be back in three days. We never saw each other again.

Had I known that there was no question of my returning in three days I would have collected some reasonable clothes. As it was, I was taken later to England in the same clothes I had been wearing when arrested in Alt Aussee. These clothes were the same as worn by everybody up in the mountains. They were the only practical clothes – short leather trousers (*Lederhosen*), a grey-and-green short jacket (*Joppe*) and all the rest that went with it. Had I taken off my 'famous' black raincoat when standing in the dock at the Old Bailey I would have cut a picturesque figure.

For some three days I remained in that miserable room in the American CIC post at Alt Aussee expecting to go at any time. I slept on a straw mattress on the floor and was kept awake most of the night by the American sentries who, feeling in need of

o

company, used to visit me with bottles of wine and talk most of the night. They were friendly enough, but it was very wearing.

On my last day in Alt Aussee, the American sentry called excitedly to me. 'Look,' he said, 'there are three of Himmler's killers down there!' He pointed out of the window.

'Himmler's killers?' I asked. 'What do Himmler's killers look like?'

'There's three of them down there, I tell you,' said the sentry waving his tommy-gun.

I had a look. There below the window sat three of the local uniformed gendarmes.

'Himmler's killers!' I said to the agitated sentry. 'Those are three village "cops". What did you want to arrest them for?'

'I tell you,' said the sentry, 'those are three of Himmler's killers. I *know* it!'

I shrugged my shoulders.

Later, as I was chatting to the sentry, I heard my interrogator and the Jewish officer talking on the landing below. One was saying: 'We'll send him down to the local lock-up in Bad Aussee. After that he'll go for a ride.'

So now I knew. I got together my few things without being told and waited. Then a jeep arrived and I found I was not to go alone; the three 'Himmler's killers' were to go with me.

It turned out that these three gendarmes had been on guard over the 'Salzberg' treasures and had deliberately refrained from carrying out Gauleiter Gruber's order for demolition. They were under arrest, it is true, but they were under arrest as witnesses.

We were herded into the waiting jeep and driven into Bad Aussee under guard. There we were lodged in a wine cellar at street level which was being used as a temporary prison. The room was already full of every type of prisoner.

There was only one small window to the place and occasionally a woman would appear and throw some food or cigarettes in through it. Our guards this time were old peasants – members of the 'Austrian Freedom Movement'. Their weapons were sporting rifles.

On the next day I was transferred to the local museum which had been turned into a prison and the following day I was moved again, this time to the local jail. Here there was an amazing throng. I arrived just as there was an issue of stew and took my place in the queue. I was surprised to see that we were mixed with the women's section. As I was waiting, a pleasant-faced woman, dressed in a nice bright *Dirndle*, started talking to me. Apparently she was on good terms with the wardress serving out the stew because she got me a second helping after whispering in the wardress's ear.

I spent only one day in this prison when I was called out again and told to prepare for departure. A jeep with three armed American soldiers in it was waiting for me. I was told to get in and off we drove.

I could tell from the expressions on the Americans' faces that this was to be no joy-ride. They clearly hated their prisoner. We had not driven far before the American sergeant in charge turned to me and said roughly: 'Take a last look at the countryside, you Nazi bastard. You ain't got so long to live.'

I said, 'Thank you', and left it at that. However, the three Yankee soldiers now warmed to the task of baiting me. I had to listen whilst, between them, they laid the blame for all the concentration camps at my door and made me generally respon-sible for all Nazi crimes, referring to me continuously as 'that Nazi bastard'. I expected any minute that they would stop the jeep and beat me up after this outburst, but, instead, there was an uneasy silence lasting for some miles. Then suddenly the Yankee Sergeant turned and said: 'Had anything to eat, recently, buddy?'

I replied stiffly that I had been used to going on short rations for some years now and that I was all right.

'Stop the car, boys,' called the American Sergeant, 'I don't think this fella has had anything to eat. We'll give him a c-ration.'

The jeep pulled up and I remained sitting, amazed at this sudden change. An American c-ration was quickly pulled out of some corner of the jeep and opened. I ate it quickly, ravenously. The Yankee Sergeant opened another and gave it to me with a: 'Here y'are, buddy, you're hungry.'

I appreciated this unexpected kindness and said so. The Sergeant grunted, climbed back into the jeep and off we drove again. The ice was now broken. From then on all three of them spoke to me in a friendly manner and commenced to show a real interest in Germany and its problems.

The German people, I stressed, were human beings just as they were. I added that the German people, too, were a kindly people.

The Yankees liked this, and very soon they discovered that all four occupants of the jeep were human beings. 'Hey, fellas,' called the Sergeant, 'I want to give this guy some beer. Pull up at the next Army store.'

We pulled up at the next store and collected some large flagons of beer which we drank liberally en route. I was beginning to like these men until, as we drove on, the Spanish-looking Corporal took a look at my wrist-watch. 'How many jewels has that got, buddy?' he asked.

Realising what might be in his mind I replied: 'Well, I don't know if it's got any. It's just an ordinary Swiss watch.' It was a present I valued greatly.

'Huh,' grunted the Corporal, and his interest subsided.

The question had rather chilled me through. I disliked this plundering.

The atmosphere cleared up again rapidly as the other two chatted away cheerfully. They could afford to be cheerful.

We passed along the same route taken by the German armies that had capitulated under orders. Along the road were notices nailed to telephone poles: *Wir sind waffenlos, aber nicht-ehrlos* (We are without weapons, but not without honour). The Americans passed these notices, unmoved and uncomprehending.

I recognised Munich as we reached it. The American Sergeant suggested we spend the night in the city in order to give me, his prisoner, 'a good time'.

But this idea was abandoned and we drove up to a military building on the outskirts where I met the heads of the Slovakian Government, including the Prime Minister. These men were to travel with us, one of them, a prisoner, coming in our jeep.

We continued the journey with the Slovakian car leading and our jeep following. My new companion was introduced to me by my jeep crew as a 'Nazi hangman', a terrible killer. I looked at him wonderingly. He did not look like a 'hangman' and looked inoffensive.

As we drove along the Americans repeated their bloodthirsty Nazi cross-talk, but this time it was tinged with humour. Every now and again they would turn to me and make signs of stringing me up. My companion, Dr K, regarded them with mild wonderment. He did not understand a word they said, although he understood their actions.

In between the Americans' sallies, I asked my companion if he really had been the 'hangman' they said he was. He was astonished. No, he had never been a hangman, he said, and asked me to inform the Americans of that fact.

I did and this so provoked them that we nearly careered off the road. 'Of course he's a hangman!' they yelled, and turned to him holding their throats, hanging their tongues out and rolling their eyes like a man on a scaffold. Dr K unfortunately had no sense of humour – and no wonder!

On we drove with this crazy gang and stopped in a field for some more rations. Here the American driver of the Slovakian car, after taking out his pistol and threatening the Slovakians with it, indulged in some pistol practice and put the fear of God into the neighbouring peasants, as well as the Slovakians who had already been frightened by the man's dirt-track driving.

From Munich we made for Vocklabruck on the Attersee. On the way Dr K had a heart attack. He asked for a cigarette from the Americans, explaining that this acted as a *Gegengift* (antidote). A literal translation of the German word is 'counter-poison'. I had forgotten the English word antidote and told the Americans that Dr K wanted a 'counter-poison'. This again sparked off the Americans.

'What!' they yelled, 'does the hangman deal in poison as well?' They then proceeded to search the Doctor, going over the whole of his person. The Americans were rough, but not unkindly, and it was only their 'sense of humour' in this instance that made them cruel.

Dr K, none the less, got his cigarette and he recovered slowly. We arrived at Vocklabruck and here I was submitted to a further interrogation. I took the opportunity of stressing my German nationality and asking the reason for my arrest and treatment. I was told that as a member of the German Government I would have been arrested in any case.

The Americans here showed the liveliest interest in my case and asked if I would talk to the Press – their Press. This I absolutely refused to do. I found it odd that military authorities of any nation should encourage their prisoners to make statements to the Press.

After my interrogation I was taken to a large room in what had previously been a school. Here I found ninety-six prisoners – men and women – crowded together, most of whom had no idea why they were being held.

As the prisoners entered the room they were relieved of their watches, which went into a sort of pool to be divided afterwards among the American guard. The head of the American guard was my Sergeant from the jeep and he was glad to see me again.

As I entered I was also told to hand over my watch. This I was loath to do and protested, explaining that it was a valued gift. To my surprise the Sergeant also joined in roughly with a 'Come on, buddy, hand over that watch. I like the look of it myself.'

I started to argue but felt a heavy foot on my toe and looked up to catch a flicker of an eyelid from the Sergeant. Realising that he was up to something, I handed over the watch and walked away to a corner of the room. In a few minutes the Sergeant sought me out and pressed the watch into my hand, saying: 'Bit slow in the uptake, aren't you, buddy?'

The American Sergeant, for whom I now had a real liking, later explained to me that only by demanding the watch for himself had he been able to rescue it from his companions. Once one of them had got it there would be no getting it back.

The Americans now proceeded to make some sort of order out of the chaos existing in our grossly overcrowded room. The guards themselves occupied a platform at one end of the room and from here the Sergeant called a roll. Or rather he started to do so and then broke down completely over the names. The prisoners had names of every description, ranging from German to Polish, Czech, Hungarian, Italian and Serbian. After only a few prisoners had answered to their names the Sergeant looked up in exasperation and shouted for me to call the roll.

Opposite many of the names were the initials SS and I noticed that this mark applied to the most unlikely people. As I called the roll, with the Sergeant looking over my shoulder, all prisoners denoted with the SS mark were made to stand in lines in front of the platform.

When I came to my own name I was astonished to note that SS also stood against mine. I stopped calling the roll and asked the meaning of the mark. The Sergeant replied: 'Well, ain't you SS, buddy? It's what the CIC in Alt Aussee marked you down as.'

I hastened to disillusion the Sergeant on this point. 'OK, buddy,' he said obligingly, 'I'll cross it out. There, that'll make you feel better now.' He crossed it out and I proceeded with the calling of the roll.

After I had finished calling the roll many of the prisoners rushed up to me. They wished to voice their needs and complaints. Some of the women were quite distracted; they had been torn from their homes, often as a result of malicious denunciations, and had not even been given the opportunity to provide for their children. Could they communicate? Could they telephone? Could they send someone?

I was compelled to return a 'dusty answer' to all the tearful complaints from those who wanted to know why they had been arrested.

Emergency rations were issued to everybody, after which the whole room was arranged for sleeping by the simple process of forming the packed multitude up in lines and then giving them the command to lie down. Only thus was it possible to arrange for sleeping space for so many. Men and women lay together, there being no chance of segregation.

I was allotted a place underneath the platform where I could be called upon at any time to interpret. In front of me lay three lines of SS.

There was no sleep that night for anyone. Firstly the American guards, who had been drinking, put on a sort of clown show up on the platform. One American dressed in his underclothes and a battered top hat which he had raked up from somewhere did a sort of ballet-*cum*-stepdance on the platform, earning the thunderous and raucous applause of his comrades.

The Slovakian Government lay in a row of their own, right out in the front. They looked so respectable and dignified in their black clothes.

The 'hangman' was deputed cleaner of the room. He still suffered very much from his heart, but was otherwise spared the attentions of the guards. 'Hangman' was the name he had been given and 'hangman' was the name he answered to.

The time came to leave the friendly Americans. Our destination was Freising in Bavaria and with two new American guards we reached there, late in the evening.

I was handed over by my escort to an American officer who, to his astonishment and amusement, received strict instructions to treat me well as I was 'OK'. My escort shook hands with me in front of the officer and wished me luck.

Later, an American officer locked me in a room where I found myself facing an enormous man dressed in Bavarian national costume. He introduced himself as Dr Martin, the Chief of Police in Nuremberg. He was my room-mate.

The Americans had so many prisoners in Freising that their system broke down. They had insisted on feeding us on old German Army rations and when they ran out we were left for a while with nothing. When this happened, Negro guards brought us food and cigarettes from their canteen and kept us going.

The day came when I was ordered to get ready to leave Freising. I said goodbye to Dr Martin and we both wished one another 'luck'. Outside the corridor I met two other prisoners who were to accompany me. One was General Ritter von Epp, an

early member of the Nazi Party. He raised sixty thousand marks
to enable Hitler to buy the then run-down *Voelkischer Beobachter*,
and made it into his official daily mouthpiece for his propaganda.
General von Epp also helped to organise Hitler's mob brawlers,
the brown-shirted SA, and it was he whom, under Hitler's
orders, in March 1933, turned out the Bavarian Government
with his storm troopers and established the Nazis in Bavaria. The
other prisoner was Ernst Wilhelm Bohle, a member of the
German Government and head of the Nazi *Auslandsorganisation*
(Organisation for Germans Abroad). They introduced themselves
and then we waited around chatting. After a while we were led
downstairs and out into a yard where a large number of Negro
soldiers were waiting for us with their cameras.

Apparently they had been told that three notorious Nazis were
about to be led away to their fate and they wished to snap the
historical occasion. A few white American officers stood around
in the background watching the scene.

The three of us were lined up to face the cameras, but I resented
being photographed, turned my back on the Negro soldiers and
started talking to my companions, but they advised me to face
the cameras, which I did unwillingly.

A lorry, used for the transport of coal, was waiting for us and
we were bundled into it. The tailboard of the lorry was snapped
up and we were ready to move off. Suddenly an American
interrogation officer came running after us, waving his hands.

'Wait a bit,' he shouted, 'you mustn't forget your surprise
packet!'

I then saw the 'surprise packet' being bundled along towards
the lorry. He was a bearded, tattered and handcuffed figure,
without a shirt and clad only in trousers and jacket. He was
tossed over the top of the tailboard like a sack of potatoes onto
the floor of the lorry.

'That is Julius Streicher,' yelled the interrogation officer. 'Enjoy his lousy company!'

We helped an almost unrecognisable Julius Streicher to his feet. He staggered as we made room for him on the wooden lockers that were covered with coal dust. A half-Negro soldier climbed in after Streicher with his tommy-gun, and he never took his finger off the trigger for the whole of the subsequent journey. He was under strict orders.

A burst of derisive cheers came from the Negro spectators as the lorry started off with the four of us. We had no idea where we were going. It was a most unpleasant journey with dust and fumes continuously flying around in the lorry.

In a depressing silence I had an opportunity for the first time of studying the miserable-looking Julius Streicher, about whom I had heard so much. Streicher, a member of Hitler's hierarchy and the Fuehrer's chief instrument for murdering and torturing Jews, broke the silence occasionally to whisper a whine about his impending fate. He brooded with his head resting heavily between his hands, his buttonless, dirty jacket exposed a hairless chest. He had no shirt or underwear. For him retribution was at hand and he knew it.

Breaking the silence, Streicher leant forward and said to me in a low whisper: 'Have you by any chance got any poison with you?' General von Epp and Bohle shifted uneasily. They did not want any dealings with Streicher. They obviously thought that friendship with a top-ranking Nazi would bring retribution from their American captors. They were taking no risks. Streicher reciprocated by ignoring them and addressing me.

As the lorry rumbled along, Streicher whimpered occasionally about the way he had been treated by the Americans. He told a tale of near-martyrdom, of sleepless nights and of being photographed in unseemly postures. Streicher extended his manacled hands and complained that his handcuffs were too tight.

Ignoring the Nazi General and Bohle, Streicher confided to me : 'They'll hang me, I know they will! What have I done? All I have done is to clarify and inform the world as to what the Jews are and what they are doing; mine has been the work of education' – this from the 'uncrowned King of Franconia', who used to laugh and boast of the personal whippings he gave to Jews.

After telling me about his 'educational work', Streicher lapsed into silent brooding and rubbed his hands against the legs of his trousers. Every few minutes the coloured guard glanced at the four of us, and fingered his tommy-gun.

As darkness fell we arrived in a town which we later learned was Wiesbaden. We drove into the grounds of a large private house which had been commandeered by the American military authorities and were lined up facing a wall. We were searched thoroughly by the American troops, apparently for poison phials.

General von Epp and I were placed in this house. Streicher and Bohle were driven off to the large city jail. Von Epp and I were received by three American soldiers who were surprised to hear that we had had nothing to eat all day. Once more we experienced the extremes in the American character, because our new custodians this time gave us every care and attention.

When one of the guards tried to remove Streicher's handcuffs before he and Bohle were taken to the city prison, he discovered that the Americans in Freising had forgotten to send the keys of the handcuffs. A guard came to the rescue and, with dexterity unusual for a normal law-abiding citizen, he proceeded to pick the lock of the handcuffs. First-aid dressings were placed on the weals on Streicher's wrists.

Von Epp and I were later taken to the city prison where we were again searched for poison. Our clothes were taken away and we were given ordinary German prison garb to wear. We shuffled to our cells in wooden clogs.

These cells were pitch dark as there was no electric bulb. I felt my way around in the darkness until I came to an iron bed against the wall. I laid out some blankets on it and slept until awakened by daylight.

I looked round the cell. There was nothing in it except primitive toilet arrangements. Outside the door I could hear voices speaking German. They were the voices of other prisoners calling to one another.

Then I heard someone calling: '*Hallo! Hallo! Sind sie da Herr Stewart? Hier ist Bohle.*'

I called back through the ventilator in German: 'Yes, here I am. Where are you?'

'In the next cell,' came the reply.

Bohle then called to me that when I wanted to communicate with him I was to shout: 'Karl.'

Then I heard the sound of clogs on stone and saw from my window the pathetic figure of Julius Streicher emerge into the exercise yard. The bearded and bandaged Streicher looked like a shambling scarecrow.

That was the last I saw of Julius Streicher, the fanatical anti-Semite. As one of Hitler's major war criminals he was hanged at Nuremberg in October 1946. He mounted the gallows in the execution chamber after Ribbentrop, Keitel, Kaltenbrunner, Rosenberg, Frank, and Frick.

Streicher's place in the exercise yard at Wiesbaden was then taken, to my surprise, by a very good-looking young girl wearing smart ordinary clothes. She was German but seemed to speak fairly good English because she had a long conversation with a hulking American guard who was clearly not averse to talking to her. She talked more than she walked.

Bohle was next to take exercise, clip-clopping around the ring. My turn would come soon, I thought. I was right. I heard a key in my door and was summoned out by a sentry. For half an hour I shuffled around the ring, Here and there I saw part of a face looking out at me through smashed window-panes. Once a hand waved. I felt a silent message which only imprisoned people can feel and which only they can communicate to one another. The American guard stood stolidly chewing his gum and twirling his wooden baton.

I was soon back in my cell where I just sat looking at nothing. There was nothing to do and not even a book to read. For hours I sat there in silence. All noise down in the yard had ceased, and a horrible silence brooded over the unhappy building. I was awakened from my nightmare thoughts by an urgent voice: '*Willi. Willi. Kommen Sie doch zum Fenster!*'

I climbed up to the window and called back: '*Hier bin ich, Karl. Was ist?*'

'Listen,' came the urgent voice of Bohle. 'You will, I hope, be released soon. I am in a different situation. I want you please to communicate with my wife and Inge – remember the name, Inge – at Franzensbad. Tell them that my honour has not been able to stand this treatment. Tell them I thought of them to the last. I am now going to take my life.'

At once I sprang into action, scarcely knowing what I was doing. Kicking off a wooden shoe I grabbed it and started to hammer on the door. I soon heard leisurely footsteps approaching. A key was inserted in the lock and the door swung open. A face expressing lazy interest appeared. I saw the American uniform and a hand resting on a pistol butt.

'Say, where's the fire?' drawled the guard.

'Listen,' I said. 'I have to speak to an officer immediately.'

'Why, what's the matter? Won't I do?' he replied.

'No,' I said emphatically. 'It is too urgent. Hurry up or it may be too late!'

The sentry stood looking for a moment with a half-smile on his face. Then he drawled: 'OK. Anything you say.'

The door was closed and locked again and I heard his far too leisurely steps departing. I had deliberately not referred the matter to a sentry. I feared that the only result of that would have been another search and general unpleasantness for Bohle. It might also have led to a tightening up with regard to the treatment of prisoners all round.

I paced my cell and waited in a fever of anxiety. Perhaps it was already too late and Bohle had found some way out of his misery.

In a short while I heard the same leisurely steps and my door was unlocked once more.

'OK, come on,' said the sentry. 'The Captain is waiting to see you.'

I was led downstairs and into an office where a swarthy, but not unpleasant-looking, officer was seated at a desk. The sentry was dismissed and I was left alone with the Captain who was also the governor of the jail.

'Well, what is it?' he enquired, looking at me with an expressionless face.

'Before saying what I am going to say,' I said to him, whilst trying to pierce his mask and discover if humanity lurked anywhere in his make-up, 'I should like to ask you, on your word as an American officer, not to take any subsequent action which will inflict further suffering and humiliation on the prisoners under your charge.'

The American officer looked at me sharply. 'I can give no guarantee of any kind,' he replied. 'I am here to serve the best interests of the United States. I act solely on that principle.'

I felt encouraged, although rather hopeless, in the face of this blunt refusal to temporise. 'In that case,' I said, 'I shall be unable to prevent what is likely to happen to someone in your charge. I myself am indifferent to my fate, but I do not know if your knowledge of the German character goes so far as to enable you to realise that if a German's honour is, may I say, deliberately outraged he is liable to take his life.'

The Captain sat up sharply. 'What is that you say? I am quite aware of the German mentality. That is why I have this job.'

'Quite so,' I said. 'In that case you will realise that certain conditions of treatment can lead to a man taking his life.'

The Captain now displayed alarmed interest. 'I am personally responsible for every man in my charge,' he said, 'and it is a serious matter if any man takes his life. Who is likely to do so? If you are serious and if you tell me, I will give you my word that I will deal with the matter as justly as possible and without any victimisation, which you apparently fear.'

I then told the American Captain of Bohle's intention and added that he had entrusted a farewell message to me.

The American Captain sprang up. 'Thank you,' he said. This time all hostility had vanished from his face. 'I shall see about this immediately.' He opened the door and called the sentry who led me back to my cell.

Later that day I awoke from a doze to find in my cell a table with books on it. An electric bulb glistened reassuringly in the socket which had once been empty and, beside me on the bed, civilian clothes – my *lederhosen* – and my ordinary leather shoes. I could hardly believe my eyes. I had interceded for Bohle and this is what had happened. I wondered what had happened to Bohle. I got my answer when I heard. 'Willi, Willi,' from the direction of the window.

I sprang to the window and climbed up. '*Gott sie dank, Karl;*

Deutsches Reich

Einbürgerungsurkunde

Der wissenschaftliche Hilfsarbeiter ‒ ‒ ‒ ‒ ‒ ‒ ‒ ‒ ‒ ‒

‒ ‒ ‒ ‒ ‒ Norman B a i l l i e ‒ S t e w a r t ‒ ‒ ‒

‒ ‒ ‒ ‒ ‒ ‒ ‒ ‒ ‒, geboren am 15. Januar   1909

in L o n d o n ‒ ‒ ‒ ‒ ‒ ‒, hat mit dem Zeitpunkt der Aushändigung

dieser Urkunde die Reichsangehörigkeit durch Einbürgerung erworben. Die Ein-

bürgerung erstreckt sich nicht auf Familienangehörige.

Berlin, den   9. Juli   1940

Der Polizeipräsident
Im Auftrage:

Gebühr: 100.‒RM.

Tgb.-Nr. II 5010 B. 4973

The certificate which granted Baillie-Stewart German naturalisation

Reichspropagandaamt
Wien

Wien, den 18. August 1939.
III., Reisnerstraße 40
Fernsprecher: B-52-5-40

Aktenzeichen: A 7020/11.8.39/2484-2.1

(In der Antwort anzugeben)

Schnellbrief

Betrifft:

Herrn

B. S t e w a r t ,

W i e n , 19.,
Hungerbergstrasse 6/13.

Über Ersuchen des Herrn S e y f e r t h vom Reichs-
propagandaministerium teile ich Ihnen mit, dass derselbe Montag,
den 21. August d.J. um Mittag hier in Wien eintreffen wird und
Sie bittet, ihn an diesem Tag abends um 19 Uhr 30 in der Halle
des Hotels "Erzherzog Karl", Wien, I., Kärntnerstrasse 31, zu er-
warten.

Ich bitte zur Bestätigung des Erhaltes dieses Schrei —
bens am Montag, den 21. ds. zwischen 9 und 10 Uhr vormittags unter der Nummer B 52-5-40 (Frau Laube) anzurufen.

Heil Hitler !

i.A.
Eduard Frauenfeld.

A photograph of one of a series of letters that passed between Baillie-Stewart and the Vienna branch of the German Propaganda Ministry before he was taken on as an English newsreader

Sie leben noch!' I called, delighted to hear his voice again.

'Willi, think what's happened,' called back Bohle. 'They have given me back my clothes; I have a table, books, a light, a typewriter and paper. I have also got a companion to share my cell.'

'That's fine,' I replied. 'Do you feel better now?'

'*Prima*' (first rate) came the reply which both pleased and surprised me. What amazing resilience man has and how swiftly can even the most dangerous moods change under the recurrence of some 'normality' in the shape of clothes, books and a light.

'And how are you?' continued Bohle.

'Thanks,' I called back, 'I've been given clothes, books and a light, too. It makes all the difference, doesn't it?'

'Indeed it does,' I heard Bohle's reply. 'I can't understand it. The change was so sudden. They are even friendly to me.'

I did not tell Bohle the reason for the change. The change, in any case, may not have been entirely to the good in his instance. The typewriter had been given to him not merely as a distraction. With the aid of this typewriter he provided the Americans with all the details of the German *Auslandsorganisation* and the part he had played in it. He was to receive five years' imprisonment. After this incident I used to hear Bohle's typewriter tapping away until late every night.

One morning my door was thrown open. 'Get ready to go. A plane is waiting for you. Hurry up!'

So this was it. I was taken downstairs to collect a few things and then escorted to a waiting jeep which was driven to the aerodrome where a British light bomber waited. Accompanied by an American escort, I was bundled into this and it took off immediately.

The fact that a bomber had been specially detailed for my transport filled me with foreboding. Apparently I was considered

P

important enough to merit such a distinguished and expensive form of transport. I was the sole prisoner in the bomber.

We flew over country which had recently been the scene of major military operations. I peered down with interest at the old battlefields and at the Rhine and its broken fortifications.

I imagined that I was being flown direct to England; but no, we landed without reaching the Channel or the sea. I was led off the aerodrome and taken to a waiting British lorry.

Charged

I HAD NO idea where I was. I was driven through cobbled streets and only noticed here and there a sign written in French. I presumed I was in France but it was, in fact, Brussels.

The lorry drove into a new prison and I was taken to a reception room where I was received by two British NCOs. I had to listen to one or two jibes; my clothes and papers were taken from me and I was handed a British private soldier's uniform to put on.

The uniform was apparently of no significance. Hadn't I been sent to Wormwood Scrubs in full officer's uniform once before, and hadn't I had to queue, whilst wearing it, with criminals, drunks and the riff-raff of the London underworld?

From the reception room I was taken into a separate block of what was a large military prison. I was led along to a tiny cell which, I found, was in perpetual gloomy twilight. The 'roof' of the cell consisted of wire netting interlaced with barbed wire. Light filtered through from the long opaque panes of glass in the roofing above. Inside the cell were a bed-board, some blankets and a bucket in the corner for the purposes of nature. Otherwise the cell was completely bare and its bareness accentuated by whitewash. There was nothing upon which one could even fix one's gaze – except the bucket in the corner.

It was difficult to know that one was surrounded by about one hundred men. Not a sound could be heard except an occasional cough or sigh. The NCOs crept up and down outside the cells in rubber gym shoes, peering in every now and again through the slits in the doors which had a shutter to them.

Occasionally a whisper would start somewhere and when this happened a volley of raucous abuse and threats resounded round the hall.

There was nothing to read and nothing to do. I just waited for nightfall. There was no mattress or pillow on the hard board and the three blankets were insufficient for any purpose. For five months I 'slept' in these conditions.

As it became dark, the guards were changed and the lights turned on – not to be turned off again for the whole night. With the changing of the guard a loud whispering started off all down the hall. This was apparently the moment waited for by all the prisoners. Suddenly I heard a loud throaty whisper from the next-door cell: 'Hey, mate. How long're you doing?'

I kept quiet, not knowing that I was being addressed. Then came a tap on the wall and a louder 'Hey, mate. Can't you hear me? How long're you doing and what did they put you in here for?'

It seemed that I was expected to reply. I whispered back: 'I don't know and I don't know why I am here.'

There followed a tee-hee from the cell on the other side: 'Blimey! We've got a duke or somebody here!'

Then from the other side again: 'Hey, you ain't a soldier, are you? What are you doing here?'

'I don't know,' I replied, 'and I'm not talking any more.'

The conversation now continued between the occupants of the two cells either side.

'Hey,' said one, 'do you hear that fellow's accent? He must be some special kind of prisoner.'

Then from the other side: 'Perhaps it's the King of the Belgians. There was a rumour he was coming here.'

Then the first one again: 'That's who he is. Blimey, it's the King of the ruddy Belgians!'

I heard the whisper going all along the line of the cells: 'The King of the bloody Belgians is here. Yes, in one of the top cells. Poor bastard!'

The whisper became a murmur and then almost a tumult. It ceased like magic as a voice like a clap of thunder roared: 'Stop that bloody noise! The next man who talks will get the fire bucket and will lose his blasted name. I'll give you King of the bastard Belgians! I'll treat you all the same – frigging royalty or otherwise!'

The last remark did it. The King of the Belgians *was* there, and for days afterwards men in that hall believed that I was the King of the Belgians.

Night – an electric light night – set in, and I stretched myself out on my board as the bell rang for 'Beds down'. It was a nightmare night and the first of many similar.

For the first four days I received no exercise at all. I was confined to the absolute blankness of my whitewashed cell. After that I was taken out for half an hour each day and made to walk in a circle on my own in a corner of a yard.

After a day or two I was issued with a 'book' which was thrown down outside the cell. These books were changed every day but remained inside the hall. Not only were the books of an utterly worthless nature, but many had pages missing and, as a result of the system, one often got the same book re-issued and re-issued. I complained about this and the reply was: 'What? A book is a book, ain't it?' Having read my book many times, I just sat on the hard board and stared – at nothing.

The only thing that was good was the food, and that was

exceptionally good after what I had been used to, even during my years of wartime Germany.

For some time I was the only political prisoner in the British military prison in Brussels. Then others started to arrive. One by one they were brought in until, in the end, there were twelve. This did not include some eleven fighters for Arab freedom who made quite a stir in the prison. Few of them could speak English, and even the British military policemen were hard put to it to preserve some kind of discipline with them.

Shortly after my arrival at the prison I was informed by the prison Commandant that an officer would be coming down very soon to interrogate me.

In due course the man arrived and I was taken to see him. He was a captain of the Intelligence Corps. He did not reveal his identity at the time but many months later I learned that he was Deputy Commander Spooner of Scotland Yard. He merely said he was a representative of SHAEF (Supreme Headquarters of the Allied Expeditionary Force) and had come to take a statement from me. After this statement, he said, it would be decided as to whether I would be charged or released.

The inducement of release was held out to me as it was until the very end of my stay in Brussels. Even shortly before I was finally flown to London to be charged with 'High Treason' the British Commandant told me that I might be putting on my little leather trousers soon and returning to the Austrian mountains.

My experience was that such 'statements' were taken down under peculiar conditions. In the first place, the prisoner due to make the statement has often been in solitary confinement for a considerable period. He has also, often as not, been subjected to unpleasant and demoralising treatment. He emerges from all this to meet a kind and friendly man who offers him a chair and cigarette (just help yourself as you feel like it, old man!).

The kindly man then starts off with: 'Now just let me run over this together before we' – yes, *we* – 'start writing in order to get the facts straight.'

I found that 'getting the facts straight' meant that the interrogator sorts them and shuffles the pack before dealing – that is to say before *he* writes the 'statement'. When the statement is then written, 'facts' have somehow taken a new order. Some are highlighted, and others are missing altogether. The prisoner is then asked in a kindly manner to sign what the other has written in his own handwriting and in his own words. The prisoner often signs to oblige. In other cases he signs because he does not know what he is doing and is not in a fit state to judge.

I found, much later, that Commander Spooner worded the statement with the purpose of my being charged and not released.

It ran, in his words: 'My present nationality is German, I having been naturalised some time at the beginning of 1940.'

This was the 'hanging' part of the statement and I did not know it, nor could I have dreamed it. In my story I had not spoken of time of naturalisation but of the time when I received my naturalisation certificate. These are two quite different things and because of subsequent events their importance cannot be over-emphasised. In fact, to me they became a matter of life and death.

The actual receipt of my naturalisation certificate was a pure matter of formality. Its despatch to me was part of an automatic process controlled only by the slow functioning of Government departments. In effect, as I learned much later, and after I had been some two years in prison in Britain, a naturalisation certificate is not even essential to naturalisation. The British Nationality and Status of Aliens Act (1914), section 13, reads:

A British subject who, when in any foreign state and not under disability, by obtaining a certificate of naturalisation *or by any other voluntary and formal act*, becomes naturalised therein, shall thenceforth be deemed to have ceased to be a British subject. [The italics are mine.]

Just as I did not know the significance of those lines in the statement I had signed, also I did not know the above extract from British law. I had, of course, undertaken a variety of positive 'voluntary and formal acts' to make myself a German citizen and at the same time to renounce my British citizenship. Official documents prove this. What is most important: I had initiated these acts before the war started.

The 'hanging' part of the statement, which I so unguardedly signed, was contained in the first relevant paragraph. The preamble to it read: 'I have been cautioned that I need say nothing unless I wish, but anything I say may be given in evidence.' The statement concluded with the words: 'This statement has been read over by me and is true,' and my signature was appended.

My error was that I did not see the mouth of the trap. I walked into it without knowing the direction I was taking.

Commander Spooner wrote a statement, which, though appearing to be fair and giving any amount of unnecessary detail, contained a 'below-the-belt' punch in the first paragraph. That was the paragraph which enabled MI 5 to catch a nigger by his toe. I was the nigger in this case.

In my case no 'exterior evidence' was produced in support of the statement that I had been 'naturalised some time at the beginning of 1940'. Not even my naturalisation certificate was produced – although it was available! I was being trapped on a statement I had never made and which could have been disproved by available official documents.

Commander Spooner should have mentioned first that I had applied for German nationality in September 1938. Chronological order was vital. Furthermore, after I had declared from the start – long before the Commander had even started to write – that I was a German citizen, that I had applied for German citizenship in 1938 and that my actual nationalisation certificate had been issued in 1940, was it not the Commander's duty, knowing that nationality obtained during war was invalid in British law, to inform me that I appeared to be under a misapprehension?

After making this initial fatal statement, I later wrote out two subsidiary statements with the object of making good the damage that had been done in the original phraseology and wording. But even so I missed the point of the 'hanging' paragraph which had been inserted.

All three statements were made as a direct result of the original inducement of release which had been held out to me and which continued to be held out to me for a period of five months. From the start it had been assumed and intimated that statements would be taken only as a matter of course. In the circumstances, I had reason to expect release.

Of the twelve prisoners in Brussels, only three were subsequently charged and these three were imprisoned.

A fleeting visitor to Brussels was William Joyce. One morning, when I was unlocked for 'stepping out' along with other prisoners, I saw an almost unrecognisable William Joyce wearing British uniform and carrying a bucket in his hand.

His fellow prisoners were laughing at him, and not without reason. His head was completely shaved and painted a bright yellow. He was still limping from the wound that had been inflicted upon him, at the time of his arrest in Germany near the Danish frontier.

The word had clearly got around the hall that he was 'Lord Haw-Haw', and he was an object of general interest. A Welsh sergeant, who was placed over us for most of the time, spotted me emerging from my cell and called me over. At the same time he called William Joyce to him. It was clear that he wanted to note our reactions to one another, since he had no pretext for calling us together.

The Sergeant was disappointed though. I ignored Joyce, as I had done for the past four years. We stood around for a few moments amidst an embarrassed silence, and then the Sergeant told us to return to our cells.

Joyce stayed some three days in Brussels during which time I only got occasional glimpses of him. He was then flown out to England to face one of the most historic and expensive trials in British history.

The solitary confinement had such an effect upon me that I once begged to be let out of my cell, even if it was only to scrub the floor of the hall. I wished to preserve my sanity. My request was granted and I duly scrubbed the floor and the empty cells. Later I was put to work in my cell polishing rusty bolts.

During my stay in the detention barracks I was put in the punishment block along with the gangsters, gunmen and razor-slashers. As soon as I arrived two of them were discovered with weapons they had manufactured to use on the prison staff. For this they were put in handcuffs for a period. I then learned that five of them were planning to escape and 'lay out' the Staff Sergeant on duty when he was on his own. I also discovered the way in which they were planning their escape. I was worried about the consequences of the whole business. These men were all potential murderers and had committed robbery with violence many times and I could see them killing the Staff Sergeant on duty. But I was a prisoner myself; what should I do? I didn't like the idea of 'sneaking' on another prisoner so I discussed the matter, at risk of punishment, with a sensible civilian prisoner whom I had befriended. He said that it was clearly my duty to report the matter since there was danger to life and, should the escape over the roof succeed, all the other prisoners would suffer for it. I therefore reported the matter to the senior Staff Sergeant. He pooh-poohed the idea and said he knew all the people concerned. I warned him, however, not to leave a staff sergeant by himself in the hall.

Six days later everything happened just as I had said it would. A staff sergeant, when he was alone in the hall, was jumped on and thrown into a cell, but since he was a small man and put up no resistance whatever he was scarcely injured. The five gangsters took their time and made their escape over the roof just as I had predicted. I rang my bell during these proceedings but with no avail since it only rang inside the building and I could only see through the spy-hole.

When the alarm was given some ten minutes later and the whole staff came down I slipped the details secretly to them by pushing a piece of paper under my door. It would have been as much as my life was worth to communicate openly. On the next day I was called up to the Assistant Commandant, a Major Shaperoni, and asked to give an account of the happenings. He was astonished to hear that I had already given warning in every detail as to the escape and asked the Staff Sergeant concerned why no notice had been taken of my warnings. The Sergeant lamely replied that he 'didn't believe anything that prisoners told him'.

However, because of the dangerous nature of the gangsters, the Assistant Commandant enlisted my aid in their recapture. One

man who would have been with the five on the run if he had not
been in hospital was transferred to the cell next door to me. From
this prisoner (a man with a particularly cowardly razor-slashing
offence to his credit) I learned about the haunts of the escaped
gangsters, their plans and their methods. I passed all this information on to the SIV (Special Investigation Branch of the Army)
and I think I helped not only in locating the bandits, but in
preventing further crimes of a major nature. The escapees were
caught one after another and were all back within five weeks.
Some of them were then shifted to gaols in England but the two
ringleaders remained and immediately announced their intention
to escape again – once more over the roof but this time by daylight. I was asked to go too, and was offered money in substantial
quantities. I interviewed the Assistant Commandant again and
warned him of another coming 'break'. I suggested the two
ringleaders should be transferred to the military DB at
Antwerp.

He told me that arrangements were already being made for
their removal but five days later I saw them making preparations
to break through the roof when they were working on some
scaffolding in the Hall. I was powerless to do anything. They had
men keeping watch all down the Hall and staff sergeants were in
the office drinking tea. I couldn't get in to them because there was
a sentry at the door. I therefore dashed back and saw the two
escapees standing in front of the glass panels in the roof which
they had broken open. Under the very noses of the gang and at
great personal risk I rang the alarm bell, which a prisoner is not
supposed to do. It was too late – they got away. I collaborated
with the Assistant Commandant once more and, whether or not
my efforts helped directly, they were caught again after a
month.

Five months had passed in the Brussels prison and all of we

prisoners felt that no action would be taken against us. I had protested officially and in writing against my imprisonment, uncharged, as a German citizen. I felt that it would never take five months to draw up a charge against me.

I was beginning to feel fairly secure when one prisoner was flown away to England to face trial. This dashed all our hopes. We all wondered who would be the next. It was not long before I found out who – it was I.

The summer had come and gone and one autumn morning I was summoned to the main office. Here a colonel and a major of the British Intelligence Corps were waiting for me. 'Sit down,' said the kindly Colonel, offering me a chair. 'I am afraid we have some bad news for you. Take it steady.'

I wondered what was to come. I experienced a sinking feeling, although by that time I should have been used to anything. The Colonel now came forward and said: 'I am afraid I must break some bad news to you. Your mother has died.'

I was stunned by the blow. I had not even known that she was seriously ill. The Colonel handed me a letter, which had been held up for eleven days, informing me of my bereavement. Another letter from my aunt, written on the day of my mother's death, was handed to me on the following day in the airplane that took me to England. This one had taken twelve days!

I thought of my mother's funeral, and a hundred-and-one things, and looked up at the Colonel, as he continued, scarcely pausing for breath: 'We are flying you to England tomorrow where you will be charged with High Treason.'

That night was a bad one. It was filled with thoughts of my mother and the pain and anxiety I so often caused her.

The following day I was met once more by the Colonel and the Major who greeted me in a friendly manner; but I ignored them. I was now wearing again my Austrian mountain dress which had been returned to me by the prison authorities. I climbed into the waiting car and was driven to the airport.

We went to the refreshment room where the Colonel and Major ordered breakfast for themselves. I stood at the window with my back towards them whilst a sergeant with a revolver stood in the offing. He was my guard to England. The Major came over to me and asked me if I would have some tea. I refused his offer without bothering to turn around.

The Major then spoke soothingly to me: 'You're taking it rather badly, aren't you? You know we are only doing our duty. We can't help it, you know.'

When the time came to board the military plane for England it appeared that the Intelligence Colonel was not going with us. Only the armed sentry and the Major were to be my escort in a plane already crowded with officers and personnel flying, perhaps, on leave to England. Before I walked up the gangway, the Colonel made a gesture which was particularly odd under the circumstances. He shook me warmly by the hand and wished me 'the best of luck'.

After take-off, the Major started to ask me about my first case which led up to the 'Tower of London' episode and my subsequent sentence. Although this officer only had the rank of major he was a senior member of the twin British 'Secret Service' organisations – MI 5 and the Special Branch of Scotland Yard. He must, therefore, have known all that MI 5 knew about the 'Marie Louise' case.

The Major wanted to know all the details of the first case and the so-called 'secrets' involved. I obliged to a limited extent. He wanted a story and he got it. All the time the Major acted the part of a sympathetic 'confessor', and he made a good but puzzling impression on me. He seemed, in fact, to be both human and genuine.

We landed at an airfield near London and I was taken into the airport waiting room. Here I was handed over to two plain-clothes Scotland Yard detectives and one of them read out several charges of 'High Treason' against me. The first charge was that I had committed an act of 'treason' in that I had become a German citizen!

As I listened I ruefully thought that I must have committed 'treason' in September 1938 when I had first applied for German nationality and had been committing it also in peacetime right up to Britain's declaration of war. The other charges concerned broadcasting.

The charge sheet was, however, changed on two sub-sequent occasions. The first charge to be dropped was the one that I had committed 'High Treason' by becoming a German citizen.

Having read the charges, the detective then warned me that anything I might say would be used in evidence against me – a warning that was not given by Colonel Syms at Aldershot in 1933. I was then asked if I had anything to say. Remembering that any word one says under such circumstances could lead an accused person into difficulties I confined myself to saying, 'I am not guilty and *cannot* be guilty'.

The detective wrote this down and, since there was nothing more to be said, led me out to a car driven by a chauffeur who politely said 'Good morning, sir' to me.

It was strange to see, as we passed through a blitzed London, row upon row of undamaged orderly buildings and houses apparently untouched by German action. After the scenes of utter desolation that I had been used to in Germany, this was like a glimpse of a new world. Hardly anywhere did I see any note-

worthy bomb damage, but then, of course, I had not passed
through the City and dock areas which had been blitzed. London
still lived – there was no doubt about that. Scarcely a town of
any kind still 'lived' in Germany. As I saw it, there was no room
for comparison between the severity of the bombing of Britain
with that of Germany.

The car took me to Scotland Yard and I was led up to a room
somewhere at the top of it. In this room were several telephones
which were in almost continuous operation. I heard some queer
names such as 'Aunt Kate' and 'Pal Jack' being used by the men
who were answering the phones in the room. I imagined that
stooges or 'narks' were at the other end of the line and were
feeding Scotland Yard with information.

A young man came up to me with some paper in his hand and
asked if I would like to write out a statement.

'What? Another one?' I asked with resentful surprise. 'Haven't
I already made statements enough?'

The young man apologised. 'Sorry,' he said, 'I didn't know
you had made one already.'

Then he asked me for my address.

'I have just, as you know, come from Austria,' I replied.

'Yes, yes,' said the young Yard man, 'but what is your address
in England?'

'I have no address in England,' I answered, amazed at such a
question. 'How can I have one? I am a German.'

'That's all right,' persisted the youth. 'Give us any kind of
address in England – it doesn't matter what. It's just a matter
of form.'

'I have no address in England,' I replied exasperated.

I had disappointed the young man. But I learned afterwards that had I given an address it would have appeared in
the charge and would also have been communicated to the

A photograph of Baillie-Stewart taken in May 1945, shortly after his arrest by the Americans (*courtesy : UPI*)

A photograph of Norman Baillie-Stewart and his family, far removed from courts martial and Nazi propaganda, taken shortly before he died. With him are his wife, Catherine, whom he married in November 1950, and their children, Grainne, aged six, and Norman, aged ten. Mrs Baillie-Stewart and the two children still live in Dublin, Ireland

Press. I would thus have appeared to be a resident British citizen.

I was then told I would have to have my fingerprints taken. I protested, but was told that if I did not submit there and then they would be taken later in prison by force.

From Scotland Yard I was taken to Bow Street police station where I spent two nights and days waiting to appear before a magistrate. The door of my cell was permanently open, the light was kept on all night and a policeman sat on a chair in front of the open door every moment I was there.

The police – the uniformed police – were both friendly and chatty. I liked them all and had long and interesting conversations with them about their work. I listened, too, to their grievances which seemed to be well-founded. They were very human men, and talking to them kept my mind off things.

I found that the cells at Bow Street were appalling. Prisoners had to lie on a long sort of wooden settee, the end of which lifted up disclosing a lavatory. One would have known that the lavatory was there without lifting the board. It stank!

I was shaken when I finally appeared before the Magistrate, wearing, incidentally, a black mackintosh over my *lederhosen*. The court was packed when I entered and who did I see seated amongst the guests of honour in front but my old friend, Major – now Brigadier – Hinchley Cooke of MI 5. His presence did not pass unnoticed by the Press, as it all helped to make my case look important and mysterious.

I was only a few minutes in the dock. I had been brought up to Bow Street for the sole purpose of being 'remanded' for a week. In reply to the charges I once more stated: 'I am not guilty and cannot be guilty.'

I took the opportunity to ask for legal aid, stating as a reason that I had no means, and had no one in England to turn to for

Q

assistance because my mother had just died. This incident was later interpreted in an unfair way by a certain woman writer who stated that I had made a cheap appeal for sympathy on the subject of my mother's death.

The application for legal aid was granted and I was led back to the cells.

The Second Trial

I WAS TAKEN from Bow Street by car and brought to Brixton where, being on a capital charge, I was housed in a cell in the prison hospital. A prisoner in one of these cells is kept in the closest solitary confinement. He exercises on his own and has to sleep looking up into an electric light bulb which burns all night.

These conditions were a great nervous strain for me, a man about to be tried for his life. I found that on occasions I was unable to think clearly but, apart from that, I found conditions reasonable.

With a few exceptions, the warders in Brixton Prison were quite fair and honourable. On several occasions they gave me cigarettes and the Chief Officer himself gave me a daily newspaper.

I had made an application for a certain solicitor, recommended by a prisoner in Brussels, to represent me, but I was told for some reason or other that I could not have him. For days I waited in a fever of anxiety to see some legal man. Nearly a week went by, and then, one morning, I was taken out of my cell and shown into the visitors' room where a man, wearing a bowler hat slightly too small for him, was waiting.

He introduced himself as a Mr Kenwright and said he had been deputed to represent me legally. We sat down and looked at one another. Mr Kenwright spoke first and spoke hopelessly. He informed me that the situation was bad indeed, indicated that there was no way out of it and that the job of defending me was difficult for him personally because his son was an officer in the RAF.

I felt quite crushed. 'But you haven't heard what I have to say,' I said. Mr Kenwright said that if I had anything to say I was to write it down and send it to him and he gave me his business address.

Mr Kenwright was my only life-line. I was fighting for my very life and my predicament was as desperate as any man's could be. I had been brought over to England on what I considered a spurious and unfounded charge and my case was being sand-wiched between the cases of William Joyce and John Amery. The public might not differentiate between my case and theirs. Were not both Joyce and Amery ringing the changes on the matter of citizenship? Was not my own clear defence based on a matter of citizenship and would not I also appear to be 'ringing the changes'?

I was called once more to Bow Street and again I was wearing my familiar black mackintosh and with my fumigated Austrian mountain dress underneath as I entered the dock.

I sat in the uncomfortable dock, the cynosure of hundreds of curious eyes. I knew, too, that my every twitch of a muscle would be faithfully reported and interpreted. I therefore contrived to remain expressionless but, none the less, I was described as 'a burly figure sitting slumped in the dock'. It was reported that every now and again I passed a weary hand across my brow – or a hand across my weary brow.

After the evidence, the Magistrate committed me for trial at the Old Bailey. The question of my citizenship was not considered at this stage.

Mr Kenwright had been joined on the defence bench by Mr Norman Parkes, the barrister who had defended me during my court martial twelve years earlier.

Mr Parkes, a most charming man, visited me in the cell before the hearing and it was then that he informed me that I was 'in a legal jam'.

After my formal reappearance at Bow Street I returned to Brixton Prison to prepare my defence. But how could I prepare any defence? Commander Spooner had promised me in Brussels that, if charged, I would be given every facility to obtain all my papers, so I asked 'spy-catcher' Spooner to go to the villa of Countess Platen in Alt Aussee to collect all my papers and documents.

There was a huge mass of them and they were of most vital importance to me because a detailed study of them would disclose to anyone almost everything that had happened to me from the time I left England in 1937 right up to the time of my arrest. Briefly, they included hundreds of letters disclosing my correspondence with German officialdom, including the broadcasting authorities, the Foreign Office, Gestapo and the German military. They also included details of my step-by-step procedure to secure German nationality; how I landed a job in the Berlin broadcasting station from Vienna; my nationalisation certificate; military call-up papers and at least two hundred records of my Berlin broadcasts to Britain.

I had discussed these with the Countess Platen and we both agreed that it would be better to preserve the lot for my eventual protection in case any unjust accusations might be made against me after the war.

Commander Spooner proceeded to Alt Aussee from London and searched the home of the Countess from top to bottom to discover my documentary belongings. But, to my utter amazement, he brought back to the public prosecutor's officer in London only the documents that suited the prosecution. Vital documents, such as my German naturalisation certificate, my Certificate of Reliability and Provisional Certificate of Citizenship that were given to me at the Gestapo HQ in the Hotel Metropole in Vienna about November 1938, and other papers that could go to prove my case, were left behind.

This was clearly a monstrous injustice because the failure or refusal of the famous 'spy-catcher' to bring back defence material might easily have cost me my life. I may mention here, incidentally, that just after the war started two German security officers took me by car to the police in the Burgstrasse. One of them went inside and came out with my naturalisation certificate. He handed it to me with a laugh and said: 'You could have got it long ago if you had only tried.' Many of these documents are probably still on my file in Scotland Yard.

It can be proved from the records of my broadcasts that at times I risked my life to give the British radio monitoring systems a variety of subtle or indirect tips. For instance, I repeatedly gave them warnings about the forthcoming 'V' bombs that Hitler was preparing to launch from the French coast for attacks on London and England's south-east coast. But my warnings were dismissed as 'intimidation' at the time. Our information in Berlin was that, when Hitler was preparing his attack with his 'V' weapons, the air-raid precautions in England were being eased, as was the black-out. Had my 'V' weapon warnings been heeded, many hundreds of civilian lives would have been saved in Britain. I made it quite clear in talk No. 183 that I loathed and deplored the war and all its tragedies. In talk No. 100 I expressed my regret that the British public was being bombed, and hinted at my real British sentiments. This is all absolutely undeniable and can be found in the archives of Scotland Yard.

I protested directly to Dr Hesse, who had much influence with Foreign Minister Ribbentrop, about the bombing of England in 1940. Putting aside humane arguments, I told him that the English were 'tough' and that the bombing would stiffen British resistance. He replied that he knew the English and they were not as tough as all that.

Not much imagination is needed to appreciate that my predicament in Brixton Prison at the time Commander Spooner set off for Alt Aussee was literally desperate. My very life was in the balance and the Commander knew it. The position was that John Amery had been taken from Brixton Prison on 28th November 1945 and hanged on charges similar to those I had to answer. Then came William Joyce, also from Brixton Prison, and he too was sentenced to be hanged. It was my turn and my life largely depended on the Alt Aussee documents which I had carefully preserved for the previous eight years.

There was a striking contrast between my attitude towards the Allied forces at the end of the war and those of Joyce and Amery. Joyce was arrested when trying to escape towards Denmark and Amery was captured when he was heading for Italy. Believing in my German citizenship, I did everything quite openly in my own name and stayed my ground in Alt Aussee. I even helped the Allied Military Government and acted as interpreter between the American forces and the local people.

I was with Countess Platen all the time I was in Alt Aussee up to the time of my arrest by the Americans. She knew of my pro-Austrian and anti-Nazi sentiments. She carefully retained all my documents until the arrival of Commander Spooner and she knew of my plan to surrender whole districts of Upper Austria without bloodshed.

It was when I was in Dublin in 1950 that I secured the help of an Irish Civil Servant to go to Alt Aussee in search of my vital documents in the home of the Countess. I gave him precisely the same instructions as I had given Spooner five years earlier. The Irishman had no difficulty whatever in picking up my German passport, German Military call-up papers and an internal German permit. The terrible significance of this must be apparent: If I had been hanged in Brixton Prison after Amery and Joyce, the perpetration of this miscarriage of justice would never have been disclosed and the tell-tale documents would never have come to light.

The result of this was that I was unable to secure my vital *Wehrpass* (German Army book) – which included the papers calling me up for registration *before* the war – or even my naturalisation certificate. Non-nationals could not have joined the German Army in peacetime. I was also unable to procure other papers which would have made my defence good in law. They would all have been links in my chain of evidence to prove my submission that I had become a German national. This was the essence of my case.

As to witnesses, how – even if I had been able to call them – could they have been traced after some six or seven months of post-war chaos in Germany and Austria? I continually pressed, whilst in prison awaiting trial, to be able to get my papers and to call witnesses.

I was, it is true, permitted to look through a suitcase full of useless letters and documents that Commander Spooner collected when he was at Alt Aussee. He was paid to travel around and collect evidence for the prosecution, but the same facilities were not allowed for the defence. I was not permitted to view my own German passport, a wrong and misleading English translation having been made of it. This passport and the misleading translation are also available for inspection, while a certificate of my citizenship, based on the original, has been presented to me since by the West German Government.

It was while I was awaiting trial in Brixton Prison that I decided to embrace the Roman Catholic faith. The reason was that I was living in a state of mortal terror, awaiting trial on charges that carried with them the death penalty. Although fighting hard for my defence with very limited scope in prison, I still believed there was no escape from the hangman's rope. Uppermost in my mind was the fact that William Joyce had been condemned to death on similar charges a short time previously. Joyce would have been hanged earlier but for the fact that he had appealed against conviction to the Court of Criminal Appeal and later to the House of Lords. These appeals took many weeks and the delay prolonged the agony and terror for me. I was, of course, waiting my turn for trial on similar charges involving broadcasting for Germany and on the issues of nationality and passports.

It was in these grim circumstances – facing the hangman – that I informed Father Vincent Ryan of Southwark, the Prison Chaplain, that I wished to become a Roman Catholic.

One Sunday when the Governor (the fairest of any prison Governor I ever met) visited me on his rounds, I expressed a wish to attend Mass. 'Good heavens!' said the startled Governor, 'you can't go there. You'd be lynched. No, no, that's impossible.'

He then departed in his usual whirlwind fashion, but I was by no means satisfied with his ruling. So I decided to put the matter up to the Chaplain and asked to see him. It was not long before he arrived. After I had explained the situation, he pondered deeply. He did not think that I would be lynched but, as far as he personally was concerned, he left the choice to me. As I told him, I would defend myself if there was a disturbance; I felt quite certain that there would be no demonstration of any kind.

I was right. I went to Mass, as I was entitled to, and apart from a few curious and friendly glances nothing untoward occurred. After that I went regularly to Mass and to Benediction.

The Governor's fear that I might be lynched by the other prisoners was quite genuine and he was anxious about my safety. Their hostility towards me was obvious and they made no secret of it. It was even worse when I was lodged in Wandsworth Prison and this attitude of the other prisoners was in strong contrast to the treatment I received from other prisoners like Clarence Hatry and Hermann Goertz in Maidstone Prison before the war. In Maidstone the prisoners and the 'screws' were quite friendly, although everybody knew me as 'The Officer in The Tower'.

No doubt the war had changed all that. In Brixton and in Wandsworth I was getting the backwash for 'Lord Haw-Haw'; the blitz on Britain; the starting of the war and the German concentration camps. The other prisoners and some of the prison staff seemed to regard me as being responsible for the lot. I was the subject of a popular myth in that nobody seemed to know that, when I was broadcasting from Berlin during the war and when I was working for the German Foreign Office in Berlin, I was a German citizen. There was the popular and widespread belief that I had committed treason against England – but how could a German citizen commit treason against England?

In passing references to me at least six British writers have stated that I was guilty of treason. It was much against my will that I had to take court actions against them and I won every time without even having to go into court personally. It was inevitable that these actions for libel had to be taken because if I had remained silent my silence would have been interpreted as having no answer to the defamation. Apart from the natural injustice of such a baseless accusation, I was never even charged in court with treason as I shall show later. Those who wrote about me never even took the trouble to look up the court records to find out exactly what happened.

Apart from defending my own character, I have always been most anxious that my children should not have to suffer any public odium for the alleged sins of their father.

That was the background to the hostility of fellow prisoners in Brixton and Wandsworth towards me. It was at times very real and frightening. I remember particularly in Wandsworth being offered cigarettes quite often by a prisoner who, I suspected, was trying to get me into trouble with the 'screws'. I refused his offers. I remember one big, hefty prisoner from the north of Scotland who became friendly with me and confided that two or three of them had been told by a hostile 'screw' to beat me up. It was just after this incident that a principal officer in Wandsworth called me into his office and said, 'I have been keeping a special watch on you because there is a plot to beat you up. Some of my staff are not exactly friendly towards you but while you are under my care you will not be beaten up.' I thanked him and left.

I made a point of associating with the few German prisoners of war in Wandsworth and, as time passed, the hostility towards me died down.

Usually I was exercised around the hospital yard alone, but on occasions, when there was a shortage of warders, another prisoner was exercised with me. When this happened my companion would be one of two Polish murderers, or a man called 'Russian Robert'. On one day it would be one of these murderers and on the next day the other. Since the two murderers entertained a murderous hatred for each other they were never allowed anywhere near each other. Both were subsequently hanged when I was in Wandsworth Prison. The smaller of the two Poles occupied the cell next door to me at Brixton. Sometimes, if I started to whistle a Hungarian tune, the Pole would take it up. He would then whistle his heart out – he could whistle well – until some clod-hopping warder would come along and ask him roughly and facetiously if his canary wanted any bird-seed. If this didn't work he would be told to stop his bloody row. The Pole knew that he was doomed, and whistling seemed to mean a lot to him.

John Amery was in another hospital cell of Brixton Prison when I was there. His cell was actually in another wing, but I had to go to that wing in order to fetch water and to have a bath. Amery's cell was almost opposite to the bathroom recess and his door, unlike mine, was never closed. Instead, the barred iron gate was closed on Amery. He could see through and be seen. and Amery and I were, therefore, able to snatch brief conversations.

Amery was indignant about my treatment. 'They're swinging it on you,' he said. He then described how, when a prisoner of the British in Italy, he had spoken to an MI 5 man who had stated: 'We can't get Baillie-Stewart; he has been too clever for us. He is a German citizen.'

I always found Amery surprisingly optimistic and cheerful and I was even able to speak to him on the evening before he went up to the Old Bailey to plead guilty and literally to ask for death. At that time he had already made his decision to plead guilty. He laughed freely and seemed almost exalted. He had indeed made a noble – and perhaps wise – decision, and the reason for this was, as he whispered to me through the prison bars in Brixton, that efforts to provide him with a faked Spanish passport had failed. In the circumstances, John Amery died with immense courage.

Joyce had previously occupied the cell in which Amery was

kept. I heard many stories about him from the warders, some of whom hated him and teased him without restraint.

The cell occupied successively by Joyce and Amery was an unlucky one. Three occupants of it were sentenced to death one after the other. The third to be sentenced – a half-German who had served in the Waffen SS – was later reprieved.

I was nearly three months awaiting trial in Brixton Prison, and it was nearly nine months since I was arrested in Austria, before I stepped into the same dock in Room No. 1 of the London Central Criminal court in which William Joyce had been sentenced to death. Joyce was executed on 3rd January 1946 and I appeared in court exactly a week later. The main reason for the long delay from the time Joyce was sentenced until his hanging was due to his appeals. My trial was accordingly delayed because of the similarity between Joyce's case and my own and I was able to follow the legal arguments in the Joyce trial and the appeals with burning interest because my own life might depend on similar submissions.

As the day of the court appearance drew nearer I got into a panic because of the apparent inaction and failure even to produce the bricks needed to build up the defence. Then, about three weeks before the day fixed for the trial, Mr Kenwright came to see me in Brixton. He had, he said, just seen MI 5 and had come from them with a 'proposition' which he wanted to lay before me.

I enquired what the proposition was and was told that the prosecution were prepared to drop the capital and treason charge, on one condition.

'That condition,' Mr Kenwright replied to my question, 'is that you agree to plead guilty to having "aided the enemy" under the Emergency Defence Regulations of 1939.'

I was stunned. 'But this is blackmail; it is putting a pistol to my head,' I protested.

Mr Kenwright shrugged his shoulders. 'Those are the terms,' he said. 'I would advise you to accept. If you fight the treason charges you will go down, and you know what that means – the hangman's rope. Any British jury would be prejudiced against you, and you wouldn't stand a chance.'

'And what if I accept?' I asked.

'You will get five years,' was the simple answer.

I was utterly stunned; first of all the threat under penalty of death and then the price demanded.

I renewed my protest but Mr Kenwright cut me short by informing me that I had been given forty-eight hours in which to come to a decision in the matter. I was to let him have an answer in a guarded, but unmistakable, form of letter. I was also warned by Mr Kenwright that I was to be most careful not to speak to anybody on the subject. If it got out to the Press, he stressed, there would be a lot of trouble and everything might be spoiled.

Mr Kenwright put the proposition to me in such a way that I was led to believe that the prosecution were doing me a great and unusual favour. He urged me to accept, stressing the alternative – hanging if convicted.

Utterly crushed at this new turn in the affair, I told Mr Kenwright that I had no choice but to accept – death being the only foreseeable alternative. He added that he would confirm acceptance in writing, as directed.

Immediately I returned to my cell I rang the bell and asked that the Chaplain should be informed that I wished to see him as soon as possible. The matter was urgent, I told the warder who answered the bell.

Mr Kenwright had warned me not to speak to anybody about the proposition that had been made, but I did not regard a Catholic priest as 'anybody'. I had no one to whom I could turn for advice and had no visitors. The Catholic priest is in most cases a man to whom one can turn at any moment of doubt and trouble in one's life. I decided to turn to him.

Within a short while, Father Vincent Ryan arrived and I wasted no time in telling him of the interview with Mr Kenwright and the proposition that had been made. I also told him of the prearranged sentence of five years which I was to receive on accepting the terms.

Father Ryan was appalled.

'But what am I to do?' I asked. 'I have to accept or refuse the proposition by letter within forty-eight hours.'

Father Ryan shook his head again. 'Choose the lesser evil,' he advised after a moment's thought. 'What other choice have you?'

Subsequent events indicated that some such behind-the-scenes 'arrangement' had been made before I entered the Old Bailey to stand my trial – or rather to hear the sentence.

Fearing any sort of delay in the post and prison censorship I immediately sat down, after Father Ryan's visit and melancholy advice, and wrote the required letter to Mr Kenwright. In it I stated that I agreed to the proposition that had been put to me. After that I wrote saying that I would regard *any* sentence of *any* kind as a gross injustice under the circumstances.

My fate was now sealed. All I had to do was to wait for my 'trial' and its inevitable result.

Before going for my trial I was interviewed by a doctor. One question I was asked stood out clearly. It was if, after emigrating to Austria and Germany, I had ever entertained the idea of returning to England even for a short holiday. The answer was emphatic: 'No, never.'

It was not long before Mr Kenwright came to see me again. He informed me that since Mr Hartley Shawcross, the British Attorney-General, was leaving shortly for Nuremberg (for the trials), my case would have to be heard sooner than had originally been arranged. He pointed out that it was wise to agree to this alteration, as there was no point in displeasing the Attorney-General.

Mr Kenwright also told me that the services of Mr Fox-Andrews, KC, had been engaged as counsel for the defence. I was to meet Mr Fox-Andrews for the first time in the cells at the Old Bailey – just half an hour before I was due to appear in the dock.

Before leaving Brixton Prison I had pointed out to Mr Kenwright that the new charges accused me of having 'entered the service of the German Propaganda Broadcasting System'. I could not have 'entered' such an amorphous institution, I stressed. Such an organisation did not exist. I had been a member of the Foreign Office and had merely carried out direct orders.

I was advised not to worry about this as there would have been no point in having the charge sheets changed at that stage.

I came to the conclusion that if anything is calculated to demoralise a prisoner about to be tried at the Old Bailey it is the cells. The prisoner is shut up in a tiny, windowless and airless cell. There is only a dirty glass ventilator that lets in a little light and air, but if one smokes a cigarette in the cell one is almost stifled. On the walls are obscene drawings and recordings of sentences and unflattering remarks about judges.

I was taken from my mouse-trap cell to meet my counsel, Mr Fox-Andrews. I found him to be pleasant and he created a favourable impression upon me.

In his short interview with me, half an hour before I was due to appear in the dock, Mr Fox-Andrews told me not to be disappointed if he did not say much that I would probably like him to say. I assumed that he knew what he was doing and did not demur.

Wasn't I pleading 'guilty', after all? I was sure that, under the particular and unusual circumstances, no one could have done better than did Mr Fox-Andrews.

Just before he left, presumably to take up his place in the court, Mr Fox-Andrews asked: 'What is this about the translation of your German passport having been altered?'

I explained the nature of the alteration and its considerable significance.

'Can you swear to it?' queried Mr Fox-Andrews.

'Yes, I can.'

'All right, I'll take the risk then,' were Mr Fox-Andrews' final words before he left.

The time came and I mounted the stairs to that dock in No. 1 Court of the Old Bailey which had held so many tragic and even desperate figures. I was wearing my black mackintosh about which the Press had written so much.

As I emerged from the darkness below I noticed that soft lighting illuminated serried ranks of white wigs in the court. The robes of the figures seated around provided a strange splash of colour.

Seated prominently in the court was a uniformed gathering of MI 5 men, amongst them was Brigadier W E Hinchley Cooke. He glanced proudly up at me, his catch, in the dock.

I looked at the man with the largest wig and the most resplendent robes and assumed that he was the Judge. I was wrong. After some mystic ceremony had been performed, this august figure got up and left the bench, followed by most of the other bewigged figures. What is happening now? I wondered. There seemed to be no one left to judge me. A small figure wearing a small wig remained. He was the Judge, I supposed. I was right this time – Mr Justice Oliver was his name.

I realised that I had no actual part to play in the proceedings so had leisure to take stock of my surroundings. This was my first

R

experience of a civil court of law. I was amazed at the formality, pomp and ceremony.

My attention was attracted by the jury. They were in for an easy time, I thought.

The proceedings started with the Clerk of the Court reading out the charges. He started with the 'treason' charges of which there were eight in all. After reading them I was asked by the Clerk: 'Are you guilty or not guilty?'

'Not guilty,' I replied, as I had been directed to say before-hand.

The Clerk then went on: 'There is another indictment against you containing three counts, charging you with doing an act likely to assist the enemy with intent to assist the enemy contrary to Defence Regulations, and the particulars in the first count are that you, being a British subject, on the 24th December 1939, with intent to assist the enemy, did an act likely to assist the enemy by broadcasting propaganda on behalf of the enemy. In the second count, the charge is that you, being a British subject, on a day in February 1940, with intent to assist the enemy, did an act likely to assist them by entering the service of the German Foreign Office. In the third count, the offence is a similar one, and the particulars are that you, being a British subject, in February 1942, with intent to assist the enemy, did an act likely to assist them by entering the service of the German propaganda broad-casting system. Are you guilty or not guilty?'[1]

I replied as arranged: 'Guilty to the second indictment.'

This seemed to displease the Clerk. He snapped at me: 'I have just read you the whole of the second indictment.'

1. The extracts from the court proceedings, which appear in quotation marks on this and subsequent pages, are taken from a handwritten copy made by Baillie-Stewart of a Home Office report. According to Baillie-Stewart, this report was obtained for him by the Freedom Defence Committee who took up his case while he was serving his second sentence.

To this I answered, wonderingly: 'Yes, the whole of the second indictment.'

Now I had done it! I had been forced to admit to being a British subject and had pleaded 'guilty' to something that I knew not to be true, as confirmed later by the Judge's remarks.

The Attorney-General now got up to speak and I quote here from the Home Office copy of the proceedings. The copy of the proceedings, however, does not contain the transcript of the shorthand notes of the trial and is an edited and abbreviated Home Office version.

The Attorney-General started by explaining why the plea of guilty to the second indictment could be accepted. My case, he said, was *not* similar to that of a person who, whilst claiming the protection of the British Crown, whilst asserting his British nationality, betrays his country.

The Judge agreed to this and gave his 'full approval' to an acceptance of the plea of 'guilty' on the second indictment.

The Attorney-General then went on to give his version of my history up-to-date and concluded by saying: 'It is true that in 1938 he applied for German nationality and it is true that in 1940 or 1941 – unfortunately we have been unable to confirm the exact date – he did in fact become a naturalised German citizen.'

Mr Justice Oliver: 'That was in 1940?'

The Attorney-General: 'In 1940 or 1941, my Lord. We think that in all probability it was in 1940, but we have been unable to confirm the exact date.'

Mr Justice Oliver: 'If that date had been before the war he would not have been guilty of any offence at all.'

The Attorney-General: 'No. If it happened that following the application, which he had made two years before the war, he had received the grant in August 1939, he would have been guilty of no offence at all. As it was, he probably did not receive it until a year later. His German passport is dated August 1940.'

Mr Justice Oliver: 'Is he a German citizen now under German law: if there is any German law?'

The Attorney-General: 'Yes, my Lord, I am so advised.'

Mr Justice Oliver: 'He is not, according to our laws, because you cannot naturalise yourself during a war.'

The Attorney-General: 'Presumably he has a dual nationality. Under our law he retains his original nationality because his attempted naturalisation was held up, but under German law, as we understand it, he does become a German citizen. We felt it not right to disregard the fact entirely that two years before the war he applied for German nationality and that he made no secret of his hostility to England and his sympathy towards Germany.'

Now, according to these statements, I was standing in that dock under false pretences. The sole reason for my presence there was the assumption that I was a British subject. But that, apart from the 'statement' I had signed but never made in that form, the prosecution had no knowledge whatsoever as to my citizenship. We find the Attorney-General saying that I had become a naturalised German in '1940 or 1941', but this was ignoring the statement I had made – my 'hanging' statement – to the effect that I had received my naturalisation certificate in 1940. The Attorney-General later admitted that my German passport was issued in August 1940. Did he think that a German passport would be issued in 1940 to a man who 'possibly' didn't become a German until 1941?

A detective inspector from New Scotland Yard was then called to give evidence.

The Attorney-General: 'Did Baillie-Stewart leave this country in August 1937?'

Detective Inspector: 'Yes, the 18th August 1937.'

Attorney-General: 'As far as is known, he has not returned until he was brought back in custody on the present charges?'

Detective Inspector: 'That is right, sir.'

Mr Justice Oliver: 'Is there any reason, so far as you know, for thinking that he ever intended to come back to England?'

Detective Inspector: 'No, my Lord, none at all.'

Mr Justice Oliver: 'None at all?'

Detective Inspector: 'None at all.'

Mr Justice Oliver: 'It is not a case like the case of Joyce which we had here at another sessions, who went backwards and forwards?'

Detective Inspector: 'No, as far as is known he never came back and had no intention of doing so.'

Mr Fox-Andrews then cross-examined the Detective Inspector and asked him if he did not know that, whilst in a British military prison at Brussels, I had 'prevented a very high German official from taking his own life'.

The reply was: 'I know nothing about it.'

The incident had happened at Wiesbaden (when I was in American custody) and not at Brussels. Mr Fox-Andrews had unfortunately muddled the facts.

The Judge now asked: 'He has been in custody nine months?'

Detective Inspector: 'That is right, my Lord.'

Mr Fox-Andrews then spoke on my behalf and spoke very well, but he was hamstrung in view of the enforced plea of guilty. A point that he stressed was that the stage of considering whether or not there was legal guilt or innocence had been passed. It was only unfortunate that he was unable to say openly just how that stage had been passed. Again quoting from the Home Office report, Mr Fox-Andrews said:

Nothing I can say to your Lordship in this Court today on

behalf of the accused can equal in potency in his favour the
fact that the Crown's advisors have thought right to accept
the position that he shall stand before your Lordship so far
as they are concerned for sentence upon the second indictment only. I hope I do not go too far, my Lord, when I
submit that I am fully entitled to say that that course could
not have been taken by the Crown's advisors unless they
had formed an opinion as to Baillie-Stewart's true intentions,
of a type which can only be, at least to a degree, highly
favourable to Baillie-Stewart. It is quite clear, is it not? The
Attorney-General has made it clear beyond possible discussion or doubt that at a time when it was perfectly lawful for
Baillie-Stewart to do it he, for reasons which were good at
any rate to him, decided not only to renounce British
nationality but to seek citizenship in another country which,
in the year 1939, became the enemy of this country for a
second time. It has just occurred to me to put the matter to
your Lordship in this way. Would a Briton, who was informed that a German had acted similarly in order to
become a British subject, regard that German as a traitor to
Germany? That would depend, my Lord, would it not,
entirely upon the circumstances in which the German so
acted? My Lord, I submit that an ordinary thinking and
well informed citizen of this country would not consider
that that German was a traitor to Germany.

From my viewpoint the matter of 'traitors' was put rather well.
    Mr Fox-Andrews then went on to say:

The Attorney-General has told you of his service and of the
fact that somewhere about 1929 or 1930 he went to South
[it was East] Africa and there fell in love with a German girl,

and certain points of view not appealing to the ordinary Englishman were put to him. In 1932, after a vist to Berlin, he was unfortunately persuaded to have dealings with German agents, which resulted in his being placed before a General Court-Martial and convicted; and, at the age of twenty-four years being sentenced to cashierment and to incarceration in penal servitude for five years. My Lord, whatever may be thought, and I am not seeking to represent to your Lordship that his offence was not of some gravity, about the desirability of such a sentence upon a man of his age, it certainly meant this, did it not, that for all time in this country he was in all respects irretrievably ruined?

The Home office version quotes the Judge as now saying: 'He would have been without the sentence .... an officer in our service was selling information to Germany.'

That is how it appears – even to the dots – in the Home Office version. What the Judge did say is engraved on my mind. He said, simply, words to the effect that the sentence had been 'unnecessary'. No word was spoken about 'selling information to Germany'. My version on this point was later substantiated by legal men and court officials.

Mr Fox-Andrews then went on to deal with the pre-war threats made to me by MI 5. He said:

Before he went [to Austria] he was told by a very high official in MI 5 that if war ever broke out again between Germany and this country he would be undoubtedly and immediately incarcerated for the duration of the war. Of course, it was quite right for that high official to say that, but I only tell your Lordship that now because your Lordship may well imagine the effect of that added threat, about which

I am not complaining in the least, upon his mind in the state in which he found himself after his release from prison. For an embittered and hopeless young man to have that hanging over his head must, must it not, have redoubled his intention never to call this country his country again, must have redoubled his intention to renounce this country for all time and to seek what salvation he could elsewhere.

Mr Fox-Andrews went on to describe my life in Austria and told of the refusal of the British Embassy in Vienna to grant me protection when it was requested. He also stressed the fact that not even the prosecution had any reason to doubt that the application for German citizenship was made in September 1938 and had been a perfectly genuine attempt to obtain German citizenship. He added:

Before this war broke out and at a time when it was absolutely lawful for him to do it, Baillie-Stewart had taken every step, formal or informal, which lay in his power to take, to become a German citizen. Nothing whatever remained to be done except that he should receive passively a piece of paper, the certificate of naturalisation.

Continuing to deal with this point Mr Fox-Andrews said:

It, therefore, boils down to this, that, but for a simple administrative act, about which there was some delay, Baillie-Stewart could never have stood in this Court today charged with any of these offences. I therefore submit, my Lord, that so far as his intentions go, and that as I have already stated, I put before your Lordship as the broad basis upon which he should be charged, he was never in any respect a traitor to this country. If that view were not accepted, the course taken before your Lordship today would never have been taken.

When Mr Fox-Andrews told the Judge that I had 'taken every step, formal and informal . . . to become a German citizen' he was expressing the same idea as is contained in the 1914 Act – 'by obtaining a certificate of naturalisation or by any other voluntary and formal act . . . shall thenceforth be deemed to have ceased to be a British subject'.

Nothing could be more definite than that I had complied fully with this clause in the British Act. As I stood in the dock of the Old Bailey, about to be sentenced on an enforced plea of guilt to a charge of helping the enemy, I was there under false pretences, for I was not British. If Mr Justice Oliver's attention had been drawn to the 1914 Act, he would have had to reject the plea of guilt and order my release; otherwise he himself would have been ignoring the law.

Unfortunately for me, not even Mr Fox-Andrews at that time seemed to have heard of the 'British Nationality and Status of Aliens Act (1914)', with its vital Section 13, which fitted in precisely with my case. It was only whilst in prison at Parkhurst some two years later that I read it, and the British Freedom Defence Committee included it in their report on my case.

Had they known of Section 13 of that Act at the time, the prosecution's case would inevitably have fallen through. But then MI 5 would probably have carried out what they later threatened – deportation to the Soviet Zone of Germany where, they asserted, 'certain death' would be my lot.

Mr Fox-Andrews then drew attention to the Attorney-General's muddled state of mind with regard to the date of my acquisition of German citizenship. The Attorney-General, it may be remembered, had spoken vaguely as to my having acquired it in 1940 or 1941. This was in spite of the clearest indications that my German citizenship dated from an earlier time. Mr Fox-Andrews said:

> The Director [of Public Prosecutions] writes: 'The enquiries in Vienna as to your client's nationality appear to show . . . no trace of your client's document has been found.' That is merely repeating what the Attorney-General said. Then comes this sentence which your Lordship may like to know about: 'It would therefore appear that the Berlin authorities were considering . . . between that month and the 5th August 1940, the date of his German passport.' I put the matter in this way, that he became a German citizen by German law before August 1940.'

It is clear that the prosecution were losing their case on the date of the acquisition of German nationality, which they did not know. This, none the less, was the 'hanging' point. Had I declared that I had received my naturalisation certificate in, let us say, August 1939, the prosecution could not have refuted it.

Mr Fox-Andrews continued by dealing next with the events that had brought me to Berlin and the Berlin *Rundfunkhaus*. Referring to the situation when war broke out and when there was no turning back or any point in appealing to the British Embassy for repatriation, even had I wished, he stated:

'An individual might feel quite honestly that a middle course in which he did not necessarily curry favour in any direction was not an impossible one to take. In those circumstances, and finding himself placed as he was, it requires very little imagination, does it not, to understand what his fate would have been if he had failed to comply with German orders?'

The Judge interrupted: 'That cannot be accepted as any sort of excuse for treason. That happens again and again. You suggest that he really had ceased to be a British citizen at the time of these events.'

Mr Fox-Andrews: 'That is really the basis of my claim. I hope your Lordship will think it is a just comment that, if a man who was technically English had formed the intention of becoming a German and had gone so far, if that man at the end of August or the beginning of September 1939 had said: "Now that war has broken out I do not wish to serve the enemies of the country of my birth", his position would have been, I submit, quite impossible in the sense that he quite obviously would have been shot or put in a concentration camp.

'I say no more about that positive aspect of the case, but I would like to add one word about the negative aspect of it. The accused British officer of a famous regiment would be the ideal individual, from the German point of view, to be put up for corrupting British prisoners-of-war. There is not even a hint of anything of that sort in this case.'

The Judge at this stage appeared to overlook Mr Fox-Andrews' assertion that I 'had ceased to be a British citizen at the time of these events'. Instead, he observed: 'He was very notorious, Mr Fox-Andrews. Do you think he would have had any chance in that way? Everybody in England, I imagine, would remember his case.'

But apart from not trying to recruit British prisoners of war into John Amery's Free Corps to get on the bandwagon and fight for the Germans, I demonstrated at Berlin University that there was a positive – not negative – aspect to my behaviour as well.

Mr Fox-Andrews next dealt with MI 5's alteration of the word 'INLAND' in the translated copy of my German passport to the far more significant word 'IRELAND'. The word appeared on the passport under the heading, 'Validity of Passport'.

As is known, many German agents were landed in Ireland during the war by submarines and parachute. Pointing to the translated copy, Mr Fox-Andrews explained: 'The reason for my reference to this is obvious.'

To this the Judge replied shortly: 'Yes.'

The inference was that in an effort to blacken the case against me, 'INLAND' had been changed to 'IRELAND' to give the impression that the Germans intended to land me in neutral Ireland as a wartime German spy. And Hitler was much in need of spies in Ireland, especially after the fall of France when he was poised to deliver the final knock-out blow by invading both Britain and Ireland.

Mr Fox-Andrews ended his speech for the defence with these words: 'I said to your Lordship that this man was never a traitor to this country by intention. I submit that is a true view and I ask your Lordship to extend mercy to him.'

The Judge then made a remark that was clearly heard by the lawyers and by others in the packed court, but which did not appear in the shortened Home Office report. It was: 'I cannot send this man to prison. It is not within my jurisdiction to do so.' To this he added a direction that I should be returned to where I had come from and that I should sign an undertaking never to set foot in Britain again.

Mr Justice Oliver then said: 'Mr Attorney, there is a view of this case which seems to me to be a possible view, that the sooner this man is got away from this country the better for this country and for him. Is there anything to prevent him returning to the country of his adoption?'

This last paragraph is the Home Office version of what was said. But if this was all that was said, the commotion that ensued would never have taken place. The Judge was now making nonsense of my plea of guilty.

There followed a most unusual scene in court because the Judge had made a pronouncement which was about to be challenged by MI 5, a body which did not belong to the court and which had – or should have had – no judicial authority.

A rapid exchange of conversation took place between the huddled crowd of MI 5 men, and then one of them got up and approached the Attorney-General. There followed a murmured conversation whilst the Judge, taking a back seat, looked on surprised.

The Attorney-General then approached the Judge and another murmured conversation took place. All these secret conversations were illegal because they should have been in open court. They could not be chronicled because no one could hear them – not even the shorthand writers.

Following this the Attorney-General turned and spoke to the 'defence'. Mr Kenwright then got up and came over to speak to me in the dock. What he had to say staggered me. He told me that MI 5 had let the Judge know that, if he insisted on releasing me and returning me to Germany, they would put me in the Soviet Zone which, they said, would be 'certain death' for me.

Could I not be permitted to go to some neutral country such as Ireland? I asked Mr Kenwright.

Mr Kenwright went over to one of the MI 5 men and spoke to him. After a few words he returned to me and informed me that MI 5 had seemed horrified at the idea and had said: 'Good Lord, no; Ireland is hostile to Britain!'

Mr Kenwright returned to his seat.

All this naturally took some time. None the less, the Home Office version gives a continuous and unbroken narrative. This is how it continues:

The Attorney-General: 'May I take instructions? My Lord, there are difficulties. I am told that his return to Germany at the present time would be extremely unacceptable to the Allied Control Commission.'

Now, presumably, although the Home Office version gives no indication that this was the case, 'instructions' must have been taken from MI 5 between the Home Office version's words 'May I take instructions?' and 'My Lord, there are difficulties'. What was said after this was that I was unacceptable in the British Zone and that the Americans refused to have me in their zone.

With what right had the Attorney-General taken instructions from MI 5 and passed them on to the Judge? This was verily something new in legal procedure and justice.

The Home Office narrative continues:

Mr Justice Oliver: 'That may force my hand, I must bear it in mind. I was considering keeping him in captivity until such time as he could return and then, upon his undertaking never to set foot in this country again as long as he lives – I was considering whether he would be willing to enter into such a contract.'

Note that the Judge admitted that his hand was being forced – and by somebody exterior to the court. The Judge also was apparently considering 'keeping' me in captivity until such time as I could return to Germany.

But under what law could any man be 'kept' in captivity? Not even a British citizen *per se* could subsequently have been deported to Germany for under British law, no British citizen my be deported. And why should any man – if he is a British citizen – be asked to sign an undertaking never to set foot in Britain again? I was a German citizen – as it was also admitted – and it had been clearly stated by members of the prosecution that I had no intention whatsoever of returning to Britain. I had been brought over to England, literally at pistol point and in spite of my protests, and now I was to sign an undertaking never to return to that country. This was pure Gilbert and Sullivan.

The Home Office version goes on:

The Attorney-General: 'My Lord, the difficulty is that in the existing state of affairs in Germany, the Control Commission apparently do not find it possible to allow persons who have active official associations with the Nazi Government in Germany of this nature to be at large.'

This was, as had been seen, quite untrue. Many members of the German Foreign Office may, it is true, have been rounded up for interrogation but, unless some charge of war crimes could be presented, they were released. As proof of this, I would point out that many wartime officials of the German Foreign Office served later in the West German Government. I was not even a 'big shot' in the German Foreign Office. I had indeed not even been a Nazi or a member of any Nazi organisation, although I had many opportunities of joining the Party.

The Home Office report continues:

Mr Justice Oliver: 'That seems to be a matter for them. I could put the man back.'

The Attorney-General: 'Yes, I should then have an opportunity of consulting those who advise me.'

Mr Fox-Andrews: 'Would your Lordship allow me to say one word. Your Lordship has power to take a certain type of course. Would it be convenient to your Lordship if I were to find out now if Baillie-Stewart would give the promise indicated?'

Mr Justice Oliver: 'By all means; I was going to suggest you should do so. I am not in the least saying what will be the result, but it is one of the things I must know before I make up my mind. If he is prepared to enter into such an undertaking, it is a matter I should like to know.'

Mr Fox-Andrews: 'If your Lordship pleases.'

Mr Justice Oliver: 'Mr Attorney-General, if I rose for a short time, would it assist you?'

The Attorney-General: 'Could your Lordship say it would be dealt with tomorrow morning?'

Mr Justice Oliver: 'Yes. Is it convenient for you to be here tomorrow?'

The Attorney-General: 'I think so, my Lord; if not Mr Howard will be.'

Mr Justice Oliver: 'Then he can stand back until tomorrow morning.'

So many whispered conversations went on that day of 9th January 1946, that nobody in court, including the Judge, could possibly have heard what was said, except those engaged in the whispering. If anyone in court is entitled to hear what is being said it is surely the accused person. It is obvious that 'something' had happened to interrupt the proceedings and I can only assume that this 'something' was to enable the Attorney-General to receive instructions from MI 5. Was MI 5 thus acting as a quasi-judicial authority?

I returned to the cells where Mr Kenwright sought me out. He formulated a statement for me to sign, undertaking never to set foot in Britain again. I duly signed.

To the surprise of everyone in the hospital of Brixton Prison, I was returned there. Some friendly warders assured me that now everything was all right and that nothing could be done to me.

For some time before my appearance in court at the Old Bailey I had been taken off the Brixton Prison 'Capital Charge' list. I was thus able to sleep without a light, but that was about the only concession. It was interesting in itself though, as showing that the arrangement whereby the Capital Charges were dropped on condition that I pleaded 'guilty' to the Emergency Defence Regulation charges had become official. On receipt of the new charge sheet, Mr Kenwright had even informed the Chief

Officer at Brixton and had asked him to relax the 'Capital Charge' restrictions and regulations.

I spent a sleepless last night in Brixton Prison. The events of that astonishing day swirled round and round in my head; I felt as if I was living in an 'Alice through the Looking Glass' world.

I was brought to court again the next day and I quote once more from the Home Office report:

Mr Justice Oliver: 'Mr Attorney-General, have you any further information?'

The Attorney-General: 'I have made further enquiry. It certainly appears it would be a matter of considerable embarrassment if he were sent back to Germany at the present time.'

Mr Justice Oliver: 'The question arises as to what zone.'

The Attorney-General: 'All sorts of questions arise as to what zone he could go to, whether he should be regarded as an Austrian national or German national. That is one of the great difficulties in the case. He is by English law a British subject. In our zone there may be great difficulty in dealing with him. There is no power to detain him here under anything but sentence of the court. It does appear he would be very unwelcome in Germany at present.'

Mr Justice Oliver: 'I can see very good reasons against sending him there now.'

Mr Fox-Andrews: 'May I inform the Court he has in fact signed an undertaking in the form which was suggested yesterday. I thought your Lordship ought to know that.'

Mr Justice Oliver: 'I am obliged. I told you yesterday I would consider this to see what I ought to do. I will deal with it now.'

This was the sentence, as recorded by the Home Office report. It bristles with ambiguities which would be meat and drink to any lawyer.

S

Norman Baillie-Stewart, you, I suggest, are one of the worst citizens that any country has ever produced. You were an officer and had a good start in life. You turned against your country when you were quite young, and that brought you in 1933 before a court martial for offences against the Official Secrets Act for which you were sentenced to five years penal servitude. In 1937 you were released. The offences you had committed up to then were washed out. I do not take any heed of them at all.

You then went as soon as you could to the Continent. You went to Austria, you went to Germany, and the learned Attorney-General has accepted, and I, now I know all about the facts, fully accept that you went. When abroad, you shook the dust of England off your feet; you desired to have nothing more to do with England.

I am satisfied from the questions asked that you had no intention of coming back here. You were not, therefore, in intention one of those despicable creatures who will go to and from a country and sell it to the enemy. You became an enemy of your country. In your heart you ceased to be British at all. You applied for naturalisation from the moment you arrived on the Continent, and the learned Attorney-General accepts, and I accept, that you did that genuinely. It was a mere accident in some sense that you had not obtained it before the war broke out. If you had you would not have been guilty of any offence at all. Nevertheless, you remained a British subject.

You committed these acts, which could well have been called acts of treason had the learned Attorney-General decided to go on with that Indictment, which were acts in betrayal of your country's interests, and you did these acts knowing quite well what you were doing.

I have to deal with you. Had it been possible, I will say at once, I would have had you sent back to Germany, a citizen of which you now are by your own act. I would have had you sent back upon the terms of your undertaking that never again would you set foot upon the soil of this country. I cannot do that, however, because it is quite impossible to send you back to Germany. I can understand it being a matter of nothing but embarrassment and possibly of international embarrassment, that you should arrive there; above all, embarrassment to the authorities of this country.

In these circumstances, I must deal with you *upon the footing* that you have quite deliberately broken one of the most serious laws of your country, and I must sentence you to a term of five years penal servitude.

But I will say this. I hope the Prison Commissioners will take note that as soon as matters in Germany are sufficiently settled in my view you ought to be sent from this country upon licence not to return. This country does not require your presence. [The italics in this quoted summing-up are mine.]

An appeal to a higher court after this would have been nonsensical in the circumstances. I could not appeal against *the conviction* because I had been induced to plead guilty to the minor charges – in order to escape a trial on the major charges that would have meant being hanged. I could not, with any hope of success, appeal against *the sentence* in view of the very strong anti-German feeling that existed immediately after the war and the demands for revenge against the Nazis. My release from prison could only have been effected by order of the Home Secretary on the grounds of a miscarriage of justice.

I have heard the view that I was lucky to get off with five

years' imprisonment when my so-called 'fellow travellers', William Joyce and John Amery, were both hanged. But that view is held by people who know little or nothing about the facts and circumstances. One of many reasons for public ignorance of my case is that at the end of the war there was a famine of newsprint in Britain. Newspapers were rationed to a few sheets daily to cover the world's news. The result was that my 'trial' was not as adequately covered by the newspapers as it might otherwise have been.

I was told that America's lenient attitude towards many of its citizens who broadcast from Germany during the war probably had an influence on the British attitude towards me. An additional reason was undoubtedly the uproar that followed the hanging of Joyce.

William L Shirer, the American radio commentator and reporter, wrote in his book *End of a Berlin Diary*[1], after discussing my case and those of Joyce and Amery:

> The United States also had its full share of radio traitors –
> a peculiar phenomenon of the Nazi war – but our Government's attitude seemed to be, in their case, to forget and forgive. Some of the most notorious of them (like Donald Day, the veteran former *Chicago Tribune* correspondent) were released outright, and there did not seem to be any undue determination in Washington to bring the rest to trial.

Every country that was engaged in the Second World War had, of course, its foreign broadcasters and Britain, like Germany, had its full quota.

Why so much fuss, then, about those who broadcast for Germany? Douglas Reed, the English author, published a book

1. Hamish Hamilton, 1941

in 1942 called, *All Our Tomorrows*[1]. On pages 294–5 of that book
appears the following:

> Quite early on (during the war) the *Evening Standard* wrote
> jestingly: 'Broadcasting House is so full of foreigners engaged
> for the expanding foreign-language services of the BBC that
> even the Press Department has been moved to another
> building to make way for the invaders; it is now proposed, I
> am told, to put a notice outside the main entrance: "English
> Spoken Here".'
>
> About all this the Government maintained a closely guarded
> silence. Mr Duff Cooper, while yet Minister for Information,
> refused 'in the public interest' to state how many persons
> employed by the Ministry of Information and the BBC
> changed their names during the last five years and to give
> their original names and nationality, when he was asked this
> on 23rd April 1941, St George's Day. On the 19th November
> 1941, Mr Brendan Bracken became Minister for Informa-
> tion, still did not give the information, but said that 61
> Germans and 303 other aliens were employed by the BBC
> at salaries ranging from £3 10s 0d a week to £1,000 a year.
> By 28th January 1942, Mr Brendan Bracken, in refusing 'in
> the public interest' to state the number of aliens or former
> aliens employed in the BBC's foreign services, said that
> 'British subjects with adequate qualifications are not obtain-
> able in the numbers required, though preference is given to
> them when they are available' – two statements which I
> hereby challenge; they are at variance with the facts.

From this it is clear that Britain had been employing German
broadcasters during the war and had, at the same time, also made
them British citizens. Incidentally, the Judge said in my case at

1. Jonathan Cape, 1942

the Old Bailey: 'You cannot naturalise yourself during a war.' I did not do so, but if the Judge's statement is true how did the atom spy Klaus Fuchs, Richard Tauber and other foreigners receive British citizenship during the war?

The Attorney-General had said that I had dual nationality. Being domiciled in Germany, subject to German laws (and a military dictatorship!), I could scarcely have been expected to conform to the laws of Britain which had become foreign to me. I could scarcely have been expected to appeal to the Nazis to send me back to Britain where I would have been automatically locked up.

I had also been called up for registration with the German Army *before* the war and I had been taxed as a German citizen before receipt of my naturalisation certificate. I say that these points are further proof of my German citizenship.

Sanctuary

AFTER JOYCE HAD been hanged, and before I appeared in the Old Bailey dock, the question was asked whether the execution was one of expedience, or had Joyce been hanged in accordance with the strict letter of the law. These questions were asked by jurists and by a section of the Press. They cropped up again when I was sent to prison for five years. The strong public criticism of the hanging of Joyce helped to save my life. I have no doubt about that.

Frankly, I know that most of the people who posed these questions did not approve of the roles played by Joyce and myself during the war, but they were honest enough and fair minded enough to try to uphold the principles of British justice at all costs.

Mr A J Cummings, the political correspondent of the *News Chronicle*, for instance, regarded the execution of Joyce 'as an act of savagery which shocked the conscience of decent people throughout the world.'

The main differences between my case and Joyce's was that I had been forced to leave England for reasons that have been mentioned, more than two years before the war started. I had applied for German citizenship a year before the first shots were fired. Joyce, however, fled from England of his own volition only a week before the bombs started to drop and at a time when he knew that the finger was on the trigger. It was, in fact, because the war was about to start that Joyce sought asylum in Germany. He wanted to climb on Hitler's bandwagon, as he thought, and as a British Fascist he wanted a place in the Nazi-Fascist victory parade in London. He would never have dashed over to Berlin on the eve of the war if he had thought for one moment that the Germans were going to be defeated.

Part-German myself, my sympathy for the Germans began a couple of years before Hitler came into power. A place on the bandwagon did not, therefore, arise. As a man without a country in Germany, it was natural that I should seek passport protection and citizenship of some kind. Not knowing the frustrating ways of bureaucracy, I was innocently under the impression when I applied for German citizenship that I would receive my certificate of naturalisation within a matter of days or weeks.

Anything I did in Germany, including broadcasting and working in the German Foreign Office, I considered I had a perfect right to do as a German citizen. I was breaking no English law.

It is wrong to suggest that I acted with enmity towards Britain when I became a German citizen. My idea was to forget Britain and many unhappy memories. Why should the peacetime adoption of German citizenship have been regarded as a hostile act by the British authorities? I simply wanted to lead a new life in another country.

After a short time in Brixton Prison I was removed to Wakefield Prison in Yorkshire. And during my entire imprisonment I never ceased to protest that I had broken no law. This was almost impossible at the beginning because I was allowed no correspondence and no visitors. I was a special prisoner with whom MI 5 were taking no chances.

It was while I was in Wakefield that a very remarkable and elderly Quaker woman came into the picture. Prim, proper and puritanical, she was Miss Mary Troughton, who visited the prisoners regularly to lecture on English literature. A head-mistress of a Yorkshire girls' school, Miss Troughton wore old-fashioned clothes, had her hair in a bun at the back and her gold-rimmed pince-nez were held with a broad, black ribbon. She was rather plump, wore a bonnet type of hat but her general appearance, demeanour and kindly manner gave little indication of her real character; for little Miss Troughton was a fierce, courageous fighter for any cause that interested her. Humanitari-anism was in her blood and she abhorred injustices. For these very good reasons, she took an interest in my case, as readily as a fish to water.

Our association began as the result of a casual remark during a conversation in her prison class. When I remarked to the likeable little lady that I was not allowed visitors as other prisoners were, an angry warder who had been standing guard over us, stepped forward with the sharp rebuke: 'Now, none of that. Stop it!'

But this intervention, unexpected to Miss Troughton, not only made her curious, but furious.

'Why can't he have visitors like the others?' she snapped.

'Governor's orders, madam,' he said, switching to a respectful tone.

'Well, if he is not allowed any visitors, I am going to visit him,' she said with a decisive air that left me gaping in amazement. I never thought that this little Quaker lady could have worked up such passion in such a short time.

Pouting her lips with obvious contempt and with a swift adjustment of her pince-nez, she marched off to the Governor's office and from there the prisoners could hear loud voices raised in an angry, shouting match.

She told me later: 'The Governor told me that I was a visiting lecturer to the prison and as such I would be forbidden to visit any prisoner. My answer took him by surprise. I said that I would resign my lectureship. He was startled by my defiance because he is so used to having his own way.'

Resign she did, and when she turned up at Wakefield to visit me, the Governor was ready for her.

'You cannot see this fellow,' he said from his office desk. 'Why, he is nothing to you. You don't even know him.'

But the Governor had not reckoned with the terrior-like qualities of tough Miss Troughton. She was on the next train to London, marched straight into the Home Office and protested to a surprised, high-ranking official that, ' "The Officer in The Tower" is suffering a terrible injustice in Wakefield.' After an argument, she won her fight to become my only visitor.

Flushed with success and sniffing something out like a bloodhound, the Quaker lady got her teeth into my problems. She went into action, all at her own expense.

First, she went to the Working Committee of the Freedom Defence Committee at their headquarters in Endsleigh Gardens, London WC I. This Committee comprised many prominent people in Britain, including Julian Huxley, Professor C E M Joad, Victor Gollancz, Emrys Jones, George Orwell, Emrys Hughes, Bertrand Russell, Augustus John, Rhys J Davies, Harold J Laski and Ethel Mannin. The Committee agreed to take up my case right away and Miss Troughton also enlisted the support of the Society of Friends and the International Red Cross.

These three organisations did not take a mere academic interest in my case; they fought long and doggedly for my release, despite constant and persistent frustration. In their view, there had been a grave miscarriage of justice and their executives included several distinguished lawyers. Frequently they sent representatives to see me in Wakefield, and later to Parkhurst, to take statements from me and to clear up points. The Freedom Committee's Secretary, Mr Laurence Hislam, brought out a special pamphlet on my case.

Mr Fredrick Bieri, chief delegate in England for the International Red Cross, which specialised in the welfare of prisoners of war, was instructed by his Geneva headquarters to take up the cudgels on my behalf. This intervention was particularly fortunate for me because when officers of the Red Cross are interviewing prisoners they are allowed to do so without the presence of warders.

But these efforts were temporarily shelved when I decided to take matters into my own hands by making an escape bid from Wakefield Prison. A seaman and I managed to make prison keys from wax impressions. We had, however, to enlist the help of a third prisoner and it was this man who double-crossed us and gave us away during a preliminary trial-run. Soon after this I was transferred to Parkhurst, Isle of Wight.

This attempt to break out of prison seemed to add zest to the activities of Miss Troughton, although I had feared, on the discovery, that she would have abandoned all interest in me. She travelled regularly from her Yorkshire home all the way down to Parkhurst to see me. She told me excitedly about the wonderful plans she was making to secure my release. Carrying on the fight, she made trips to London from Yorkshire to have talks with executives of the three welfare organisations, and to see Members of Parliament.

But the bureaucrats were also at work – in their usual negative manner – deliberately standing in the way of the efforts of the humanitarian organisations. Months went by, for instance, before the Home Office replied to simple letters seeking information – replies that could have been given without difficulty in a few days.

It took two whole years to obtain a transcript of the statements that were made during the Old Bailey proceedings, and it was two years before the existence of the British Nationality Act, 1914, was accidentally discovered. It was an extraordinary discovery for it might have played a dominant part in my fight for freedom at the Old Bailey.

Whilst I was in prison, the Defence Committee was constantly pleading with the British Government for my release. This was done in personal interviews with the Home Secretary, Mr J Chuter Ede, and in many letters to him. These letters are now in my possession and one of them to Mr Ede, dated 9th October 1947, clearly delineates the Committee's policy towards me.

On 6th June last my Committee received a communication from Mr Norman Baillie-Stewart, Parkhurst Prison, who was sentenced to five years' imprisonment on 10th January 1946, on charges of assisting the enemy, with a view to having his position clarified.

Our efforts in obtaining a clear picture of the situation had not been facilitated by the considerable delay to which letters to and from Mr Baillie-Stewart have been subjected, and by reason of the fact that we are informed by him that a copy of the verbatim report of his trial has been denied him. In connection with the former point, we communicated with you on 29th July but your reply of the 18th August does not explain the reasons for the consistent delay in our correspondence, which is not apparent with other correspondence in H M Prisons. With regard to the verbatim report, my Committee is anxious to have a copy or at least to have sight of a copy, and your advice on this matter would be appreciated.

In the course of the past two years during which our Committee has had occasion to communicate with you, we trust we have convinced you that we have always suppressed our personal opinion in considering whether the principles of justice were involved in cases to which our attention had been drawn. In view of statements you have made to the House in defence of freedom of speech, we are confident that you will endorse this principle which is fundamental to this Committee's activities. Unfortunately, in the case of Mr Baillie-Stewart, it appears to us, judging from the information at our disposal, that the principles of justice have been sacrificed to expediency and prejudice. We, therefore, propose to take up this case and would be obliged if you would give answers to the following questions:

1) Does the Government accept the fact of Baillie-Stewart's German nationality?

a) Mr Justice Oliver, addressing Baillie-Stewart, stated: '. . . you applied for naturalisation from the moment you arrived on the Continent. The Attorney-General accepts, and I accept, that you did this genuinely. It was a mere accident in some sense that you had not obtained it before war broke out. If you had, you would not have been guilty of any offence at all. Nevertheless, you remained a British subject . . .'

and later:

b) 'If it had been possible I would have you sent back to Germany, a citizen of which you now are by your own acts, on terms of your undertaking that never again would you set your foot on the soil of this country. I cannot do that because it is quite impossible to send you back to Germany now . . .'

In a letter my Committee has received from Baillie-Stewart dated 19th December, he states that MI 5, with whom he has been in correspondence for the return of his property, give as the reason for not returning his German passport, a) It does not belong to him but to the German Government which issued it, and b) that in any case it has expired. We need hardly say that we do not think these valid reasons for withholding the passport, but the decision of the MI 5 (which we assume has received your sanction) is more serious since Baillie-Stewart has informed the representative of the International Red Cross that '. . . in spite of all the findings of the Court and Judge as to my nationality – the British Government now regards me as 'British'.

We feel that the very least Baillie-Stewart can expect is that this point of nationality should be cleared up once and for all.

2) There can be no doubt about the fact that, but for the Attorney-General's statement 'It certainly appears it would be a matter of considerable embarrassment if he [Baillie-Stewart] were back in Germany at the present time', the Judge would not have sentenced Baillie-Stewart. Indeed, in sentencing him, he referred to the Attorney-General's remarks and concluded:

> In these circumstances I must deal with you on the foot-ing that you have quite deliberately broken one of the most serious laws of your country, and I must sentence you to a term of five years penal servitude.

Our Committee views this concluding remark of the Judge with considerable misgivings for, in effect, the Attorney-General's advisors (who, in this case, would appear to be the

MI 5) have been permitted to reverse the Judge's original decision regarding Baillie-Stewart's future.

In view of the foregoing, does the British Government propose that Baillie-Stewart should serve his full sentence (less remission)? If so, what does the Government propose to do with him when he is due to be released?

Since my Committee cannot proceed further in this case until a clear ruling is given on the matters raised in this letter, it would be much appreciated if you would oblige me with an early reply.

Yours faithfully, Laurence Hislam, Secretary, Freedom Defence Committee.

On 15th December 1947 the Defence Committee received a letter from the Home Office in reply to the letter of 9th October. This stated that the Secretary of State could not give advice on my nationality. The letter went on: 'Although he may be under German law a German national, Baillie-Stewart is, in the laws of this country, a British subject . . .' A British subject! Yet I had to sign a statement for Mr Justice Oliver that I would leave Britain and never return! The Judge would have sent me, a British subject, back to Germany but for the unsettled immediate post-war conditions there. Mr Ede refused to order my release.

In a letter to me in Parkhurst on 18th May 1948, Mr Hislam, for the Committee, stated: 'We ourselves quite agree that logic and the Judge's remarks indicate that you became a German citizen and that it was nothing short of political expedience which brought about your imprisonment.' He further stated: 'We are going very thoroughly into the question of "dual nationality" in so far as it is possible to pin down the rights of anyone who suffers under such an absurd condition. In this connection, we are very pleased that you drew our attention to the British

Nationality and Status of Aliens Act, 1914, which clearly states that obtaining a certificate is not essential in establishing nationality; although it is still essential to prove that you did become naturalised before 3rd September 1939.'

He stated that it was the view of his Committee that this situation, coupled with the fact that I had been called up for German military service before the war, was circumstantial evidence that my naturalisation had been accepted in Germany. Mr Hislam added: 'Even the Attorney-General would, I think, have difficulty in avoiding the logic of this sequence of events.'

In a further letter to me on behalf of his Committee, Mr Hislam observed: 'With regard to the British Nationality Act, 1914, quite frankly we never suspected that such a glaring loophole in the prosecution's case could have failed to have been referred to by Mr Fox-Andrews in what was, apparently, a fairly comprehensive final speech (within its limits, of course), or in later correspondence.'

The fight for freedom went on almost up to the time of my release, after remission, in May 1949.

For some months before the time of my discharge from Parkhurst, London newspapers and book publishers had been contacting me in prison through friendly 'screws'. They were offering big sums of money for my story. But I rejected the lot. I had had more than my share of publicity and I wanted to fade into oblivion for at least some years. The 'screws' worked for both sides – me and the Press representatives – and they gave me the tip-off that an army of reporters and photographers would be waiting for me on my release. Representatives of the Press had also contacted Miss Troughton and Mr Hislam to use their influence with me to obtain interviews and photographs immediately the prison gates clanged behind me. One particularly enterprising reporter had gone up to Yorkshire to see Miss

Troughton with the idea of making arrangements in advance for him to see me through her. Mr Hislam and I were strongly opposed to this proposal, although the Fleet Street man and Miss Troughton had already engaged a room in a Southsea hotel for my reception. It was a rather slick bit of organisation.

For a week or so before my release, Mr Hislam and I worked out a cat-and-mouse plan to dodge the newsmen. Hislam and I were about the same build so we decided to adopt a disguise to deceive the Press. We both grew beards. At the same time, Hislam made a few quasi-furtive appearances before the Press representatives who had been keeping a round-the-clock vigil outside the prison days before the expected release. But our trump card was a three-seater airplane which we hired from an aerodrome about five miles away from the prison. This master stroke of organisation avoided the sea crossing from the Isle of Wight to the mainland and a certain encounter with the newsmen.

Long before daybreak on the morning of 19th May 1949 a taxi drove up to the prison. Within seconds I was inside with Hislam and we were off to the aerodrome, turned into a side road en route and waited there for a few minutes to find out if we were being followed. Just before dawn broke we were airborne and within minutes had made a perfect landing at Southsea.

Because of a frantic appeal to me by Miss Troughton – who was furious about our evasive tactics – I agreed to the secret meeting with her Fleet Street reporter. Ever helpful, Miss Troughton had given her word to the Fleet Street man that she would obtain the interview for him, and I had no wish to run counter to the appeals of this wonderful Quaker lady who had fought for me for years and who had befriended me when I was friendless. So one newspaper got a scoop, but the other reporters and photographers soon ferreted out our location, probably as

T

a result of a tip from a 'screw', and descended upon the hotel like an avalanche.

Still sporting our beards, Hislam and I dashed out of the back entrance of the hotel, but on our way to a waiting car, we were cornered. With a considerable amount of force we literally smashed our way through the crowd of Press men. We started off at top speed for London – followed by an imposing cavalcade of Press cars. At one stage during the cross-country chase, I stopped at a police station and asked for protection, but the police said they were powerless.

Reaching the outskirts of London, I decided that our car was too slow so, at a garage, we changed into a more powerful limousine. Soon the long line of Press cars was far behind and out of sight. By arrangement, our next stop was at the YMCA headquarters in London – where we were greeted by another army of reporters and photographers who had been waiting cheerfully for some hours outside.

There was so much jostling outside the building when word was passed that it was 'The Officer in The Tower' that eventually the police had to be called to keep order. I dashed up to the YMCA bathroom and quickly shaved off my beard, leaving on a slick, cavalry moustache. As I changed into a smart new suit that had been given to me, I noticed that the red hairs from my rich, flowing beard were now blocking the plughole in the basin.

Now I needed steady nerves and some courage for the next part of the act. At the main door, I stepped out as nonchalantly as possible and with the superior air of a Guards officer walked into the street. With head erect, as if oblivious of them all, I walked through the crowd. It worked – there was not a sign of recognition. Around the corner I stepped into a waiting car and was immediately driven off by the faithful Miss Troughton. Our next step was at the Quaker guest house at Jordans in Bucking-hamshire.

I had succeeded at last in eluding the Press and, for two weeks, lay low with the Quakers. With their approval, I assumed the name of 'James Scott'.

When the dust had settled and I appeared to be assured of some peace, I was put on the pay-roll at Jordans. I earned my keep gardening and working as a guest-house employee. Then I got a job on a nearby farm at thirty shillings a week and my food with a Quaker family who were unaware that I was 'The Officer in The Tower'. Life among the Quakers was not easy – I had to work twelve hours a day, milking cows, gardening and doing odd jobs – but I was certainly glad of their sanctuary at the time.

One day I shocked and alarmed the wife of my employer when she walked unexpectedly into my bedroom to find me wearing earphones. I had made my own crystal wireless set but she thought I was some sort of subversive agent, in touch with a foreign power. She reported me to her husband, so 'James Scott' was sacked on the spot.

Again the faithful Miss Troughton came to my rescue and found accommodation for me near Skipton in Yorkshire. After a few weeks in Yorkshire, the idea of getting to Ireland appealed to me. Wartime travel restrictions were, however, still in force and without an official travel permit, I could not land legally in Ireland. Once more the Quakers came to my aid. A false travel permit was obtained and, as 'James Scott', I arrived in Dublin.

Within a short time, Special Branch detectives were on my track, but I was allowed to remain in Ireland without further difficulty. It is in Ireland that I have been able to settle down – to a job, a wife, a family and to a life of tranquillity.

And it is in Ireland that I intend to spend the rest of my days.

Epilogue

UNDER THE NAME of 'James Scott', Norman Baillie-Stewart sailed into Dublin on the cross-channel ferry from Liverpool on 15th October 1949 to start a new life.

From the day he became the mysterious 'Officer in The Tower' of London in January 1933 he had had an overdose of adverse publicity, not merely in Britain, but throughout the world. And with the publicity went the indelible, soul-branding ignominy of two terms of penal servitude of five years each in English prisons. In prison he mixed with criminals of all sorts from common thieves and confidence men to murderers.

On arrival in Dublin he had no friends and no money, but he was helped with food and shelter, confidentially, by a few friendly Quakers. All he wanted in Ireland was to settle down to a quiet life; to earn a decent living and to forget the long nightmare of his past life. His sense of realism told him that under the name of Baillie-Stewart (a name to remember) he would never get a chance to earn a living. So he adhered to 'James Scott', a name he had used on a forged travel permit to enter Ireland from Britain, wartime travel restrictions being still in force in 1949.

Life was beginning to look more promising for him than for many years when he became associated with an Irish-German export-import venture with a Dublin office. But the halcyon days for 'Mr Scott' were numbered – Aliens Branch detectives were on his trail. Deportation back to Britain seemed a certainty, but the situation was saved when friends appealed to the Irish Government to give him a chance. The result: he was allowed to remain in Ireland, but he lost his job.

Almost destitute and with no home, he managed to get a job as a stationery salesman. He dropped 'James Scott' and registered his name for business as 'Patrick Stewart'. Then, on his own, he started in a small, unpretentious office in Parliament Street, Dublin, working as a manufacturers' agent.

Baillie-Stewart, although a blue-blooded aristocrat with an English public school education, had never known home life. This came to him for the first time in November 1950 when, aged forty-one, he married a pretty, chestnut-haired Dublin girl, Miss Catherine Molloy, a counter employee in a Dublin draper's. They had two children, a boy and a girl.

Baillie-Stewart always had a hankering after inventions, even from the days when he was a cadet at the Royal Naval College, Dartmouth. In Dublin he invented many gadgets, some for the British and United States armed forces and some of major commercial importance – always under the name of 'P Stewart' or a commercial friend. One of these was a revolutionary type of 'kangaroo ship' – a ship within a ship – the patent rights for which he sold to Harland and Wolff, the Belfast shipbuilders.

By choice he had few friends in Dublin and was personally little known. He abhorred publicity. Despite this his name was seldom out of the newspapers because of libel actions he was constantly taking in the English and Irish courts against authors and publishers who got certain vital aspects of his extraordinary career mixed up. He instigated ten libel actions in as many years – winning the lot without even having to go into court himself.

One of these actions was against Chief Superintendent Spooner of the Special Branch, Scotland Yard, a wartime MI 5 man. It was Spooner who interrogated Baillie-Stewart in Brussels military prison, as a result of which Baillie-Stewart appeared at the Old Bailey, charged under the Official Secrets Act, in 1946.

Three more were pending at the time of his sudden and unexpected death in Dublin on the afternoon of 7th June 1966. He was fifty-seven.

He asked me to help him write the story of his career and the manuscript was completed about seven weeks before his death. He never ceased to protest his innocence and decided to publish his story to defend his name for the sake of his two children. By the publication of *The Officer in The Tower*, he wanted to absolve his children from the stigma that had haunted him for more than thirty years – the stigma of a 'traitor'.

JM

Index